THE HOUSE
OF ATREUS

THE HOUSE OF ATREUS

*Abortion as a
Human Rights Issue*

James F. Bohan

PRAEGER

Westport, Connecticut
London

Library of Congress Cataloging-in-Publication Data

Bohan, James F., 1964–
    The House of Atreus : abortion as a human rights issue / James F.
    Bohan.
        p.   cm.
    Includes bibliographical references and index.
    ISBN 0–275–96282–2 (alk. paper)
    1. Abortion—United States.   2. Right to life—United States.
    3. Abortion—Law and legislation—United States.   I. Title.
    HQ767.5.U5B65   1999
    363.46′0973—dc21   98–38280

British Library Cataloguing in Publication Data is available.

Library of Congress Catalog Card Number: 98–38280
ISBN: 0–275–96282–2

First published in 1999

Praeger Publishers, 88 Post Road West, Westport, CT 06881
An imprint of Greenwood Publishing Group, Inc.

Printed in the United States of America

The paper used in this book complies with the
Permanent Paper Standard issued by the National
Information Standards Organization (Z39.48–1984).

10 9 8 7 6 5 4 3 2 1

Copyright Acknowledgments

The author and publisher gratefully acknowledge permission for use of the following material:

Excerpts from *The Holocaust and the Crisis of Human Behavior*, Revised Edition, by George M. Kren and Leon Rappoport (New York: Holmes & Meier, 1994). Copyright © by Holmes & Meier Publishers, Inc. Reproduced with the permission of the publisher.

Excerpts from Brenda Shafer, "What the Nurse Saw," *National Right to Life News*, July 18, 1995: 23; and excerpts from Governor Robert Casey, "America Is Returning to Its Senses," *National Right to Life News*, January 1995: 16+. Reprinted by permission of *National Right to Life News*.

Judgment of February 25, 1975. Translated in Robert W. Jonas and John D. Gorby, "West German Abortion Decision: A Contrast to *Roe v. Wade*," *John Marshall Journal of Practice and Procedure* 9 (1976): 605–684. Reprinted by permission of the *John Marshall Law Review*.

> . . . and readily Thyestes took
> What to his ignorance no semblance wore
> Of human flesh, and ate. . . .
> Aeschylus, *Agamemnon*

Contents

Preface

Several years ago, after having found myself in numerous discussions on abortion, I decided to make a rough outline of my thoughts on the topic. I felt I could articulate my position more clearly if I had time to organize my thoughts beforehand. The project I thought would take a weekend soon took on a life of its own. This book is the result.

The House of Atreus aims to stimulate a re-evaluation of abortion and its place in American society. Rather than developing a new code of ethics specifically for abortion, I have striven to show that abortion is irreconcilable with principles that we already regard as almost universally accepted. I attempt to do this by framing abortion as a *human rights* problem, rather than merely an abstract philosophical, theological, or medical issue. I have also tried to present the issue in a manner that is unique and thought provoking, and accessible to lay persons as well as scholars.

Although *The House of Atreus* occasionally refers to some of the better-known arguments on both sides of the abortion debate, I have consciously tried to limit my discussion of them. There are already many fine books discussing these arguments, and I wanted to develop a slightly different perspective on the issue. I have also deliberately avoided the theological arguments made against abortion. While theological appeals are important—very important—they tend to be effective only to the extent that they are based on a shared theological foundation. I wanted to concentrate on arguments that would be persuasive regardless of the reader's religious beliefs.

Where possible, I have tried to avoid certain terms which have themselves become a source of controversy in the abortion debate. I generally refer to the "unborn," for instance, rather than to the "embryo," "fetus," "baby," "child," and so forth. (The term "unborn" has its own problems but carries fewer connotations than the other alternatives.) Similarly, to avoid the problems associated with referring to the sides in the abortion debate as "pro-life" and "pro-choice"— both terms the other side finds objectionable—I generally refer to those individuals opposed to abortion as "abortion opponents" and those in favor of legalized abortion as "abortion proponents" or "supporters of abortion." These terms will not be acceptable to everyone—no terms I could select would be—but I hope that they are, at least, sufficiently neutral to allow readers to evaluate the underlying arguments on their merits.

Acknowledgments

I am grateful to my family and friends for their support, understanding, and encouragement, and to the following individuals who graciously took the time to review my manuscript in its formative stages and offer their advice: Charles Rice, Professor of Law at the University of Notre Dame Law School; Matthew Bohan; Patricia Bohan; Francis Fusco; Joseph Allen; and Fr. Orestes Binkewicz. Most of all, I am indebted to the help, judgment, and patience of my brother Edward, who served as a sounding board and source of sage counsel from this project's inception.

PART I

This book is divided into two major parts: one which focuses on changing the way we *think* about abortion, and one which concentrates on changing the way we *feel* about it. Part I of this book aims to change the way we think about abortion. It begins with a discussion of the Supreme Court's best-known abortion decision, *Roe v. Wade*, the 1973 case which held that the unborn are not "persons" and that there is a constitutional right to abortion. Since *Roe* framed many of the issues—and was fraught with many of the fallacies—which have since become permanent fixtures in the abortion debate, any re-evaluation of our attitudes about abortion should probably start with a discussion of *Roe*. With that case as a backdrop, the remaining chapters in Part I explain why we should recognize the right to life of the unborn.

My thesis is simple: The unborn are living human beings, and, as such, they have a right to life. Although many today regard the issues of whether the unborn are living or human as issues which are hopelessly abstract, they are not. One can show that the unborn are alive and human from conception onward without resorting to arcane or controversial principles of theology and philosophy. The second chapter, "Living," explains why the unborn are living. The third, "All Too Human," explains why they are human beings.

But simply proving that the unborn are living human beings will not persuade all abortion proponents that the unborn have a right to life. Although some in the "pro-choice" movement may believe that every human being has a right to life, many do not. Those who do not fall into one of two schools of thought. Some believe that all *persons* have a right to life but that some human beings are not persons. Others believe that even some persons have no right to life. The fourth chapter, "Persons," explores the pitfalls inherent in refusing to recognize the right to life of the unborn on the theory that they are not "persons." The fifth chapter, "Drawing the Circle," explains why we should recognize a right to life in every human being. The sixth chapter, "The Objections," examines the other principal arguments raised by abortion proponents to justify the destruction of the unborn, particularly those that assert that a woman has a right to abort her young even if the unborn are persons.

Many will find the idea that the unborn are human beings, and the conclusions that follow from that proposition, profoundly disturbing. It would be much easier to believe that the unborn are not humans. But truth—not expedience—is the foundation of any truly ethical decision. We must look to the facts rather than our inclinations. "Sit down before a fact as a little child," T. H. Huxley once wrote, "be prepared to give up every preconceived notion. Follow humbly wherever and to whatever abysses nature leads you."[1]

NOTE

1. Leonard Huxley, *Life and Letters of Thomas Henry Huxley* (New York: Appleton, 1900), 235.

1

Roe v. Wade

O liberté! comme on t'a jouée.
O liberty! how they have fooled with you.

Mme. Jeanne (Manon) Roland de la Platiére

[I]t is assailed and sneered at and construed, and hawked at and torn, till, if its framers could rise from their graves, they could not at all recognize it.

Abraham Lincoln

On January 22, 1973, the Supreme Court issued its decision in *Roe v. Wade*,[1] holding that women have a constitutional right to abort their young—at least during certain stages of pregnancy. The ruling was destined to become one of the most controversial ever handed down. With the possible exception of *Dred Scott v. Sandford*,[2] no other decision has so polarized the public or so transformed the landscape of national politics. Over two decades later, the controversy over *Roe* still shows no signs of subsiding. The anniversary of the decision is marked with demonstrations and counter-demonstrations, and abortion figures as a prominent issue in virtually every state and national election. Although the Court has seemed poised to overrule *Roe* on several occasions, it recently reaffirmed what it refers to as *Roe*'s *"essential holding."*[3] For better or for worse, much of *Roe* remains good law.

While the constitutional ramifications of the decision are profound, the import of *Roe* stretches far beyond the case's legal significance. *Roe* and its progeny precluded states from regulating many aspects of abortion, thrusting those issues into the national political spotlight. The issues the Court addressed in *Roe*—and the fallacies the Court subscribed to—have framed much of the succeeding abortion debate. Perhaps most important, *Roe* has transformed the way our society regards the morality of abortion. We have increasingly come to regard our courts as moral institutions, not merely legal ones. Particularly where constitutional issues are concerned, we assume that the law accords with our intuitive sense of justice: If something *ought to be* protected by the Constitution, then it must be a constitutional right, and if something is constitutionally protected, then it ought to be. By holding that abortion is a "fundamental right" protected by the Constitution, *Roe* served to erode much of the moral onus which had previously attached to abortion. An entire generation has come of age thinking of abortion as a "constitutional right."

I

The Supreme Court's rationale for recognizing abortion as a constitutional right in *Roe* was that state regulation of abortion interfered with a woman's "right to privacy." Before we examine *Roe* itself, some background about this "right" may be helpful.

As the Supreme Court acknowledged in *Roe*, neither the Constitution nor its amendments expressly mention a right to privacy.[4] References to this "right" gained currency in the legal community only after Samuel Warren and Louis Brandeis published a law review article entitled "The Right to Privacy" in 1890.[5] The article did not pertain to constitutional law, much less assert that the Constitution contained a right to privacy; it discussed tort law, examining a number of decisions in lawsuits involving the publication of letters, portraits, and the like, where courts had awarded relief on the basis of defamation, breach of confidence or implied contract, and other theories. Warren and Brandeis suggested that, despite the different legal bases identified by the courts, the cases stood for a broader proposition: that persons subjected to unauthorized publicity of their private affairs should have a legal remedy, just as they would for defamation, assault, and other torts traditionally recognized as common law. Over time, many state courts adopted this rationale and began to award damages to plaintiffs who established that a defendant had divulged certain private information without authorization.

The Supreme Court transmogrified Warren and Brandeis' suggestion for common law tort relief into a rule of constitutional law in the 1965 case *Griswold v. Connecticut.*[6] *Griswold* involved a challenge to a Connecticut statute prohibiting the use of contraceptives and forbidding the counseling of others in their use. The appellants, a director and a physician from a Planned Parenthood chapter in New Haven, argued that the statute violated their rights under the 14th Amendment. The Supreme Court struck down the statute but declined to decide the specific question of whether the Connecticut law violated the 14th Amendment. Instead, the Court held that several of the Bill of Rights' guarantees protected privacy interests and that the contraceptives statute infringed upon the "penumbra" or "zone" of privacy protected by those guarantees. In his opinion for the majority, Justice Douglas wrote, "We deal with a right to privacy older than the Bill of Rights—older than our political parties, older than our school system."[7] He neglected to explain where the "right" came from if not from the Bill of Rights, or why—if the right were so ancient and revered—no court had ever previously struck down a statute on account of it. Nor did Douglas explain just how the Connecticut statute violated this "penumbra" of privacy.

The specific textual basis for the "right" to privacy remained unclear until the Court handed down its decision in *Roe v. Wade.* There, the Court stated that the right to privacy fell within the "Fourteenth Amendment's concept of personal liberty and restrictions upon state action."[8]

II

Roe v. Wade involved a constitutional challenge to Texas abortion laws by a pregnant woman—identified as "Jane Roe" in the pleadings—and a physician-abortionist.[9] The Texas laws, typical of those on the books in many states at the time, made it a crime to "procure an abortion" except "by medical advice for the purpose of saving the life of the mother."[10] The appellants argued that whether a pregnant woman decided to abort her young fell within her right to privacy and, therefore, the government could not regulate abortions—regardless of how or why a woman decided to have one, and regardless of the point in the pregnancy. The state of Texas contended that the unborn were "persons" and that the state had a compelling interest in protecting their lives from conception onwards.[11]

Contrary to its usual custom, the Court's opinion did not proceed directly to the legal analysis of the issues raised by the parties. Instead, Justice Blackmun's majority opinion asserted that laws proscribing abortion were of "relatively recent vintage,"[12] and then digressed to outline various theological, philosophical, and medical positions propounded on abortion since antiquity. After noting that abortion was punished in the Persian Empire and barred by the Hippocratic Oath, the Court explained that abortion was commonplace in Greece and Rome; it outlined Saint Augustine's views on when men acquired souls; it sketched the legal and philosophical positions on when the unborn became fully human that developed during the Middle Ages and the Renaissance; and it traced the development of the common and statutory law on abortion to the present.[13]

Most of this survey, of course, had nothing to do with the question before the Court: whether the Constitution protected either abortion or the unborn. Instead, the Court included the history lesson to allay any controversy which might arise because its ruling was at loggerheads with the Hippocratic Oath and certain religious beliefs. Quoting the language of the Oath—"I will neither give a deadly drug to anybody if asked for it, nor will I make a suggestion to this effect. Similarly, I will give no woman an abortive remedy"—the Court conceded that the Oath barred physicians from performing abortions.[14] But the Court did not find this to be a real obstacle. Referring to one commentator's suggestion that the Oath was "a Pythagorean manifesto and not the expression of an absolute standard of medical conduct," the Court wrote, "This, it seems to us, is a satisfactory and acceptable explanation of the Hippocratic Oath's apparent rigidity. It enables us to understand, in a historical context, a long accepted and revered statement of medical ethics."[15] So much for the long accepted and revered statement of medical ethics.

As for religion, *Roe* contained the blanket assertion, "Ancient religion did not bar abortion."[16] But many ancient religions *did* bar abortion. It was considered the unforgivable sin by ancient Indians, for instance, regarded as unthinkable by ancient Jews, and condemned in the Zoroastrian *Avesta* and Buddhist *Vinayas*.[17] Although *Roe* correctly noted that the Greeks and Romans practiced abortion freely, one would think that the Court would have been reluctant to look to societies which killed even their *born* young without scruple for guidance on how to treat the unborn.[18]

When the Court finally got to the *legal* analysis of the issues raised by the parties, it resolved the question left unanswered by *Griswold*: the textual basis of the newly recognized right to privacy. Although the Court acknowledged that the "Constitution does not explicitly refer to any right of privacy,"[19] it stated that the right fell within the "liberty" guaranteed by the Due Process Clause of the 14th Amendment, which provides that no state shall "deprive any person of life, liberty, or property without due process of law."[20] Thus, the Court viewed the arguments raised by both sides in *Roe* as involving different constructions of the Due Process Clause: If abortion fell within the right to privacy, then it was within the "liberty" protected by the Due Process Clause; if the unborn were "persons," then their lives were protected by the word "life" in the same clause.

The Court concluded that the term "liberty" in the Due Process Clause encompassed abortion but provided scant explanation of its rationale. Then the Court went on to consider whether the unborn were "persons" so that their lives were protected by the Due Process Clause. The fact that the Court even addressed this issue is important, for it shows that while the Court had determined that women had a "liberty" right to abort the unborn, the Court did not necessarily regard that right as trumping the unborn's right to life. Indeed, the Court stated that if the unborn were "persons," then their right to life would necessarily prevail over any right pregnant women might have to abort them. Referring to the argument that the Due Process Clause protected the lives of the unborn because they are persons, the Court wrote, "If this suggestion of personhood is established, the appellants' case, of course, collapses, for the [unborn's] right to life is then guaranteed specifically by the Amendment."[21]

The Court held, however, that the unborn are *not* persons. In his majority opinion, Justice Blackmun noted that while the Constitution does not define the term "person," the word does appear elsewhere in the document:

> ... in the listing of qualifications for the Representatives and Senators, Art. I, s. 2, cl. 2, and s. 3, cl. 3; in the Apportionment Clause, Art. I, s. 2, cl. 3; in the Migration and Importation provision, Art. I, s. 9, cl. 1; in the Emolument Clause, Art I, s. 9, cl. 8; in the Electors provisions, Art. II, s. 1, cl. 2, and the superseded cl. 3; in the provisions outlining the qualifications for the office of President, Art. II, s. 1, cl. 4; in the Extradition provisions, Art. IV, s. 2, cl. 2,

and the superseded Fugitive Slave Clause 3; and in the Fifth, 12th, and 22nd Amendments, as well as in s. 2 and 3 of the Fourteenth Amendment.[22]

After listing these other references to "person" in the Constitution, Blackmun wrote:

[I]n nearly all of these instances, the use of the word is such that it has application only postnatally. None indicates with any assurance that it has any possible prenatal application.

All this, taken together with our observation that throughout the major portion of the 19th century prevailing legal abortion practices were far freer than they are today, persuades us that the word "person," as used in the Fourteenth Amendment, does not include the unborn.[23]

That left Texas's second line of defense: its assertion that it had a compelling interest in protecting the lives of the unborn because they are living throughout pregnancy. The Court rejected that argument but also declined to accept the appellants' position that women have a constitutional right to abortion on demand.[24] Instead, the Court divided pregnancy into three trimesters and promulgated a different standard for each. During the first trimester, states could not ban, or even regulate, abortions.[25] In the second trimester, states could protect their interest in the *mother's* health by regulating abortion procedures in ways reasonably related to her health.[26] Only during the third trimester could the state protect the life of the unborn. During that trimester, the Court reasoned, the state had a compelling interest in protecting the unborn because they are viable—potentially able to live outside the womb. So long as the state permitted abortion where necessary to preserve the life or health of the mother, it could regulate abortions during the third trimester.[27] But, while a state had the *option* to protect the lives of the unborn in the third trimester, it was not *required* to do so. If it were so inclined, a state could allow abortion at any time during pregnancy, and for any reason. Because the Court deemed the unborn not to be "persons," our young have no recognized right to life until they emerge from the birth canal—or, in the case of cesarean section, until they are lifted from the womb.

III

The majority opinion in *Roe* declared that a state has "an important and legitimate interest in protecting the health of the pregnant woman, . . . and that it has still another important and legitimate interest in protecting the potentiality of human life."[28] But the abortion cases decided following *Roe* showed that the Court considered the state's interest in the unborn to be far less "important and legitimate." The Court held that states could not require that a woman be informed of the risks associated with abortion and of the assistance available to her if she decided to give birth;[29] that states could not require that second-trimester abortions be performed in hospitals;[30] that states could not require that postviability abortions be performed using the technique which would provide for the best chance of survival for the unborn;[31] and even that states could not require that abortionists "insure that the remains of the unborn child are disposed of in a sanitary manner."[32]

The dissents in these cases argued that the Court was not merely applying *Roe* but expanding it, imposing ever greater restrictions on the states. But as old Justices retired from the Court and new ones were appointed, the dynamics on the Court shifted. By the time the Court heard *Planned Parenthood v. Casey*, many suspected that the Court would use the opportunity to overturn *Roe*.

Those who suspected that the Court was poised to overturn *Roe* were wrong, however. Rather than abandoning *Roe* in *Planned Parenthood v. Casey*, the Court expressly reaffirmed what it referred to as *Roe*'s "essential holding": that a woman has a right to decide to have an abortion before the unborn are viable and to obtain it without "undue interference" from the state; that the state has the power to restrict abortion after viability, so long as it affords exceptions for pregnancies endangering a woman's life or health; and, that the state has a legitimate interest from the outset of pregnancy in protecting the health of the woman and the unborn.[33]

The Court did backpedal with respect to one aspect of *Roe*, however. At least three of the five Justices who decided to reaffirm *Roe* stated that they rejected *Roe*'s trimester framework and did not consider it part of *Roe*'s "essential holding."[34] Justices O'Connor, Kennedy, and Souter, who together wrote a joint opinion, explained: "A logical reading of the central holding in *Roe* itself and a necessary reconciliation of the liberty of the woman and the interest of the State in promoting prenatal life, require . . . that we abandon the trimester framework as a rigid prohibition on all previability regulation aimed at the protection of fetal life."[35]

IV

Neither *Roe* nor its progeny held that the unborn are not human beings. The Supreme Court has *never* addressed that question. When the Court held in *Roe* that the unborn were not "persons," its analysis of the question turned solely on whether the *framers intended* that the word "person" apply to the unborn. Based upon the context surrounding the word in other parts of the Constitution, and the fact that fewer states regulated abortion when the 14th Amendment was ratified than at the time of *Roe*, the Court concluded that "person" in the Due Process Clause does not include the unborn.[36]

It is essential to recognize that when the Court construed the word "person" in *Roe*, the Court read the word as a legal term of art. In everyday usage, "person" means "a living human being."[37] When used as a legal term of art, however, the word distinguishes those who have certain rights and duties under the law from those who do not. An entity which possesses particular rights is a "person"; one that does not possess those rights is not. Thus, when the courts read "person" as a term of art, they have held that the word refers *to corporations* as well as to people.[38]

Under the rationale laid out in *Roe*, whether the unborn are living human beings is irrelevant to whether they are "persons." The Court never considered whether the unborn are human. It concluded they were not "persons" simply because there was no evidence that the framers had the unborn in mind when they drafted the constitutional protections for "persons." (Had the Court followed the same approach with respect to the other half of the inquiry, and made a woman's "right" to abort turn on whether the framers had abortion in mind when they drafted the "liberty" guarantee in the Due Process Clause, the Court would have concluded that there was no constitutional right to abortion.[39]) As John Noonan has observed, *Roe* subscribed to the notion that a person is simply a construct of the law: "[E]ven the apparently natural physical person is a construction of juristic thinking. . . . [J]ust as we personify a corporation for legal purposes, so we personify natural physical beings. There are no independent, ontological existences to which we respond as persons."[40]

The implications of the rationale used in *Roe* are clear and profound: In the eyes of the American judicial system, all men are *not* necessarily created equal. Human beings do not have a right to life simply by virtue of being human.

To the extent the Court's construction of "person" in *Roe* rested on the use of the word elsewhere in the Constitution, the Court based its holding on a false premise. The Court's line of reasoning was straightforward: "Person" appears elsewhere in the Constitution where it is clear from the context that the word refers only to born human beings; therefore, "person" as used in the Due Process Clause does not include the unborn. The implicit premise underlying the Court's approach is that the word "person" means the same thing everywhere it appears in the Constitution. That premise is false, however. "Person" does *not* mean the same thing everywhere it appears.

Consider the use of "person" in the Apportionment Clause,[41] which governs how taxes and members of the House of Representatives are apportioned among the states. After listing the Apportionment Clause in *Roe*, Justice Blackmun included a sardonic footnote: "We are not aware that in the taking of any census under this clause, a fetus has ever been counted."[42] That may well be true. Like virtually all of the references to "person" Blackmun cited from the Constitution, it appears from the context that the framers were thinking of born human beings only—not the unborn and not corporations. The problem with the Court's reasoning is that, long before *Roe*, the Court held that it did not construe "person" in the Due Process Clause so narrowly.

Corporations are not considered "persons" for the sake of apportioning taxes and Representatives—or for purposes of most of the other provisions Blackmun listed. Nevertheless, the Court has consistently held that corporations are "persons" for purposes of the Due Process Clause.[43] Significantly, in these earlier cases even those Justices who argued that "person" in the Due Process Clause should be read narrowly—as not including corporations—conceded that all human beings were "persons" within the meaning of the clause. In his dissent in *Wheeling Steel Corp. v. Glander*, for instance, Justice Douglas wrote, "the submission of the Fourteenth Amendment was on the basis that it protected human beings."[44] Justice Black was more emphatic. In his dissenting opinion in *Connecticut General Life Insurance Company v. Johnson*, he argued that the clause "nor shall any State deprive any person of life, liberty, or property without due process of law" must be read as "nor shall any State deprive any *human being* of life, liberty, or property without due process of law."[45] In support of his position that corporations were not "persons" within the meaning of the Due Process Clause, Black wrote, "The history of the Amendment proves that the people were told its purpose was to protect *weak and helpless human beings.*"[46]

The irony of the current state of the law is that the Amendment is deemed to exclude those human beings who are most weak and helpless. The Due Process Clause—at least as it is presently construed—affords more protection to an incorporated tattoo parlor than to a child moments before birth.

As noted earlier, the Court also asserted in *Roe* that its construction of the word "person" was appropriate because "throughout the major portion of the nineteenth century prevailing legal abortion practices were far freer" than they were in 1973, when *Roe* was decided.[47] This argument does not stand close scrutiny, however. In terms of construing the language of the Constitution, the regulation of abortion in the nineteenth century is relevant only insofar as it sheds light on the framers' intent, or on what the states understood the Due Process Clause to mean at the time the Amendment was ratified. Did the framers mean for the unborn to be protected as "persons"? Did they mean for abortion to be protected as "liberty"? Or did they mean for the Due Process Clause to protect neither abortion nor the unborn?

The assertion that abortion practices were "far freer" in the nineteenth century is deceptive. The implication is that abortion was much less regulated when the 14th Amendment was drafted than when the Court decided *Roe*.[48] But if the regulation of abortion was *less* stringent at the time the 14th Amendment was drafted, it was stringent nonetheless. When Congress passed the Amendment in 1866, 28 of the then 36 states had laws restricting abortion: seven prohibiting abortion after quickening, and 21 prohibiting it at all stages of pregnancy.[49] Two additional states enacted legislation restricting abortion between the time the Amendment passed Congress and when it was finally ratified.[50] Indeed, although the majority opinion in *Roe* characterized legislation restricting abortion as "of recent vintage,"[51] Justice Rehnquist pointed out in his dissent that no less than 21 of the state abortion statutes *in effect* at the time of *Roe* had been enacted *prior to the ratification of the 14th Amendment.*[52]

The Court's assertion that abortion practices were "far freer" in the nineteenth century than when *Roe* was decided is deceptive in another regard as well. Even assuming state regulation was less restrictive when the 14th Amendment was drafted than at the time of *Roe*, why are the state abortion statutes in effect at the time the Amendment was ratified relevant? The Amendment, after all, made many existing state statutes

unconstitutional. An amendment to the Constitution controls in all instances where it conflicts with state or Federal statutes. To reason that
the 14th Amendment should be read in the manner most consistent
with contemporaneous state legislation is to have the tail wag the dog.
Furthermore, the implicit premise behind the Court's reasoning is that
interpreting the Due Process Clause as protecting abortion—as opposed to the unborn—is more consistent with the state legislation gov-
erning abortion at the time the Amendment was ratified. Yet, if this was
the Court's rationale, it is wrong. Every single one of the statutes per-
taining to abortion at the time of ratification *limited* access to abortion;
none guaranteed it. Had the Court in *Roe* construed the Due Process
Clause as protecting *the unborn*, all of the state abortion statutes on the
books at ratification would have remained constitutional. By construct-
ing the Due Process Clause as *protecting abortion*, however, the Court
adopted a position inconsistent with every one of these state laws. The
statutes in effect at the time of ratification fell into two categories: those
prohibiting abortion at all stages of pregnancy, and those prohibiting
abortion only after "quickening"—the first recognizable movement of
the unborn *in utero*.[53] While *Roe* did permit limited regulation of abortion under the specific circumstances set forth earlier in this chapter,
both types of abortion statues in effect at ratification would have been
unconstitutional under *Roe*.

Few would argue that the framers of the 14th Amendment had either abortion or the unborn specifically in mind when they drafted the
Due Process Clause. But the Supreme Court does not necessarily view
the intent of the framers as controlling. In recent years, and especially
from the time of the Warren Court, the Supreme Court has exhibited
an increased inclination to view the meaning of the Constitution as
changing with time. Justice Powell explained the rationale succinctly in
an interview shortly after retiring from the Court:

> If one speaks broadly, original intent is relevant if you can ascertain
> it. It is perfectly clear that the Founding Fathers believed in free
> speech and freedom of religion. But when you get right down to
> the specifics, it was impossible for the Founding Fathers to antici-
> pate the developments of civilization. So I don't think that anyone
> gains by saying original intent controls. Whether they were en-
> dowed with unique wisdom or very good luck—or both—the
> Founding Fathers blessed us with a Constitution that is brief and
> broadly phrased.[54]

Justice Powell's reference to the Constitution as being "broadly phrased" is important, for it is the textual foothold of the approach he describes. According to that approach—sometimes called the "open-ended phraseology theory"—the framers deliberately decided against "specific" terms and opted for "far more elastic language—language . . . more 'capable of growth' and 'receptive to "latitudinarian" construction.'"[55]

Constitutional scholars disagree on whether the Constitution should be read as the framers intended, or more expansively, to account for changes in society since ratification. We need not become entangled in that controversy here, however. Even construing the text of the 14th Amendment more broadly to allow for changes in society since ratification, the unborn are entitled to constitutional protection before abortion. The reason is simple. Those who would read more into the Constitution than the text meant at framing do so on the theory that, to return to Justice Powell's words, "it was impossible for the Founding Fathers to anticipate the developments of civilization." The question becomes, therefore, What developments in civilization have occurred from the time of framing that dictate that the Due Process Clause protect abortion as "liberty" rather than the unborn as "persons"?

Those who drafted the Due Process Clause were certainly aware of abortion. Far from being a product of modern medicine, abortion has been known for thousands of years. It was outlawed in Assyria, abhorred as the practice of heathens in Judea, treated as a capital crime in Persia, and regarded as a crime as serious as killing a Brahman in ancient India.[56] Indeed, the fact that abortion was well known from antiquity is evident even from the history of abortion sketched in *Roe* itself.[57]

The case for developments in civilization which dictate that the unborn be protected as persons is stronger. The scientific understanding of the particulars of human reproduction remained rudimentary at the time the 14th Amendment was framed and ratified. The role of spermatazoa in fertilization, for instance, was not proven until 1879, a full decade after ratification.[58] Science has advanced by leaps and bounds since then, yet even today many lay people (like some Justices on the Supreme Court) labor under the misconception that the unborn are not alive or not human.

There is something terribly perverse, moreover, about reading the word "person" in the Due Process Clause as excluding the unborn. The 14th Amendment was drafted, in large part, to undo the Supreme Court's infamous decision in *Dred Scott v. Sandford*. In *Dred Scott*, decided four years before the Civil War, the Court held that the Constitution excluded blacks when it referred to "people" and to "citizens."[59] The majority opinion, written by Chief Justice Roger Taney, stated that the framers of the Constitution regarded blacks as "beings of an inferior order; . . . and so far inferior, that they had no rights which the white man was bound to respect."[60] Taney concluded, therefore, "It is obvious that they were not even in the minds of the framers of the Constitution when they were conferring special rights and privileges."[61]

The primary purpose of the due process and equal protection guarantees in the 14th Amendment was to ensure that the amended Constitution would protect the lives, liberty, and property of those even many abolitionists believed to be "beings of an inferior order."[62] When the framers referred to "persons" in the Amendment, they did not use the term narrowly. At the time the Amendment was drafted, scientists could not agree on whether blacks and whites were even members of the same species. Louis Agassiz, America's most prominent biologist in the mid-1800s, argued that they belonged to different species.[63] German biologist Ernst Haeckel, Darwin's most famous adherent on the Continent, maintained that a greater difference existed between Germans and Hottentots than between sheep and goats.[64] Indeed, historian Keith Thomas writes that "in the mid nineteenth century it became anthropological orthodoxy" to regard the different races as separate species.[65] Nevertheless, the framers referred to both blacks and whites as "persons" in the Amendment. The fact that they did so shows that the framers used the word "person" generically, to embrace all members of the human family—even those regarded by many as "beings of an inferior order."

Did the framers have the unborn specifically in mind when they drafted the Due Process Clause of the 14th Amendment? Perhaps not. Then, as now, many were under the impression that the unborn are not living human beings.[66] But that does not necessarily mean that the unborn are not "persons" within the meaning of the Due Process Clause—even if the framers' intent controls. One must ask whether, when the framers referred to "persons" in the 14th Amendment, they meant to extend the Amendment's protections only to particular *subsets* of the human family or whether they meant for the word to embrace *all* human beings. There is no indication that the framers meant to exclude any human beings from the protections afforded to "persons" in the Amendment. The framers may not have been thinking specifically of the unborn, but nor were they thinking specifically of the Ainu, or pygmies, or the members of the stone-age tribes subsequently discovered in the Amazon. If the only individuals who are "persons" under the Due Process Clause are those the framers specifically had in mind when they drafted the Amendment, then an Ainu, or pygmy, or a member of the Amazon tribes would have no right to life if he moved to the United States. If, on the other hand, the framers meant to include all human beings when they referred to "persons," then the unborn are protected by the Amendment so long as they are humans—whether the framers had them specifically in mind or not.

VI

Finally, one seemingly insignificant aspect of *Roe* deserves special mention, though it is seldom addressed in analyses of the decision. As noted earlier, the Supreme Court referred to Roman free-abortion practices during the course of its opinion in *Roe*. This is no coincidence. If one had to select a model for our thinking when it comes to abortion, ancient Rome is the place to look. It is true, as the Court noted in *Roe*, that the Romans felt the unborn had no right to life. But the Court neglected to mention that the Romans also regarded *born* children as having no right to life. Under the Roman right of *patriae potestas*, a father had absolute authority over the members of his household, including the right to put young children to death.[67] Prohibitions on infanticide "were thought to be an unjust infringement of the state into the sphere of paternal discretion and liberty."[68] *Roe* held, in essence, that prohibitions against killing the unborn are unjust infringements of the state into the sphere of *maternal* discretion and liberty.

Nor was *Roe* the first instance where the practices of the Romans were invoked to support the recognition of a constitutional right to abortion. The appellants in *Roe* argued, among other things, that the meaning of "human life" is a relative one which depends on the purpose for which the term is being defined.[69] In support of that proposition, they cited a dissent written by Judge Fred Cassibry in another abortion case, *Rosen v. Louisiana State Board of Medical Examiners*.[70] There, Judge Cassibry wrote:

> The meaning of the term "human being" is a relative one which depends on the purpose for which the term is being defined. To the scientist a "human being" may be no more than union of sperm and egg; to the poet or to society as a whole the term may

connote something else. Science at best marks the outermost limits of life; it cannot tell us nearly so well what a human being *is*, as it can what a human being definitely *is not*. The Romans, for example, practiced infanticide with indifference. No doubt the science of the Romans regarded the infant as a human being; but can one say the Romans did?[71]

In other words, one can be a human being in the biological sense, and yet still not be a "human being."

That Judge Cassibry could embrace the notion that "human being" means whatever we decide it means is startling, especially given his frank admission that the Romans butchered their children while subscribing to the same view. The Roman experience, like so many other sad chapters in our history, should be compelling evidence that we should err on the side of caution when deciding who is "human" and that we tend to rationalize the killing of the inconvenient on the basis that they are inhuman. Nevertheless, fully cognizant of the dangers that can result from classifying human beings as non-human, Judge Cassibry argued that whether a human being is human turns on whether society regards him as human. It is a terrifying proposition. According to Cassibry's reasoning, it is impossible for a society to engage in the mass murder of human beings: once the annihilation begins, the victims cease to be "human."

The notion that one can be a human being for some purposes but not for others may strike many of us as nonsensical. But it is representative of the thinking underlying much of the abortion movement. There is an aversion to calling things what they are. An 1871 report from the American Medical Association's Committee on Criminal Abortion ended with the observation, "We had to deal with human life. In a matter of less importance we could entertain no compromise. An honest judge on the bench would call things by their proper names. We could do no less."[72]

Sadly, we do not place the same value on calling things by their proper names today—nor do our judges. As we shall see in more detail in succeeding chapters, rather than acknowledging that we are dealing with human life, we resort to doublespeak: some living beings are not alive, some human beings are not human, some persons are not persons, some killing is not killing.

NOTES

1. *Roe v. Wade*, 410 U.S. 113 (1973).

2. *Dred Scott v. Sandford*, 60 U.S. (19 How.) 393 (1857).

3. *Planned Parenthood v. Casey*, 505 U.S. 833, 846 (1992).

4. 410 U.S. at 152.

5. See Samuel Warren and Louis Brandeis, "The Right to Privacy," *Harvard Law Review* 4 (1890): 193–220.

6. *Griswold v. Connecticut*, 381 U.S. 479 (1965).

7. 381 U.S. at 486.

8. 410 U.S. at 153.

9. The name "Jane Roe" was a pseudonym. In special circumstances, the courts allow parties to use a pseudonym to protect their privacy. More than a decade after the Supreme Court handed down its decision in *Roe*, a single woman, Norma McCorvey, admitted that she was "Jane Roe." Although she had initially claimed that she became pregnant as the result of a gang rape, she later admitted that she had made up that story to increase her chances of getting an abortion and had actually become pregnant in a failed relationship. Ironically, McCorvey never got an abortion (the Supreme Court case was decided after she gave birth) and has since reconsidered her support for abortion. See "Roe v. Wade," *The Oxford Companion to the Supreme Court of the United States*, ed. Kermit Hall (New York: Oxford University Press, 1992), 740; and Steven Waldman and Ginny Carroll, "Roe v. Roe," *Newsweek*, August 21, 1995: 22–24.

10. 410 U.S. at 117–118.

11. The premise Texas proposed, treating the unborn as persons, was not a novel one. The unborn are considered "persons" for purposes of remedies given for personal injuries, for instance; the child may sue for them after birth. See William L. Prosser, *Prosser and Keeton on the Law of Torts*, gen. ed. W. Page Keeton, 5th ed. (St. Paul: West, 1984) 367–370. And a viable child who would have been born alive but for the negligence of another is considered a person for purposes of many states' wrongful death statutes. Prosser 370.

12. 410 U.S. at 129.

13. 410 U.S. at 130–141.

14. 410 U.S. at 131.

15. 410 U.S. at 132.

16. 410 U.S. at 130.

17. Eugene Quay, "Justifiable Abortion—Medical and Legal Foundations (Part II)," *Georgetown Law Journal* 49 (1961): 402–405. (Abortion was also prohibited by the Babylonians, Assyrians, and Hittites. Quay, 399–403.)

18. Quay, 413–414, 421–422; and Will Durant, *The Life of Greece* (New York: Simon, 1939), 287.

19. 410 U.S. at 152.

20. The Due Process Clause in the 14th Amendment applies only to states and their subdivisions. There is another Due Process Clause in the Fifth Amendment which, in virtually identical language, affords individuals the same protection against the Federal government.

21. 410 U.S. at 156–157.

22. 410 U.S. at 157–158.

23. 410 U.S. at 157–158.

24. 410 U.S. at 153.

25. 410 U.S. at 164.

26. 410 U.S. at 164.

27. 410 U.S. at 164.

28. 410 U.S. at 162 (emphasis omitted).

29. *Thornburgh v. American College of Obstetricians and Gynecologists*, 476 U.S. 747 (1986); *Akron v. Akron Center for Reproductive Health, Inc.*, 462 U.S. 416 (1983).

30. *Akron.*

31. *Thornburgh*; *Colautti v. Franklin*, 439 U.S. 379 (1979).

32. *Akron*, 462 U.S. at 451 (internal quotation marks omitted).

33. 505 U.S. 833, 844–869.

34. 505 U.S. at 893.

35. 505 U.S. at 893.

36. 410 U.S. 113, 158.

37. See, for example, *The American Heritage Dictionary*, 2d College ed. (1985).

38. See, for example, *Wheeling Steel Corp. v. Glander*, 337 U.S. 562 (1949).

39. *Doe v. Israel*, 359 F.Supp. 1193 (D.R.I.), *aff'd* 482 F.2d 156 (1st Cir. 1973), *cert. denied*, 416 U.S. 993 (1974), a case decided soon after *Roe*, underscored the fact that whether the unborn are human has nothing to do with whether they are "persons" under the holding in *Roe*. In *Doe v. Israel*, the American Civil Liberties Union challenged a Rhode Island statute that recognized the unborn as persons. Relying upon the Supreme Court's decision in *Roe*, the Federal District Court in Rhode Island held that the statute was frivolous and refused to hear the biological evidence supporting it.

The Supreme Court of Tennessee came to a similar conclusion in *Davis v. Davis*, 842 S.W.2d 588 (Tenn. 1992), *cert. denied sub nom. Stowe v. Davis*, 507 U.S. 911 (1993), a case involving the fate of frozen embryos made from the eggs and sperm of a couple who later divorced, Mary Sue Davis wanted to have the embryos implanted so she could bring them to term. Junior Davis, her ex-husband, insisted that the embryos never come to term. Based upon expert scientific testimony, the trial court concluded that the embryos were human beings from conception onward and awarded custody of them to Mary Sue on the theory that implantation was in the embryos' best interest. 842 S.W.2d at 594. The Supreme Court of Tennessee disagreed with that conclusion, however, and held that Junior Davis had a "constitutionally protected" right to prevent the embryos from coming to term. 842 S.W.2d at 589. Pointing to the U.S. Supreme Court's decision in *Roe v. Wade*, the court concluded that, regardless of the scientific evidence introduced at the trial, the embryos were not "*legally* recognizable as human life." 842 S.W.2d at 596 (emphasis added).

40. John T. Noonan, Jr., "The Root and Branch of *Roe v. Wade*," *Nebraska Law Review* 63 (1984): 670.

41. U.S. Const. art. I, § 2, cl. 3.

42. 410 U.S. 113, 157 n. 53.

43. See, for example, *Minneapolis R. Co. v. Beckwith*, 129 U.S. 26 (1889), *Connecticut General Life Insurance Co. v. Johnson*, 303 U.S. 77 (1938); *Wheeling Steel Corp. v. Glander*, 337 U.S. 562 (1949).

44. 337 U.S. 562, 576 (1949).

45. 303 U.S. 77, 87 (1938).

46. 303 U.S. at 87 (emphasis added).

47. 410 U.S. 113, 157–158.

48. Justice Blackmun fostered this notion by writing in *Roe* that most states did not enact legislation restricting abortion until after the Civil War. 410 U.S. at 139. That assertion is false, however. More than two-thirds of the states in the Union (26 of the then 34 states) had legislation restricting abortion before the war began. (For a list of the abortion statutes enacted in the United States until 1961, see Quay 447–520.)

49. Statutes in Alabama, California, Connecticut, Georgia, Illinois, Indiana, Iowa, Louisiana, Maine, Massachusetts, Nevada, New Hampshire, New Jersey, Ohio, Oregon, Pennsylvania, Texas, Vermont, Virginia, West Virginia, and Wisconsin prohibited abortion at all stages of pregnancy. Legislation in Arkansas, Kansas, Michigan, Minnesota, Mississippi, Missouri, and New York, meanwhile, prohibited abortions after quickening. Quay, 447–520. Justice Rehnquist lists the abortion legislation in effect in the states and territories at the time of the Amendment in a footnote to his dissent in *Roe*. See 410 U.S. at 175–176 n. 1.

50. Florida barred abortion after quickening; Maryland prohibited it at any point in pregnancy. See 410 U.S. at 175–176 n. 1; Quay 457–458, 479–480.

51. 410 U.S. at 129.

52. 410 U.S. at 176–177 n. 2.

53. The Supreme Court noted in *Roe* that quickening typically occurs between the sixteenth and eighteenth week of pregnancy. 410 U.S. at 132.

54. "Interview: The Marble Palace's Southern Gentleman," *Time*, July 9, 1990: 12–13.

55. See *Oregon v. Mitchell*, 400 U.S. 112, 263 (1970) (Brennan, J., concurring in part and dissenting in part) (quoting Alexander M. Bickel, "The

Original Understanding and the Segregation Decision," *Harvard Law Review* 69 (1955): 1, 61, 63).

56. Will Durant, *Our Oriental Heritage* (New York: Simon & Schuster, 1954), 275, 334, 376, 489.

57. See, for example, 410 U.S. at 130 (referring to free-abortion practices prevailing in ancient Greece and Rome).

58. "Biological Sciences," *Encyclopaedia Britannica: Macropaedia*, 15th ed. (1995).

59. 60 U.S. (19 How.) 393, 411.

60. 60 U.S. (19 How.) at 407.

61. 60 U.S. (19 How.) at 411–412.

62. For a discussion of abolitionists' views of blacks at the time of emancipation, see Raoul Berger, *Government by Judiciary: The Transformation of the Fourteenth Amendment* (Cambridge, MA: Harvard University Press, 1977), 10–16.

63. Stephen Jay Gould, *Ontogeny and Phylogeny* (Cambridge, MA: Belknap-Harvard University Press, 1977), 127.

64. Daniel Gasman, *The Scientific Origins of National Socialism: Social Darwinism in Ernst Haeckel and the German Monist League* (New York: American Elsevier, 1971), 40.

65. Keith Thomas, *Man and the Natural World: A History of the Modern Sensibility* (New York: Pantheon, 1983), 136.

66. See, for example, the 1859 statement of the American Medical Association's Criminal Abortion Committee quoted in Chapter 2.

67. Earl E. Shelp, *Born to Die? Deciding the Fate of Critically Ill Newborns* (New York: Free Press, 1986), 160–161.

68. Shelp, 160–161.

69. Brief for Appellants at 122–123, reprinted in Philip B. Kurland and Gerald Casper, eds., *Landmark Briefs and Arguments of the Supreme Court of the United States: Constitutional Law*, vol. 75 (Washington, D.C.: University Publications of America, 1975), 202–203.

70. *Rosen v. Louisiana State Board of Medical Examiners*, 318 F. Supp. 1217, 1232 (1970 E.D. La.), *vacated* 412 U.S. 902 (1972).

71. 318 F. Supp. at 1236–1237 (footnotes omitted).

72. *Roe v. Wade*, 410 U.S. at 142 (quoting *Transactions of the American Medical Association* 22 (1871): 258).

2

Living

Reverence for life is the highest court of appeal.
                    Albert Schweitzer, *The Philosophy of Civilization*

Alice laughed. "There's no use trying," she said; "one can't believe in impossible things."
"I dare say you haven't had much practice," said the Queen.
                    Lewis Carroll, *Through the Looking-Glass*

Of all the fallacies involved in the abortion debate, none is more persistent than the notion that science has not yet determined when life begins. This misconception is widespread but utterly absurd. For well over a century, biologists have known that the unborn are living throughout pregnancy. It is the inescapable conclusion of a tenet as central to biology as gravity is to physics or the heliocentric solar system is to astronomy.

Outside the field of biology, however, an astounding amount of confusion remains on the question of whether the unborn are living. On July 4, 1989, the *Los Angeles Times* conducted a telephone poll of 792 Americans nationwide. The persons surveyed responded to a number of abortion-related questions, including one asking when life begins. Forty-seven percent of those surveyed said life begins at conception; 25 percent said at the first signs of life; and 13 percent said at birth.[1] Assuming the results of this polling are representative, less than half the population believes that the unborn are living throughout pregnancy.

Those confused about whether the unborn are living are not necessarily ignorant. Some of our most educated citizens have also fallen prey to the notion that the unborn are not alive from conception onward or that scientists have not yet resolved the issue. In his opinion for the Supreme Court in *Roe v. Wade,* Justice Blackmun wrote, "We need not resolve the difficult question of when life begins. When those trained in the respective disciplines of medicine, philosophy, and theology are unable to arrive at any consensus, the judiciary, at this point in the development of man's knowledge, is not in a position to speculate as to the answer."[2]

Similar notions have infected other Justices on the Court. In one recent case alone, *Planned Parenthood v. Casey,* six Supreme Court Justices referred to the unborn as "*potential* life."[3] In his dissenting opinion to another decision, *Webster v. Reproductive Health Care Services,*[4] Justice Stevens argued that the preamble of a Missouri statute violated the First Amendment's guarantee against laws respecting the establishment of religion because the preamble contained language stating that the life of a human being begins at conception.[5] According to Stevens, the statement that human life begins at conception constituted an "unequivocal endorsement of a religious tenet of some . . . Christian faiths."[6] Justice White, meanwhile, seems to have believed that science not only *has not* determined when life begins, but that it *cannot* do so. In his dissent to the Court's opinion in *Thornburgh v. American College of Obstetricians and Gynecologists,* White refers to the "*unanswerable* question of when human life begins."[7]

I

Much of the confusion over whether the unborn are alive results from the fact that we tend to view the issue as a philosophical or religious question, not a biological one. The Supreme Court's approach to the issue in *Roe* is illustrative. The Court did not treat the issue of whether the unborn are living as a straightforward biological question; it devoted much of its discussion to the history of Western philosophical thought on the issue. The Court outlined the positions of the Pythagoreans and the Stoics.[8] It traced evolution of the common law "mediate animation" view from philosophical, legal, and theological concepts developed during the Renaissance, when life was thought to begin when the unborn became recognizably human (were "formed") or when they received souls (became "animated").[9] As noted previously, the Court ultimately concluded that it need not resolve the "difficult question of when life begins" because there was no consensus on the subject in the fields of medicine, philosophy, and theology.[10] The Court then wrote:

[I]t should be sufficient to note briefly the wide divergence of thinking on this most sensitive and difficult question. There has always been strong support for the view that life does not begin until live birth. That was the belief of the Stoics. It appears to be the predominant, though not unanimous, attitude of the Jewish faith. It may be taken to represent a large segment of the Protestant community. . . . [T]he common law found greater significance in "quickening." Physicians and their scientific colleagues have tended to focus either on conception or on live birth, or on the interim point at which the fetus becomes viable.[11]

Roe's analysis of whether the unborn are alive is typical of those which conclude that we do not—or cannot—know when life begins. The Court devoted more of its attention to philosophy and religion than to biology, and it confused the issues of whether the unborn are infused with souls with whether they are living. The most extensive biological discussion of whether the unborn are living consists of a discussion of Aristotle's theory that human life passes through three stages: vegetable, animal, and rational.[12] And the Court devoted more of its opinion to analyzing when Renaissance theologians thought the unborn received souls than to modern scientific opinion on whether the unborn are alive. Although the Court asserted that scientists disagree on whether the unborn are alive from conception onwards, the Court was horribly mistaken.

What is the problem with turning to theology or philosophy to determine whether the unborn are living? If we were concerned with when we get souls, or how to live, or the nature of the afterlife, then theology or philosophy would be relevant. However, the question of whether the unborn—or any other organism—is living is a biological question. The theological and philosophical positions discussed in *Roe*—and those common in the abortion debate since then—seek to explain when the unborn are alive in the biological sense. To resort to non-biological answers to this biological question is as ridiculous as turning to philosophy or theology to determine the configuration of the solar system. Diderot and Spinoza were both eminent philosophers during the time the common law on abortion developed in England, yet both believed that rocks and other inanimate objects were alive.[13] Biological questions demand biological answers.

II

And what is the biological answer to the question of whether the unborn are living? Prominent scientists, like Dr. Jerome Lejeune, the discoverer of the cause of Down's syndrome, have testified that human life begins at conception.[14] Indeed, despite the Court's assertion to the contrary in *Roe*, there has been a consensus for well over a century that the unborn are living throughout pregnancy.

Consider, for instance, the report prepared by the American Medical Association's Committee on Criminal Abortion and presented at the Association's annual meeting in 1859. Two of the three reasons the report identified for the prevalence of abortion pertained to misconceptions about whether the unborn are living:

> The first of these causes is widespread ignorance of the true character of the crime—a belief, even among mothers themselves, that the foetus is not alive until after the period of quickening. . . .
>
> The third reason . . . is found in the grave defects of our laws, both common and statute, as regards the independent and actual existence of the child before birth, as living being. These errors . . . are based, and only based, upon mistaken and exploded medical dogmas.[15]

The fact that the unborn are living throughout pregnancy necessarily follows from a tenet accepted as dogma by biological scientists for generations: *living beings do not arise from non-living matter*. To hold that the unborn is not alive at any point from conception to birth—that a living being somehow arises from non-living matter during the course of a pregnancy—one must subscribe to the now thoroughly debunked theory of spontaneous generation.

The idea that living beings arise from inanimate matter no doubt seems ridiculous to most of us—at least outside the context of pregnancy. But to early naturalists it seemed the only plausible way to explain how maggots materialized in rotting meat, how locusts sprouted from the soil, and how a variety of other organisms seemed to issue from non-living substances. Some even believed that a lock of lady's hair, placed in a rain barrel, could become a snake.[16] One by one, however, scientists demonstrated that in each of these cases of supposed spontaneous generation, the organisms actually arise from living—not inanimate—matter.

Italian biologist Francisco Redi exposed the first chink in the theory of spontaneous generation in 1668. Using jars of meat, Redi showed that maggots arise from flies, not from inanimate matters as his contemporaries supposed.[17] He placed various types of meat in eight jars, four of which he left open and four of which he sealed. Only meat in the open jars developed maggots. To demonstrate that fresh air did not account for the difference in results between the jars, Redi repeated the experiment using four open jars and four jars covered with netting that would let in air but not flies. Again, maggots infested only the meat in the open jars.

The microscope provided the means for laying to rest many of the remaining spontaneous generation myths. Antony van Leeuwenhoek, the Dutch microscopy pioneer, showed that fleas arise from minuscule eggs laid by other fleas, not from inanimate matter as was previously thought. Succeeding investigators proved that many of the organisms previously believed to develop by spontaneous generation grew from eggs or larvae too small to be seen with the naked eye.

The theory of spontaneous generation was remarkably resilient, however. Undeterred by the accumulating scientific evidence against the theory, a significant portion of the scientific community subscribed to the idea of "free cell formation" in the early 1800s. According to this spin-off of spontaneous generation, cells developed out of an unformed, non-living substance. Ironically, many of the proponents of free cell formation had witnessed cell division through their own microscopes.

In January of 1860, after a number of further investigations had failed to resolve the spontaneous generation problem, the French Academy of Sciences announced a prize for contributions that would shed light on the question. Louis Pasteur responded with an experiment that provided conclusive evidence that even the most minute creatures come from other living cells. Biologists who subscribed to the spontaneous generation theory had argued that the appearance of microbes in wine and other fermentable mixtures demonstrated that the microbes arose from the mixtures themselves and not from other cells. Pasteur showed that if fermentable mixtures were protected from contact with air, fermentation would not take place. Even air minus the particulate matter or preheated air with particles would not cause fermentation. Therefore, the microbes causing fermentation arose from germs floating in the air—not from the inanimate mixtures. In the eyes of the scientific community, Pasteur delivered the *coup de grâce* to theories that living organisms arise from non-living matter.[18] Pasteur himself declared, "Never will the doctrine of spontaneous generation recover from the mortal blow of this simple experiment."[19]

III

The ramifications of Pasteur's experiment are profound if not intuitively obvious. Life does not *begin* when organisms reproduce; it is *continued*. No break in the chain of life occurs between one generation and the next. Fertilization takes place when the living sperm and living egg cells fuse. The fertilized egg then divides and differentiates. In humans, the offspring will continue to develop—inside the womb initially, and later outside of it—and, if all goes well, will eventually develop into a mature man or woman. To maintain that the unborn are not alive at any point during pregnancy is to believe in spontaneous generation, for if the unborn are not living throughout pregnancy, then living newborns must arise from non-living matter.

Whatever else abortion is, therefore, it is an act of killing. This may be unpleasant, it may be inconvenient, it may be unfortunate, but it is indisputably true. It cannot be changed by characterizing the unborn as "potential life," or abortion as "choice" or a "termination of pregnancy." The "right" to abort is a right to kill. Even Ron Fitzsimmons, the executive director of the National Coalition of Abortion Providers, has admitted what abortion is in this regard. "It is a form of killing," he has said. "You're ending a life."[20]

Perhaps no one has addressed the "life or death" aspect of abortion more eloquently than Pearl Buck, the Nobel-prize-winning author of *The Good Earth*. In her foreword to *The Terrible Choice*, Buck reflected on abortion in light of her experience as the mother of a child with phenylketonuria. She wrote that, even had she known beforehand that her daughter would be gravely retarded and the burdens that would entail, she would not have aborted her child.[21] Her daughter's life had not been meaningless, she argued; it had been worthwhile for her to have lived.[22] "[I]n this world where cruelty prevails in so many aspects of our life," Buck wrote, "I would not add the weight of choice to kill rather than to let live."[23] She explained:

I fear the power of choice over life or death at human hands. I see no human being whom I should ever trust with such power—not myself, not any other. Human wisdom, human integrity are not great enough. Since the fetus is a creature already alive and in the process of development, to kill it is to choose death over life. At what point shall we allow this choice? For me the answer is—at no point, once life has begun. At no point, I repeat, either as life begins or as life ends, for we who are human beings cannot, for our own safety, be allowed to choose death, life being all we know. Beyond life lie only faith and surmise, but not knowledge. Where there is no knowledge except for life, the decision for death is not safe for the human race.[24]

NOTES

1. Bill Boyarski, "Public Is Deeply Divided Over Ruling on Abortion," *Los Angeles Times*, July 4, 1989, Part I: 1+.

2. *Roe v. Wade*, 410 U.S. 113, 159.

3. See *Planned Parenthood v. Casey*, 505 U.S. 833 (1992) at 871 (O'Connor, J., Kennedy, J., and Souter, J., in their opinion for the Court), 929 (Blackmun, J., concurring in part and dissenting in part), 914 (Stevens, J., concurring in part and dissenting in part), and 949 (Rehnquist, J., concurring in part and dissenting in part) (emphasis added in each instance).

4. *Webster v. Reproductive Health Care Services*, 492 U.S. 490 (1989).

5. 492 U.S. at 566–569.

6. 492 U.S. at 566. This "religious entanglement" theory is popular with many commentators. See, for example, Robert L. Maddox and Blaine Bortnick, "Do Legislative Declarations that Life Begins at Conception Violate the Due Process Clause?" *Campbell Law Review* 12 (1989): 1–21; David R. Dow, "The Establishment Clause Argument for Choice," *Golden Gate University Law Review* 20 (1990): 479–500; and Laurence Tribe, "Foreword: Toward a Model of Roles in the Due Process of Life and Law," *Harvard Law Review* 87 (1973): 18–22, 24–25.

7. *Thornburgh v. American College of Obstetricians and Gynecologists*, 476 U.S. 747, 800 (1986) (emphasis added).

8. 410 U.S. 113, 130–132.

9. 410 U.S. at 132–134.

10. 410 U.S. at 159.

11. 410 U.S. at 160.

12. See 410 U.S. at 133 n. 22.

13. Robert H. Haynes and Philip C. Hanawalt, introductory essay, *The Molecular Basis of Life: An Introduction to Molecular Biology*, Haynes and Hanawalt, eds. (San Francisco: W. H. Freeman, 1988), 2.

14. See *Davis v. Davis,* 842 S.W.2d 588 (Tenn. 1992), *cert. denied sub nom. Stowe v. Davis,* 507 U.S. 911 (1993); and Tamara L. Davis, "Comment: Protecting the Cryopreserved Embryo," *Tennessee Law Review* 57 (1990): 529–530.

15. *Roe v. Wade,* 410 U.S. 113, 141 (quoting *Transactions of the American Medical Association* 12 (1859): 73–78).

16. Helena Curtis, *Biology,* 4th ed. (New York: Worth, 1983), 238.

17. Redi's experiment is described in Isaac Asimov, *Asimov's Chronology of Science and Technology* (New York: Harper, 1989), 159–160; and at "Francesco Redi," *Encyclopaedia Britannica: Micropedia,* 15th ed. (1995).

18. Pasteur's experiment is described in Asimov, 338; and in "Biological Sciences," *Encyclopaedia Britannica: Macropedia,* 15th ed. (1995).

19. Quoted in Curtis, 78.

20. David Stout, "An Abortion Rights Advocate Says He Lied about Procedure," *New York Times,* February 26, 1997: A-12.

21. Pearl S. Buck, foreword, *The Terrible Choice,* by Robert E. Cooke et al. (New York: Bantam, 1968), xi.

22. Buck, xi.

23. Buck, xi.

24. Buck, xi.

3

All Too Human

"The nature of man is his whole nature," said Pascal. I accept that proposition. To strip the human being, for example, of all his attributes save his logical or calculating powers is an unwarrantable mutilation. Nature is asserting herself in him, and you must take into account not one or two, but all of her assertions.

W. Macneile Dixon, *The Human Situation*

The beginning of wisdom is to call things by their proper names.

Confucius, *Analects*

It may strike many of us as odd that there could be serious disagreement about whether a particular organism is a human being or not. We regard the differences between human beings and other animals as so obvious that no one could really mistake one for the other. Indeed, one philosopher recently wrote, "It must be extremely rare, if it ever happened at all, that anyone would have some doubt whether a specimen being examined was human or not."[1] A large part of the current debate over abortion, however, revolves around precisely that question. Abortion opponents assume that the unborn are human beings; abortion proponents generally maintain that they are not.

I

The implication that the unborn are not human underlies much pro-abortion rhetoric. Abortion proponents tell us that abortion is a matter of "individual morality," that a woman should have control over "her own body," and that whether a woman aborts her young is by right a "personal choice." The precise formulation of the arguments varies, but the clear import of the language is that whether a woman aborts her young affects only one human being: the woman.

When they expressly argue that the unborn are not human beings, abortion supporters typically support their position by pointing to ways the unborn differ from born human beings. There are a number of different variations of this argument. Sometimes they focus on the anatomical complexity of the unborn or some other aspect of their *physical development*, arguing, for instance, that the unborn cannot be human early in pregnancy because they look similar to the unborn of other animals. Sometimes they maintain that *the nature of the relationship between the pregnant women and the unborn* demonstrates that the unborn are not human. The argument that the unborn cannot be human beings until they are viable, or until they are born, falls into this category. And sometimes they point to still *other differences between the born and unborn* which supposedly show that the unborn are not human beings. For example, abortion proponents contend that whether one is human depends on whether—or how—one reasons, feels pain, interacts, is "self-aware," or manifests a personality. Supreme Court Justice John Paul Stevens utilized this last approach in some of his opinions in cases involving abortion. In his concurring opinion to *Thornburgh v. American College of Obstetricians and Gynecologists*, for instance, Stevens wrote that abortion was permissible because "[t]here is a fundamental and well-recognized difference between a fetus and a human being."[2] While Stevens never identified just what this difference is, he did write that "the State's interest in the protection of an embryo . . . increases progressively and dramatically as the organism's capacity to feel pain, to experience pleasure, to survive, and to react to its surroundings increases day by day."[3]

There is a logical problem, however, with these and all other arguments that assert that the unborn are not human because they differ in some way from born human beings. The arguments beg the question.

Consider, for purposes of illustration, the argument made by abortion proponent Dr. Arthur Frederick Ide in his *Abortion Handbook*: "Separating the fetus from the human is simple inasmuch as human beings have brains complete with nerve endings that can sense and feel pain, while the fetus does not have this bodily development and function until late in the gestation-development period."[4] How did Ide determine that this criterion separates humans from non-humans? Simple. He looked for characteristics which are present in born human beings but not the unborn. The problem is that Ide's argument rests on the very premise it attempts to prove. Ide assumes that all humans have brains with complete nerve endings that can sense and feel pain. But one cannot conclude that all human beings have brains with complete nerve endings unless one first assumes that the unborn are not human beings. The other arguments that assert that the unborn are not human suffer from the same problem: they assume the characteristics of born human beings define those of all human beings.

If the logical flaw inherent in such reasoning is not immediately apparent, it can easily be illustrated in another context, one with which we are more familiar. Consider the following line of reasoning:

IF all white people are humans,
AND black people differ from white people,
THEN black people are not humans.

The argument assumes that the properties of *some* members of a class (white people) define those of *all* members of that class (all humans). But we cannot conclude that black people are not human because they differ from whites unless we first assume that only whites are human. Similarly, we cannot conclude that the unborn are not human because they differ from born human beings unless we first assume that only born human beings are human.

II

Those who contend that the unborn *are* human beings cite a number of reasons in support of their position. Some, based on religious conviction, maintain that the unborn are human because they have souls or are made in the image of God. Others argue that the unborn are human simply because they are potentially capable of thinking a human thought, feeling a human emotion, or performing a human act. Still others insist that the fact that the unborn contain a complete genetic blueprint is determinative. In his dissent to the Supreme Court's opinion in *Thornburgh v. American College of Obstetricians and Gynecologists,* for instance, Justice Byron White wrote:

> However one answers the metaphysical or theological question whether the fetus is a "human being" . . . one must at least recognize, first, that the fetus is an entity that bears in its cells all the genetic information that characterizes a member of the species homo sapiens [sic] and distinguishes an individual of that species from all others, and second, that there is no nonarbitrary line separating a fetus from a child or, indeed, an adult human being.[5]

The arguments typically used to show that the unborn are human beings tend to have their own problems, however. Theological appeals are persuasive only to the extent that others share the theological foundation upon which the appeal is based. (For instance, if I do not believe in God, the argument that the unborn are made in His image will not persuade me that they are human.) As for the non-theological arguments, they leave a number of questions unanswered: Does the fact that the unborn *will be* humans after birth necessarily mean that they *are* human beings beforehand? And is the issue of whether the unborn are human beings a "metaphysical or theological question" as Justice White suggests?

III

Before turning to the specific question of whether the unborn are human beings, we should dispense with one preliminary issue. Discussions of whether the unborn are human are often encumbered with the ruminations of philosophers, theologians, writers, and others on the question of what it means to be human. We need not revisit those positions here, for they are utterly irrelevant to the question of whether the unborn are human beings. We are interested in what *is* a human being, not what *it means to be* human. The first is a question of classification; the second is a question of the human condition. The two questions are as different as "Who is an American?" and "What does it mean to be an American?" or "Who is a woman?" and "What does it mean to be a woman?"

While the question of whether an organism is a human being is more mundane, it has its own complications. Having come to regard Man as the measure of all things, we find it difficult to measure Man. Nowhere is our confusion more evident than in our approach to whether the unborn are human. If someone were to ask whether an aged woman or newborn is human, we would not throw up our hands and exclaim that this is a matter of opinion, or that the subject might be human for some purposes but not for others. Yet this is precisely how we tend to respond to the question with respect to the unborn. Celeste Michelle Condit, for instance, seems to feel that whether the unborn are human is a matter of popular opinion. In *Decoding Abortion Rhetoric*, she writes, "Ultimately . . . we may *choose* to classify the fetus as human. Our choice to do so, however, will be based on the weighing of similarities between the 'fetus' and the 'human being/person' against the differences. To this point, there has been no public consensus (nor much discussion) about this weighing process."[6]

Other abortion proponents assume that one can be human for some purposes but not for others. The appellants in *Roe v. Wade*, for instance, argued that "the meaning of 'human life' is a relative one which depends on the purpose for which the term is being defined."[7] Mary Anne Warren argues that abortion is ethical because one must distinguish between humans "in the genetic sense" and humans "in the moral sense."[8] According to Warren, the former comprise all members of the species *Homo sapiens*, but only the latter are "full-fledged members of the moral community."[9]

The problem with these arguments, and others which assert that the unborn are not "human beings," is that they do not really refer to *human beings* at all. Instead, they fashion new and self-serving definitions for the term, tailoring them to exclude the unborn. But whether one is a human being is not simply a question of opinion, where one view is as legitimate as another; it is a question of biological fact. A human being is a particular type of animal. One can no more change humans into non-humans—as Condit suggests—simply by "choosing" not to classify them as human, than one can change cats into dogs by calling cats "dogs." Language can disguise reality but not transform it. A rose by any other name is still a rose. While abortion proponents tend to assume that the unborn cannot be humans if many do not perceive them as "humans," that assumption is fallacious. The fact that many people believe whales to be "fish" does not make whales fish; the fact that many people believe the unborn are not "humans" does not make the unborn non-humans. As for Warren's distinction between "humans in the genetic sense" and "humans in the moral sense," though she frames her argument in terms of "human beings," she never really argues that the unborn are not full humans. Terminology aside, she simply argues that there are some human beings ("genetic human beings") whom one has no moral obligation to treat like human beings.

IV

The first step in resolving whether the unborn are humans is to determine what makes an organism a human being. There is a tendency for some reason to treat this as something other than a biological issue. In the closing paragraphs of *Notes from Underground*, Dostoyevsky writes, "It is a burden to us even to be human beings—men with our own real body and blood; we are ashamed of it, we think it a disgrace and try to contrive to be some sort of impossible generalized man."[10] Unwittingly, he described the major impediment in our quest to determine who or what is human: our reluctance to treat the issue as one of "body and blood," as a matter of biology. Even Carolus Linnaeus, the eighteenth century Swede who pioneered the scientific classification of organisms, fell victim to this temptation. In the definitive edition of *Systema Naturae*, Linnaeus detailed other creatures in terms of their size, shape, and other physical characteristics; human beings he described only with the Socratic maxim: *nosce te ipsum*—"know thyself."[11]

But the question of who is a human being is necessarily a biological question. A human being is a particular type of animal. Were we to discover the existence of a disembodied spirit, or a dachshund with the capacity to reason, we might want to afford each some sort of legal or ethical recognition, but certainly neither could be considered a human being. The term "human being" by definition refers to any member of the species *Homo sapiens*. *The American Heritage Dictionary*, for instance, only attributes one definition to "human being": "A member of the genus *Homo* and esp. of the species *Homo sapiens*."[12] While *The Oxford English Dictionary* does not define "human being," it does define "human" and "*Homo sapiens*":

human   n. A human being, a member of the human race.

Homo sapiens   n. The human species, the forms of man represented by the surviving races and varieties.[13]

Even under the *Oxford* definition, therefore, one is a "human being" if a member of the species *Homo sapiens*. (Anyone who believes that this definition is too expansive—that non-humans could fall within its terms—necessarily believes that some members of the human species are not human beings.)

Non-biological traits have, of course, been advanced to distinguish human beings from other animals. No other animal reasons, we are told, or communicates through symbols, or passes significant knowledge from one generation to another. But relying on such non-biological criteria to determine whether an individual is human is problematic. The fact that only human beings engage in an activity does not mean that an individual must presently be engaged in that activity to be human. Only human beings reason, for example, but we do not become non-humans when we sleep. Furthermore, the sheer extent of variation within the human family makes it difficult to derive non-biological generalizations which apply to all humans all the time. Indeed, some prominent philosophers in this century have even challenged the idea that there is such a thing as human nature. Maurice Merleau-Ponty declared that "it is the nature of man not to have a nature."[14] Simone de Beauvoir referred to human beings as "the being whose essence lies in having no essence."[15]

Some scientists are also beginning to challenge the idea that the non-biological dividing lines between humans and other animals are as bright as we once supposed. Researchers now speak of "animal reasoning," for instance.[16] Anthropologist Elizabeth Marshall Thomas, author of *The Hidden Life of Dogs*, attributes a variety of human characteristics to canines. "Each species has its own version of thoughts and feelings," she maintains. "Dogs think dog thoughts and sometimes those coincide with humans."[17] Psychologist Theodore X. Barber, meanwhile, author of *The Human Nature of Birds*, argues that birds "speak" with their eyes, beaks, and feathers about "important daily events."[18] "They can be contented and happy and even ecstatic as well as sad and hopeless and forlorn," he contends. "They can manifest parental love, close friendships, and erotic love."[19]

By defining "human being" as "any member of the species *Homo sapiens*," we avoid the vagaries inherent in the non-biological definitions. We also use the commonly accepted definition for the term—unlike many abortion proponents, who invent new definitions for "human being" specifically tailored to support the conclusion that the unborn are not human.

The definition "any member of the species *Homo sapiens*" is preferable in other respects as well. Confining our attention to those individual organisms whose humanity is not in dispute, for instance, we find that the criterion "a member of the species *Homo sapiens*" always embraces those organisms regarded as human and always excludes those regarded as non-human. There are no exceptions. The definition also avoids the more sinister problems that can accompany subjective definitions of the word "human." During the struggle for women's rights in the early decades of this century, Suzanne La Follette observed, "Most people . . . , when they espouse human rights, make their own reservations about the proper application of the word 'human.' "[20]

History attests to the fact that we tend to rationalize the elimination of the inconvenient on the grounds that they are inhuman. The exploitation of the indigenous peoples of the New World, the slave trade, the annihilation of the Jews in Germany—all were justified on the basis that the victims were not human. Given the potential consequences of categorizing some human beings as non-humans, we dare not define who is "human" using criteria which are narrow, subjective, or ephemeral. We need a bright-line standard.

How does one determine whether a subject is a member of the species *Homo sapiens*?

The "species" is the fundamental unit in taxonomy, the branch of biology devoted to naming and organizing living things according to their relatedness. Certain similarities and differences exist between any two organisms. For instance, a mushroom and a humpback whale both consist of cells. "Identical" twins, meanwhile, differ slightly from one another. Even the same organism can change markedly during the course of development: consider the difference between a tadpole and a frog, or a caterpillar and a butterfly. The taxonomist's task is to group organisms into hierarchical categories according to their similarities and differences. A "species" consists of all organisms which can potentially breed and produce fertile offspring. Fox terriers and Gordon setters, for example, are the same species—*Canis familiaris*—because they can mate and produce fertile progeny. Other groupings are conjectural. Scientists must rely on circumstantial evidence—the specimen's genetically-determined features, and anatomical, biochemical, and physiological similarities—to piece together the relationships between organisms. Species are different. They can be objectively defined. In the words of biologist Stephen Jay Gould: "The category of species has a special status in the taxonomic hierarchy. Under the tenets of the 'biological species concept,' each species represents a 'real' unit in nature. Its definition reflects this status: 'a population of actually or potentially interbreeding organisms sharing a common gene pool.'

Above the species level we encounter a certain arbitrariness. One man's genus may be another man's family."[21]

The unborn are humans—members of the species *Homo sapiens*—because they can potentially interbreed with other humans. The phrase "*potentially* interbreed" in the definition of species is important. The unborn are not able to mate while within the womb, obviously. But that does not mean that they are not members of the species *Homo sapiens*. If an organism could have the capability, at some point in its life, to mate with a human and produce human offspring, then that organism is a human being. The *potential* to produce fertile offspring is enough; the organism need not necessarily possess the present ability to do so. Since the unborn can potentially mate with a human being during their lives and produce fertile offspring, they must be human beings.

Indeed, odd as it may seem at first, it now appears that an unborn female could be a mother even if she lives only weeks after conception. Human females have all of their eggs within 10 weeks of being conceived.[22] Scientists have already successfully transplanted eggs from unborn female mice into adult, barren females, allowing the adult mice to become pregnant.[23] They anticipate having the technology to implant eggs scavenged from aborted human young into sterile women within a few years.[24] The reason these scientists propose to use eggs from aborted female unborn is precisely because those eggs are produced by *human beings*. (Scientists are especially interested in other human "fetal tissue" for the same reason: it comes from *human beings*.) Could the eggs from any other organism give rise to a human child? Can a human being have a mother who is not herself a human being?

V

Abortion proponents are fond of arguing that the fact that something is living and human does not necessarily make that entity a human being. For instance, Jane English writes, "[S]ome have mistakenly reasoned from the premise that a fetus is human (after all, it is a human fetus rather than, say, a canine fetus) to the conclusion that it is a human. Adding an equivocation on 'being,' we get the fallacious argument that since a fetus is something both living and human, it is a human being."[25]

An entity can be both living and human and yet not a human being. I have five fingers on each hand, and each is both human and living. But my fingers are not each human beings. The critical distinction between what *is* a human being ("human" used as a noun) and what is simply *part of* a human being ("human" used as an adjective) is that only the former can potentially reproduce with a member of the species *Homo sapiens* and produce fertile offspring. A woman's hand, or appendix, or even one of her eggs does not fulfill this criterion. Neither does a man's sperm.

The unborn, especially in their early stages of life, do appear quite different from adult humans. But that does not mean that they are any less members of the species *Homo sapiens* than we are. A monarch caterpillar is as much a member of the species *Danaus plexippus* as the butterfly that emerges from the chrysalis; an American bullfrog tadpole does not change species when it metamorphoses into an adult frog.

The fact that the unborn do not visually resemble born human beings for some time after fertilization—a point frequently made by abortion proponents—is neither relevant nor, indeed, surprising when one considers the process of development. Vertebrates face a challenge when they reproduce. All vertebrates—from eels to polar bears, from parrots to humans—arise from the fusion of two cells: one sex-cell from each parent. The fused cell, or zygote, will develop into the adult multicellular organism. Since they all consist of two fused cells, vertebrate zygotes appear fairly similar under a microscope. But that appearance is deceiving. Each zygote contains, among other things, a detailed biochemical blueprint for the eventual adult organism. Species which appear dissimilar as adults develop along diverging pathways. The more closely related the species, the longer into development their appearances will remain similar. But the fact that these organisms appear similar early in their development does not mean that the immature organisms are more closely related than the adults of their respective species. For example, a newborn gorilla may resemble a human infant more than their respective mothers resemble one another, but the newborns are no more closely related than the adult gorilla and the mother of the child. Similarly, the zygotes of different animals appear more similar than adults, but they are no more closely related.

In the words of Richard John Neuhaus, "If someone objects that, at five or 15 days, the embryo does not look like a human being, one has only to point out that this is precisely what a human being looks like at five or 15 days of development."[26]

VI

While many abortion proponents seem to regard the words "fetus" and "human being" as mutually exclusive, they are not. Indeed, the retention of fetal traits is one of the very characteristics that make us human. One of the prominent developmental features that distinguishes humans from other animals is our tendency to retain fetal traits long after we are born. In the 1920s, after investigating the extensive similarities between humans and the juveniles—but not the adults—of primates and certain other mammals, Dutch anatomist Louis Bolk concluded that human beings evolved as the result of retarded development, or "neoteny."[27] In Bolk's view, the dominant motif in human development is that humans retain juvenile traits as adults. He wrote, "If I wished to express the basic principles of my ideas in a somewhat strongly worded sentence, I would say that *man, in his bodily development, is a primate fetus that has become sexually mature.*"[28]

While few scientists today believe that the evolution of humans proceeded as the result of retarded development alone, most experts in the field acknowledge that neoteny plays a central role in human development. Primates in general exhibit delayed development compared to other animals of similar size. They tend to live longer, mature more slowly, and have longer gestation periods.[29] And, unlike other animals, primates' brains continue to develop even after birth.[30] But human development is protracted even by primate standards: we have longer life spans, we mature later, and our bones take longer to ossify.[31] Indeed, the physical characteristics most often identified as distinguishing us as human beings—our upright posture, the shape of our face and head, and the size of our brain—are the result, at least in part, of retaining the traits of primate fetuses further into our development.

Like humans, embryonic apes and monkeys have a big toe which is not opposable, a bulbous cranium, a small jaw, and a large brain relative to body size.[32] Humans retain these traits throughout their lives, resulting in a strong foot (necessary for walking on two feet), a large brain, and the characteristic shape of our face and head.[33] During the development of apes and monkeys, the big toe rotates to the side, where it can be placed opposite the others and used for grasping; the jaw grows faster than the rest of the body, producing a pronounced muzzle; and the rapid fetal growth rates of the cranium and brain drop off shortly after birth.[34] Because our cranium and brain continue to grow at rapid fetal rates for significantly longer into development, our cranium and brain are larger, relative to our body size, than those of apes and monkeys.[35] The brain in chimps and gorillas attains 70 percent of its final size by early in the first year.[36] Ours does not reach the same figure until two years later.[37]

The retention of juvenile traits even plays a role in humans' unique social structure. Because humans develop at a slower rate than other animals, we take longer to mature.[38] The protracted nature of our development necessitates a stronger tie between parents and offspring than that found in other species, a tie that anchors families and increases the opportunities for our young to learn.[39] Gould writes that our tendency to retain juvenile traits

> has reacted synergistically with other hallmarks of hominization—with intelligence (by enlarging the brain through prolongation of fetal growth tendencies and by providing a longer period of childhood learning) and with socialization (by cementing family units through increased parental care of slowly developing offspring). It is hard to imagine how distinctive a suite of characteristics could have emerged outside the context of human development. This is what Morris Cohen, the distinguished philosopher and historian, had in mind when he wrote that prolonged infancy was "more important, perhaps, than any other anatomical facts which distinguish *homo sapiens* [sic] from the rest of the animal kingdom."[40]

VII

We noted earlier in this chapter that when abortion proponents argue that the unborn are not "human beings," they are not really referring to human beings at all. They maintain that one can be a human being for some purposes but not for others, or that whether the unborn are human turns on personal or public opinion. But the term "human being" is not so conveniently protean. It is more than simply a fiction to distinguish those whose right to life we choose to recognize from those we do not. The word "human being" has meaning, and it refers by definition to the unborn.

Why do proponents of abortion argue that the unborn are not "human beings" if that is not really what they mean? The logic behind such arguments may be fallacious, but it is also revealing. Most abortion proponents who use these arguments would find it troubling that abortion involves the death of human beings. By convincing themselves that the unborn are not human, they quell the jarring dissonance inherent in accepting the propositions that all human beings have a right to life and that abortion should be a "fundamental right." True, many of these same individuals argue elsewhere that women should be allowed to abort even if the unborn *are* human beings. But why do they devote so much attention—and contorted reasoning—to the issue of whether the unborn are human if they are really comfortable with the idea that abortion involves killing human beings?

Over a century ago, Frederick Douglass charged that *Dred Scott* would not stand because it was "an attempt to undo what God has done, to blot out the broad distinction instituted by the Allwise, between men and things."[41] The current acceptance of abortion is the result, in large part, of a similar attempt to blot out the distinction between human beings and mere things. In its decisions upholding the "right" to abortion, the Supreme Court has continually tried to downplay, and even deny, the fact that abortion involves the death of human beings. Unlike Douglass, the Court recognizes no "broad distinction" between human beings and other forms of life. Explaining why it believes the right to abortion is guaranteed by language in the Constitution providing that no person can be deprived of "liberty" without due process of law, the Court recently wrote:

> Our cases recognize "the right of the *individual*, married or single, to be free from unwarranted governmental intrusion into matters so fundamentally affecting a person as the decision whether to bear or beget a child" . . . These matters, involving the most intimate and personal choices a person may make in a lifetime, choices central to personal dignity and autonomy, are central to the liberty protected by the Fourteenth Amendment. *At the heart of liberty is the right to define one's own concept of existence, of meaning, of the universe, and of the mystery of human life.*[42]

The last sentence is a chilling—and unintentionally accurate—summation of the Court's view of "liberty" when it comes to abortion: *You can deny the existence of life itself; you can sculpt your own meaning for "human being"; you can subscribe to beliefs as ridiculous as the notion that the sun revolves around the earth; and you can take the lives of those you refuse to label "humans."*

Ultimately, however, the fact that much of the support for abortion is premised upon denying the humanity of the unborn may prove the undoing of the abortion movement. Many abortion proponents have not renounced the principle that every human has a right to life. They are simply unaware that the unborn are human beings. If these individuals can be persuaded to seriously re-examine the question of whether the unborn are humans, many will realize that their positions on abortion and on the right to life of all human beings are mutually exclusive. Some of these individuals may continue to support abortion, but many—perhaps even most—will hold true to the principle that every human being has a right to life and reverse their position on abortion.

In a recent address at the United States Holocaust Memorial Museum, Supreme Court Justice Ruth Bader Ginsburg said, "One of the lessons of this . . . [m]useum for people like me is the necessity of holding tight to our humanity, our human decency, so that never in the name of law, will we codify and preside over a legal regime that denies the humanity of others."[43] Justice Ginsburg believes that women have a constitutionally protected right to abort their young. But her eloquent statement about the meaning of the Holocaust Museum shows that she supports abortion only because she does not realize that the unborn are human beings. Could one hold tight to his humanity and yet insist that some human beings have no right to life? Could one hold tight to his "human decency" and yet insist that some human beings have no intrinsic worth? No. Justice Ginsburg has not renounced the view that all human beings have a right to life. Not yet. But by assuming that the unborn are not human, she has unwittingly become a principal player in her own worst nightmare: a legal regime that denies that some human beings are human.

NOTES

1. Mortimer J. Adler, *Ten Philosophical Mistakes* (New York: Macmillan, 1985), 157.

2. *Thornburgh v. American College of Obstetricians and Gynecologists,* 476 U.S. 747, 779 (1986).

3. 476 U.S. at 778.

4. Arthur Frederick Ide, *Abortion Handbook: The History, Legal Process, Practice and Psychology of Abortion,* 3rd ed. (Las Calinas, TX: Liberal Press, 1988), 22.

5. 476 U.S. 747, 792.

6. Celeste Michelle Condit, *Decoding Abortion Rhetoric: Communicating Social Change* (Urbana: University of Illinois Press, 1990), 213. (Con-

dit's argument also falls into the begging-the-question fallacy discussed previously.)

7. Brief for Appellants at 122–123, reprinted in Philip B. Kurland and Gerald Casper, eds., *Landmark Briefs and Arguments of the Supreme Court of the United States: Constitutional Law*, vol. 75 (Washington, D.C.: University Publications of America, 1975), 202–203.

8. Mary Anne Warren, "On the Moral and Legal Status of Abortion," *Ethical Issues in Modern Medicine*, eds. John Arras and Robert Hunt (Palo Alto, CA: Mayfield, 1977), 168.

9. Warren, 168.

10. Fyodor Dostoyevsky, *Notes from Underground*, in *Notes from Underground, Poor People, The Friend of the Family; Three Short Novels*, trans. Constance Garnett (New York: Dell, 1960), 140.

11. Stephen Jay Gould, "Biological Potentiality vs. Biological Determinism," *Ever Since Darwin: Reflections in Natural History* (New York: Norton, 1977), 251.

12. *The American Heritage Dictionary*, 2d College ed. (1985).

13. *The Oxford English Dictionary*, 2d ed. (1989).

14. Quoted in Adler, *Ten Philosophical Mistakes*, 157.

15. Quoted in Gould, "Biological Potentiality," 259.

16. Viva Hardigg, "All in the Family?" *U.S. News & World Report*, November 1, 1993: 69.

17. Quoted in Hardigg, 73.

18. Hardigg, 69.

19. Quoted in Hardigg, 69.

20. Suzanne La Follette, "The Beginnings of Emancipation," *Concerning Women* (1926; New York: Arno, 1972), 13.

21. Gould, "Why We Should Not Name Races," *Ever Since Darwin*, 232.

22. Gina Kolata, "Fetal Ovary Transplant Envisioned," *New York Times*, January 6, 1994: A-16.

23. Kolata, "Fetal Ovary Transplant Envisioned."

24. Kolata, "Fetal Ovary Transplant Envisioned."

25. Jane English, "Abortion and the Concept of a Person," *Canadian Journal of Philosophy* 5 (1975): 235. (The argument that the unborn is simply "part of the woman" falls into the same category.)

26. Richard John Neuhaus, "Don't Cross This Threshhold," *Wall Street Journal*, October 27, 1994: A20.

27. Stephen Jay Gould, *Ontogeny and Phylogeny* (Cambridge, MA: Belknap–Harvard University Press, 1977), 356–362.

28. Louis Bolk, *Das Problem der Menschwerdung* (Jena: Fischer, 1926), 8, quoted in Gould, *Ontogeny and Phylogeny*, 361 (emphasis added).

29. Gould, *Ontogeny and Phylogeny*, 366.

30. Gould, *Ontogeny and Phylogeny*, 371–372.

31. Gould, *Ontogeny and Phylogeny*, 366–369.

32. Gould, *Ontogeny and Phylogeny*, 372–375, 381–382.

33. Gould, *Ontogeny and Phylogeny*, 372–375, 381–382.

34. Gould, *Ontogeny and Phylogeny*, 371–372.

35. Gould, *Ontogeny and Phylogeny*, 372.

36. Gould, *Ontogeny and Phylogeny*, 372.

37. Gould, *Ontogeny and Phylogeny*, 372.

38. Gould, *Ontogeny and Phylogeny*, 396–400.

39. Gould, *Ontogeny and Phylogeny*, 402–404.

40. Gould, *Ontogeny and Phylogeny*, 400 (quoting Morris Cohen, *The Meaning of Human History* [La Salle, IL: Open Court, 1947], 174).

41. Frederic M. Holland, *Frederick Douglass: The Colored Orator*, 2d ed. (New York: Haskell, 1969), 258.

42. *Planned Parenthood v. Casey*, 505 U.S. 833, 851 (citations omitted) (last emphasis added).

43. *United States Holocaust Memorial Museum Update*, January/February 1995: 2.

4

Persons

"When *I* use a word," Humpty Dumpty said, in a rather scornful tone, "it means just what I choose it to mean—neither more nor less."

"The question is," said Alice, "whether you can make words mean so many things."

Lewis Carroll, Through the Looking-Glass

In the modern social order the *person* is sacrificed to the *individual*. The individual is given universal suffrage, equality of rights, freedom of opinion; while the person, isolated, naked, without the social armor to sustain and protect him is left to the mercy of all the devouring forces which threaten the life of the soul, exposed to the relentless actions and reactions of conflicting interests and appetites. . . . It is a homicidal civilization.

Jacques Maritain, Three Reformers

In the two preceding chapters, we examined whether the unborn are alive and whether they are human beings. At least one other major issue concerning the status of the unborn inevitably surfaces in discussions of abortion: whether the unborn are "persons." The attention devoted to this issue is largely attributable to the logic the Supreme Court used in *Roe v. Wade*. In *Roe*, the Court concluded that, regardless of whether the unborn were living human beings, they had no right to life because they were not "persons."[1] The implication behind the Court's reasoning is that a living human being is not necessarily a "person." A significant number of abortion proponents have seized upon this argument and taken the position that, even if the unborn are human beings, they are not "persons" and therefore women should be free to abort them.

The first step in determining whether the unborn are persons is to establish just what the word "person" means. "Person" derives from the Latin *persona*, a term which originally referred to an actor's mask.[2] In medieval Latin, *persona* came to mean "a human being" as well. The word "person" itself did not appear until Middle English, where it referred both to a human being and to "a character assumed in a play or actual life." By the fifteenth century, "person" had also taken on a legal meaning: entities recognized by law as having rights and duties—like corporations—were referred to as "persons" to distinguish them from entities without legal rights and duties. In modern usage, the word "person" means:

1. A living human being, esp. as distinguished from an animal or thing. 2. The composite of characteristics that make up an individual personality. 3. An individual of specified character: *a person of importance.* 4. The living body of a human being: *searched the prisoner's person for drugs.* 5. Guise; character: *"Well, in her person, I say I will not have you. . . . "* 6. Physique and general appearance. 7. *Law.* A human being or organization with legal rights and duties. 8. *Theol.* The separate individualities of Father, Son, and Holy Spirit, as distinguished from the essence of the Godhead that unites them. 9. *Gram.* a. Any of three groups of pronoun forms with the corresponding verb inflections that distinguish between the speaker (first person), the individual addressed (second person), and the individual or thing spoken of (third person). b. Any of the different forms or inflections expressing these distinctions.[3]

Of these various meanings of "person," only three—the first, second, and seventh—are arguably relevant to the issue of abortion. And only the first and second definitions are germane to the particular question that concerns us here: whether the law should protect the lives of the unborn. The seventh definition of "person"—"a human being or organization with legal rights and duties"—lists the meaning of the word as a legal term of art. When used as a legal term of art, "person" distinguishes entities that possess legal rights or duties from those that do not. If the law recognized the rights and duties only of corporations and women with gray hair, then only corporations and women with gray hair would be "persons" in this sense of the word. The meaning of "person" as a legal term of art is irrelevant for purposes of our analysis because we are concerned not with whether the unborn *have* legal rights, but whether they *should* have them. As a matter of logic, one cannot validly conclude that the unborn should have no rights simply because they do not have them now.

That leaves the first and second definitions of "person." When abortion proponents assert that the unborn are not "persons," what are they arguing? Are they maintaining that the unborn are not "living human beings?" Are they arguing that the unborn lack "the composite of characteristics that make up the individual personality?" Or, are they mistakenly using the word "person" to point to some other difference which they feel distinguishes the unborn from born human beings? The answer depends upon whom one asks, but all three approaches are well represented among proponents of abortion.

"LIVING HUMAN BEINGS"

Take, for instance, the argument that the unborn are not "persons" because they are not "living human beings." Justice John Paul Stevens, a member of the Supreme Court who is generally predisposed to affording broad constitutional protection to "abortion rights," is one proponent of this view. The fact that Stevens considers "person" to be synonymous with "human being" is clear from his concurrence in *Thornburgh v. American College of Obstetricians and Gynecologists.*[4] There, he wrote, "[U]nless the religious view that a fetus is a 'person' is adopted . . . , there is a fundamental and well-recognized difference between a fetus and a human being; indeed, if there is not such a difference, the permissibility of terminating the life of the fetus could hardly be left to the will of the state legislatures."[5]

Most lay people—whether they identify themselves as pro-choice, pro-life, or something in between—ascribe the same meaning to "person" that Justice Stevens does. They assume that the word means "living human being." The problem with arguing that the unborn are not persons because they are not living or not human, however, should be obvious to anyone who has read the two preceding chapters: the unborn are indisputably living human beings.

Before we turn our attention from this meaning of "person" entirely, however, we should note one respect in which this definition of "person" differs from the others. When abortion proponents argue that the unborn have no right to life because they are not "persons," there is a fundamental difference between those who mean "persons" in the sense of "living human beings"—the definition we have just discussed—and those who attribute some other meaning to the word. Those who treat "person" and "living human being" as equivalent may still believe that society should protect the lives of all human beings. Those who do not treat "person" and "living human being" as equivalent—such as those who resort to any of the following definitions of person—necessarily believe that the unborn have no right to life *whether they are human beings or not.*

"THE COMPOSITE OF CHARACTERISTICS THAT MAKE UP AN INDIVIDUAL PERSONALITY"

We turn our attention now to the last of the "official" definitions of "person": "the composite of characteristics that make up an individual personality." Do abortion proponents mean to assert that the unborn lack this "composite of characteristics" when they assert that the unborn are not persons? If so, how persuasive is their position?

Arguments that rely on this definition of "person" are more difficult to refute because they are intrinsically more vague. One can scientifically determine whether an organism is living or a human being. More latitude exists in determining whether one possesses "the composite of characteristics that make up an individual personality."

Nevertheless, some grave problems exist with this position. First, do we really know that the unborn have no personalities? We manifest our personalities through our behavior: by what we say, what we wear, and through a myriad of other ways we interact with one another and our surroundings. Assuming, for the moment, that the unborn do have personalities, how would we know given their environment? They rest in a confined space, surrounded by amniotic fluid and darkness, and do not know how to communicate with us. Kindergartners certainly have personalities, but if one bound and gagged a kindergartner and locked him in a trunk, would those who saw the trunk know that an organism with a personality lay inside? If one could get some crude sort of ultrasound pictures of the inside of that trunk and compare it to one of a trunk containing a baboon, would we be able to tell which of the two organisms had a personality based solely on their behavior inside the trunks?

The notion that human beings have a right to life only when they exhibit the attributes of an individual personality is problematic in other respects as well. If one need only have the *potential* to manifest a personality, then the unborn have a right to life: whether or not they have a personality in the womb, they clearly have the potential to manifest one in the future. If, however, the right to life extends only to those who *presently* manifest the characteristics of a personality, then we must have no right to life if we are unconscious or even asleep.

Furthermore, if the right to life turns on whether a human being has the attributes of an individual personality, is it clear that infants necessarily possess those attributes from the moment of birth? Not according to Germany's highest court. During the course of ruling that Germany's constitution protected the lives of the unborn, the Federal Constitutional Court wrote, "The process of development . . . is a continuing process which exhibits no sharp demarcation and does not allow a precise division of the various steps of development of the human life. The process does not end even with birth; *the phenomena of consciousness which are specific to the human personality, for example, appear for the first time a rather long time after birth.*"[6]

A certain amount of experience—and particularly interaction with others—is probably required before a newborn acquires the attributes of an individual personality. For instance, suppose that seconds after delivery, a newborn infant is placed in a completely dark, soundproof room. Fresh air is pumped in so the child has plenty of oxygen, and intravenous tubes supply his or her nutritional needs. Otherwise, however, the child is sealed off from all human interaction for the next three years. Will the child that emerges at the end of that period have any more of the "composite of characteristics that make up the individual personality" than a typical newborn? For that matter, will the child after two years in the room have more of a personality than an unborn at six months?

If a certain amount of human interaction (or other experience outside the womb) is required before a child possesses the attributes of an individual personality, and those attributes must be present before the child has a right to life, then a child has no right to life when born.

ALTERNATIVE DEFINITIONS OF "PERSON"

Readers familiar with abortion-related literature will probably have realized that certain definitions of "person" advanced by abortion proponents do not fit within any of the definitions of the word discussed thus far. I will refer to these purported definitions of "person" as "alternative definitions." Before examining the flaw inherent in arguments that rely on these definitions, it might be helpful to examine some of the definitions that fall into this category.

Examples of Some Alternative Definitions

Michael Tooley argues that whether an entity is a person depends on whether it has a right to life. He writes, "How is the term 'person' to be interpreted? I shall treat the concept of a person as a purely moral concept, free of all descriptive context. Specifically, in my usage, the sentence 'X is a person' will be synonymous with 'X has a (serious) moral right to life.' "[7] According to Tooley, any organism that is a person must possess "the concept of a self as a continuing subject of experiences and other mental states, and believe that it is such a continuing entity."[8] He argues, therefore, that some infants are not persons—they have no right to life—but certain non-human animals may be persons.[9]

Mary Anne Warren utilizes a different alternative definition. She writes that whether one is person depends upon the presence of five factors:[10]

1. consciousness (of objects and events external and/or internal to the being), and in particular, the capacity to feel pain;
2. reasoning (the *developed* capacity to solve new and relatively complex problems);
3. self-motivated activity (activity that is relatively independent of either genetic or direct external control);
4. the capacity to communicate, by whatever means, messages of an indefinite variety of types, that is, not just with an indefinite number of contents, but on indefinitely many possible topics; and,
5. self-concepts and self-awareness, either individual or racial or both.

Based upon these criteria, Warren argues, "Some human beings are not people, and there may well be people who are not human beings. A man or woman whose consciousness has been permanently obliterated but who remains alive is a human being who is no longer a person; defective human beings with no appreciable mental capacity, are not and presumably never will be people."[11] With regard to the unborn, she writes, "[I]n the *relevant* respects, a fetus, even a fully developed one, is considerably less personlike than is the average mature mammal, indeed the average fish. . . . [I]f the right to life is based upon [the unborn's] resemblance to a person, then it cannot be said to have any more right to life than, let us say, a newborn guppy."[12]

Peter Wenz's definition of "person" attributes more significance to the physical appearance of the unborn. According to Wenz, the unborn are "persons" with a right to life only when they become "substantially similar" to newborns. "Zygotes and embryos are not people," he argues, "whereas eight-month fetuses (usually) are people."[13] Wenz maintains that the reason for the distinction is the biological complexity of the unborn:

They [zygotes and embryos] do not have the organs or sensitivities of newborns. Zygotes and embryos lack the right to life because they are so unlike other human beings.[14] Their current state of being is much more primitive than birds or mammals which lack the right to life in our law. . . . As long as an embryo is still an embryo its rights are the same as those of other comparably simple organisms. In short, it has no rights at all because its degree of biological complexity is similar to that of insects, to whom we ascribe no rights at all.[15]

Problems with the Alternative Definitions

The definitions Tooley, Warren, and Wenz advance each have their own particular weaknesses. Tooley frankly admits that newborns are not "persons" within his definition of the term.[16] In his view, killing a child becomes wrong only after a child acquires "morally significant" properties, an event he argues occurs approximately three months after birth.[17] As the child grows older, according to Tooley, its "destruction becomes more and more serious until eventually it is comparable in seriousness to the destruction of a normal adult human being."[18]

Warren makes the fatal assumption that the characteristics of *some* persons define those of *all* persons (a variation of the "begging the question" fallacy we discussed in the last chapter). She might as well have reasoned that men cannot be persons because women are persons and men differ from women. Furthermore, like Tooley, Warren acknowledges that newborns do not fit within her definition of "person" and contends they have no right to life.[19]

Wenz's "biological complexity" argument also begs the question. When he argues that the unborn are not persons until late in their development because they do not resemble born human beings, Wenz assumes that the characteristics of born human beings define those of all persons. His argument also relies on some faulty biological assumptions. For instance, Wenz argues that the law should not protect human beings until they are more anatomically complex than other organisms. But, even as adults, humans are no more anatomically complex than apes and many other animals. Under Wenz's approach, the law would protect these animals as much as adult humans. In fact, the young of certain animals might be entitled to *more* protection than human newborns and toddlers. As noted in the previous chapter, humans develop more slowly than other animals. Biologist Stephen Jay Gould writes that human growth and development proceeds "at a snail's pace" compared to that of other primates and that development in humans during the year after birth resembles the growth and development of primate and mammalian *fetuses*—not their newborns.[20]

In addition to their individual weaknesses, all three positions—Tooley's, Warren's, and Wenz's—share a common flaw, one that plagues every argument that utilizes one of the "alternative" definitions of "person." Although nominally these arguments assert that the unborn are not "persons," the arguments are not really referring to persons at all. If they were, their definitions of "person" would comport with one of the actual definitions of the word set forth earlier in this chapter. Instead, the proponents of these arguments are attempting to create new definitions for "person"—definitions tailored to exclude the unborn. In most instances where it is used in these arguments, "person" is devoid of any meaning save "a being with a right to life." If an organism has a right to life then it is a "person"; if not, it must be something else.

If the abortion proponents who resort to these arguments are not really referring to whether the unborn are persons, if they are simply attempting to distinguish which forms of life society should protect and which it should not, why do they cast their arguments in terms of whether the unborn are "persons"? In most instances, they are probably not trying to be deceptive. Rather, they argue that the unborn are not persons for much the same reason they argue that the unborn are not "human beings": there is a pervasive tendency in modern society—even among many supporters of abortion—to assume that every person has a right to life. Since they are convinced that the unborn have no right to life, many abortion proponents reason backward and conclude that the unborn cannot be persons. They shore up their position by inventing their own definitions of "person"—definitions that exclude the unborn and any others they feel have no right to life. These linguistic contortions serve only to switch the labels, of course. But they do provide a convenient—if illogical—means of reconciling the irreconcilable notions that all persons have a right to life and that a woman must be allowed to rid herself of her unborn young if she has the inclination.

Assuming that we are in fact talking about "persons"—and not simply using the term as a code word to distinguish between those whose right to life we recognize and those we do not—which definition of "person" is most germane when we discuss whether we should recognize the right to life of the unborn? Is it whether the unborn are "living human beings" or whether they possess "the composite of characteristics which make up the individual personality"?

If every living human being is a "person," then one is a person simply by virtue of being a human. If, however, "persons" must presently manifest the attributes of an individual personality, then some human beings are not persons. Given the seriousness of the consequences that can follow from classifying human beings as non-persons, there is good reason to err on the side of inclusion. Those most aware of the perils of depriving human beings of even the title of "persons" are those who have been branded non-persons themselves. During his struggle against apartheid in South Africa, Archbishop Desmond Tutu reminded an audience, *"A person is a person because he recognizes others as persons."*21 Holocaust survivor Elie Wiesel makes a similar point. In his introduction to a book on the atrocities perpetrated by Nazi doctors at the concentration camps, he warns:

When human beings become abstractions, what is left? . . . [T]hose who, in the 1920s or 1930s, studied how to reduce life and the mystery of life to abstractions, were perhaps not equipped to resist the temptation of evil, for to them, it wasn't evil. . . . [The Nazis] knew how to differentiate between good and evil. Their sense of *reality* was impaired. Human beings were not human beings in their eyes. They were abstractions. . . . [W]e must not see *any* person as an abstraction. Instead we must see in every person a universe with its own secrets, with its own treasures, with its own sources of anguish, and with some measure of triumph.[22]

Human beings—not personalities—are the morally significant entities here. Many people believe that infants do not possess the attributes of an individual personality when first born, but how many believe that they have no right to life? Do any of us seriously believe that a psychological patient with two distinct personalities has more of a right to life than a man or woman with only one?

Finally, in the event that we decide that whether an individual is a "person" turns on some criterion other than whether he or she is a human being, we should at least be honest with ourselves. We should openly admit that whether the unborn are "persons" has nothing to do with whether they are human beings; we should purge ourselves of the notion that every human being is a person simply by virtue of being human; and we should disclose just which definition of "person" we mean when we assert that it excludes the unborn, rather than simply using "person" as a code word to distinguish those human beings whose right to life we choose to recognize from those we do not.

These measures will seem reasonable if there is nothing wrong with how we define "person." However, if we cannot justify our position without cloaking it in euphemisms, obscurities, or half-truths, then perhaps we should choose new criteria—criteria we can defend even when it is clear what they stand for.

"Eriptur persona, manet res," Lucretius wrote: "The mask is torn off, the reality remains."[23]

NOTES

1. *Roe v. Wade*, 410 U.S. 113, 157–158.

2. The history of "person" is based on the history for the word in *Webster's Word Histories* (Springfield, MA: Merriam-Webster, 1989), 353–354.

3. *The American Heritage Dictionary*, 2d College ed. (1985). This definition does not materially differ from the definitions attributed to "person" in other dictionaries. See, for example, *The Oxford Dictionary of Modern English*, 2d ed. (1986) and *Webster's New World Dictionary*, 3rd College ed. (1986).

4. *Thornburgh v. American College of Obstetricians and Gynecologists*, 476 U.S. 747 (1986).

5. 476 U.S. at 792. The Tennessee Supreme Court attributed the same meaning to the word "person" in the "frozen embryos case," *Davis v. Davis*, 842 S.W.2d 588 (Tenn. 1992), *cert. denied sub nom. Stowe v. Davis*, 507 U.S. 911 (1993). That case involved a dispute between a divorced couple as to who had the right to determine the fate of some frozen embryos prepared from the woman's eggs and man's sperm when the couple was still married. The Tennessee Supreme Court held that, where there was no agreement between the couple, the party wanting the embryos destroyed must prevail over the party wanting the embryos implanted and brought to term. In reaching that conclusion, the court determined that the trial court had erred by relying on expert testimony that human life begins at conception. Because the unborn were not treated as "persons" under either Federal or Tennessee law, the Tennessee Supreme Court explained, they were "not yet legally recognizable as human life." 842 S.W.2d at 594–596.

6. *Judgment of February 25, 1975*, 39 BVerfGE 1, translated in Robert E. Jonas and John D. Gorby, "West German Abortion Decision: A Contrast to *Roe v. Wade*," *John Marshall Journal of Practice and Procedure* 9 (1976): 638 (emphasis added).

7. Michael Tooley, "Abortion and Infanticide," in *The Ethics of Abortion*, eds. Robert M. Baird and Stuart Rosenbaum (Buffalo, NY: Prometheus, 1989), 47.

8. Tooley, "Abortion and Infanticide," *The Ethics of Abortion*, 49.

9. Michael Tooley, *Abortion and Infanticide* (Oxford, England: Clarendon-Oxford University Press, 1983), 411–412.

10. Mary Anne Warren, "On the Moral and Legal Status of Abortion," *Ethical Issues in Modern Medicine*, eds. John Arras and Robert Hunt (Palo Alto, CA: Mayfield, 1977), 170.

11. Warren, 171.

12. Warren, 172–173.

13. Peter Wenz, *Abortion Rights as Religious Freedom* (Philadelphia: Temple University Press, 1992), 77.

14. Wenz's reference to zygotes and embryos being "so unlike *other human beings*" suggests that he himself believes that the unborn are—or at least may be—human beings.

15. Wenz, 66–67.

16. Tooley, *Abortion and Infanticide*, 411–412.

17. Tooley, *Abortion and Infanticide*, 411–412.

18. Tooley, *Abortion and Infanticide*, 411–412.

19. Warren, 175.

20. Stephen Jay Gould, "Human Babies as Embryos," *Ever Since Darwin: Reflections in Natural History* (New York: Norton, 1977), 73.

21. Address at enthronement as Anglican Archbishop of Capetown, 7 September 1986, quoted in James B. Simpson, comp., *Simpson's Contempo-*

rary Quotations: The Most Notable Quotes Since 1950 (Boston: Houghton Mifflin, 1988), 243 (emphasis added).

22. Elie Wiesel, foreword, *The Nazi Doctors and the Nuremberg Code: Human Rights in Human Experimentation*, ed. George J. Annas and Michael A. Grodin (New York: Oxford University Press, 1992), ix.

23. Lucretius, *De Rerum Natura*, Bk. iii., c. 58, quoted in Burton Stevenson, ed., *The Home Book of Quotations: Classical and Modern*, 10th ed. (New York: Dodd, Mead, 1967), 2050.

5

Drawing the Circle

[T]hough I am more closely connected and identified with one class of outraged, oppressed, and enslaved people, I cannot allow myself to be insensible to the wrongs and sufferings of any part of the great family of man. I am bound to use my powers for the welfare of the whole human brotherhood.

Frederick Douglass

Will you decide what men shall live and what men shall die? It may be that in the sight of Heaven, you are more worthless and less fit to live than millions like this poor man's child. Oh God! to hear the Insect on the leaf pronouncing on the too much life among his hungry brothers in the dust.

Charles Dickens, *A Christmas Carol*

It should be obvious by this point that there are grave problems with denying the unborn a right to life on the theory that they are not living, human, or—in any meaningful sense of the word—not "persons." It remains for us, however, to make the affirmative case for why the unborn should have a right to life: to explain why, when society draws the circle around those whose lives it will protect, the unborn should fall inside—not outside—that circle.

As a strictly logical matter, I doubt whether one can *prove* that every human being—or for that matter even every born human being—should have a right to life. Reaching such a conclusion requires more than simply working through a series of value-neutral syllogisms. Certain value judgments factor into the equation. The notion that some—or all—human beings have a right to life benefits each of us to the extent that others must recognize our right to life, but, at the same time, it curtails our freedom to the extent that we have to recognize that right in others. There is a trade-off. Whether an individual deems the benefits of that trade-off to outweigh the costs depends on the relative importance he or she ascribes to these competing interests.

Most people are willing to recognize a right to life in others so long as their own right to life is recognized; they are willing to trade some freedom for a little security. Civilized society is based upon that very principle. However, there are exceptions. Newspapers regularly detail the tragic stories of individuals willing to take the lives of others even if they forfeit their own in the process.

Though it may be impossible to construct a value-neutral proof to show that every human being has a right to live, the conclusion that the unborn (and all other human beings) have a right to life necessarily follows from a principle that is almost universally accepted in our society: One cannot believe that all humans are created equal and that each is endowed with an inalienable right to life and yet deny that the unborn have a right to life. The unborn, as we have discussed in previous chapters, are incontrovertibly living human beings.

I

The principle that all "men" have a right to life and are created equal has been one of our nation's ideological cornerstones since its inception. The Declaration of Independence proclaims, "We hold these Truths to be self-evident, that all Men are created equal, that they are endowed by their Creator with certain unalienable Rights, that among these are Life, Liberty, and the pursuit of Happiness."[1]

Most Americans—even those who support abortion—agree that all "men" are equal and that each has a right to life. The question is, what do we mean when we say "all *men*." *Webster's Third New International Dictionary* provides only three definitions of "man" which could be relevant here: "an adult male human being," "any male human being," and "any human being."[2] Since we all agree that women are equal and have a right to life, presumably we refer to "all human beings" when we say that "all *men*" are equal and have a right to life.

The issue of whether all human beings are entitled to the inalienable rights listed in the Declaration troubled America long before the Supreme Court handed down its opinion in *Roe v. Wade*. The battle over slavery, which raged throughout much of the nation's first century, was understood by those on both sides to be a battle over whether all human beings had these rights. The abolitionists typically maintained that all humans had rights simply by virtue of being human beings. "The Constitution knows all the *human* inhabitants of this country as 'the people,' " Frederick Douglass argued. "It makes . . . no discrimination in favor of, or against, any class of the people, but is fitted to protect and preserve the rights of all."[3] Those proponents of slavery who recognized blacks as human rejected the notion that all human beings had rights. "[A]s long as false and pernicious theories are cherished respecting the inherent equality and rights of every human being," one Southern editor wrote on the eve of the Civil War, "there can be no satisfactory political union between the two sections."[4]

Both the abolitionists and their opponents addressed the specific language in the Declaration of Independence proclaiming that all men are equal and have certain inalienable rights. Chief Justice Roger Taney confronted the issue in his opinion for the Supreme Court in *Dred Scott v. Sandford*, the infamous 1857 case which held that blacks were not citizens and stated that it was unconstitutional for the Federal government to compel—or even allow—a state to ban slavery within its borders. After quoting the language in the Declaration stating that all men are created equal and have certain inalienable rights, Taney explained that the Declaration did not refer to "all *human beings*" when it said "all *men*":

> The general words . . . seem to embrace the whole human family, and if they were used in a similar instrument of this day would be so understood. But it is too clear for dispute, that the enslaved African race were not intended to be included, and formed no part of the people who framed and adopted this Declaration; for if the language, as understood in that day, would embrace them, the conduct of the distinguished men who framed the Declaration of Independence would have been utterly and flagrantly inconsistent with the principles they asserted. . . .

Yet the men who framed this Declaration were great men—high in literary acquirements—high in their sense of honor, and incapable of asserting principles inconsistent with those on which they were acting. They perfectly understood the meaning of the language they used, and how it would be understood by others; and they knew that it would not, in any part of the civilized world, be supposed to embrace the negro race.[5]

In a speech given in Springfield, Illinois that same year, Abraham Lincoln explained his conception—an entirely different one—of what the Declaration meant when it proclaimed all men equal and endowed with certain inalienable rights:

I think the authors of that notable instrument [the Declaration of Independence] intended to include all men, but they did not mean to declare all men equal in all respects. They did not mean to say that all were equal in color, or size, or intellect, moral development, or social capacity. They defined in tolerable distinctness in what respects they did consider all men created equal—equal with "certain inalienable rights, among which are life, liberty, and the pursuit of happiness." This they said and this they meant. They did not mean to assert the obvious untruth that all men were then actually enjoying that equality, nor yet that they were about to confer it immediately upon them. . . .

They meant to set up a standard maxim for a free society, which should be familiar to all, and revered by all; constantly looked to, constantly labored for, and even though never perfectly attained, constantly approximated, and thereby constantly spreading and deepening its influence and augmenting the happiness and value of life to all people of all colors everywhere.[6]

There can be no doubt that, when Lincoln read the proclamation that "all men" are created equal, he understood the words "all *men*" to be synonymous with "all *human beings.*" Moments after he had articulated his own view of the Declaration's language, Lincoln referred to the proposition advanced by Justice Taney, and echoed by Stephen Douglas, that the Declaration did not refer to blacks when it referred to "all men." Lincoln said he rejected that assertion because it "*dehumanized*" blacks and suggested they were not "*human beings.*"[7]

Philosopher Mortimer Adler referred to Lincoln's speech in a book he authored commemorating the 200th anniversary of the Constitution. There, Adler writes, "Lincoln insisted that the language of the Declaration should be interpreted as including all human beings without regard to sex or color or other traits that differentiate one group of human beings from another. Lincoln pointed out that . . . all human beings are equal not only in their humanity, but also in having by virtue of their common humanity, the same human rights."[8]

Adler goes on to write that there is one, and only one, respect in which all men are created equal:

> It is that they are all human, all members of one species, called *Homo sapiens*, and all having the same natural and thereby specific attributes that differentiate them from the members of all other species. . . .
>
> When this is understood, it will be seen that there is no conflict or contradiction between saying (1) that all human beings are equal in respect of their common humanity, and (2) that all human beings are also unequal, one with another, in a wide variety of respects in which they differ as individual members of the human species.
>
> Their equality lies in the fact that humans all belong to the same species, possessing the traits common to all members of that species. Their inequality lies in their individual differences as members of that species. All being human, they are all persons, not things; and as persons they all equally have the dignity that inheres in their being persons. But each is not only a person, each is also a uniquely individual person.[9]

Adler's comments are significant in themselves, but especially noteworthy in light of the foreword to his book. The author of that foreword could barely contain his enthusiasm for Adler's work: "When Mortimer Adler writes, his observations are always deserving of the fullest consideration. . . . But when Dr. Adler writes about the Constitution of the United States at this bicentennial time, it may properly be said that one has nothing less than a duty to read and to learn."[10] Ironically, the person who wrote that foreword also wrote the Supreme Court's opinion in *Roe v. Wade*: Justice Harry Blackmun. One cannot help but wonder whether he read Adler's book before penning the foreword. Certainly Adler's view that all human beings are equal and each a "person" is irreconcilable with *Roe*.[11] In *Roe*, Blackmun wrote that the unborn were not persons—and therefore had no right to life—without ever resolving whether they were human beings.

II

But why *should* we have a society built upon the principle that all human beings are created equal and that each has an inherent right to life? Why not recognize a right to life only in *born* human beings? Or, for that matter, why not recognize a right to life only in human beings that are more than three months old?

We must confront some fundamental questions. Is humanity, as Mohandas Ghandi believed, "one undivided and indivisible family?"[12] Do we believe that "no man is an island" and that the death of any human being diminishes us? Do we believe in *human* dignity—that every human being has worth simply by virtue of being human—or do we believe that some human beings are merely "clumps of tissue" or "life unworthy of life"?

No society that truly believes in *human* rights can fail to recognize the right to life of the unborn. Human rights are, by definition, rights which inhere in one simply by virtue of being a human. There are no conditions precedent that must be fulfilled before these rights vest. Explaining why she felt "*Roe v. Wade* has deformed a great nation," Mother Teresa wrote in 1994:

> The so-called right to abortion has pitted mothers against their children and women against men. . . . It has portrayed the greatest of gifts—a child—as a competitor, an intrusion, and an inconvenience. It has nominally accorded mothers unfettered dominance over the independent lives of their physically dependent sons and daughters. And, in granting this not inconsiderable power, it has exposed many women to unjust and selfish demands from their husbands or other sexual partners.
>
> Human rights are not a privilege conferred by the government. They are every human being's entitlement by virtue of his humanity. The right to life does not depend, and must not be declared contingent, on the pleasure of anyone else, not even a parent or sovereign.[13]

The United States often calls attention to the human rights abuses tolerated in other countries, but, by recognizing abortion as a "fundamental right," we have enshrined one in our own. The notion that unborn human beings have no right to life flies in the face of numerous human rights treaties.

The right to life of *all* human beings is protected by the United Nations' Universal Declaration of Human Rights (1948) and the United Nations' International Covenant on Civil and Political Rights (1966). The preamble of the Universal Declaration proclaims that "recognition of the inherent dignity and of the equal and inalienable rights of *all members of the human family* is the foundation of freedom, justice and peace in the world."[14] And article 3 of the same document provides, "Everyone has a right to life." If "all members of the human family" possess "equal and inalienable" rights under the Universal Declaration, then presumably the Declaration refers to "all members of the human family" when it states that "everyone" has a right to life.

The International Covenant on Civil and Political Rights is more straightforward. Article 6 of the Covenant states, "Every human being has the inherent right to life. This right shall be protected by law."[15] And article 2 provides, "Where not already provided for by existing . . . measures, each State Party to the present Covenant undertakes to take the necessary steps . . . to adopt such legislative or other measures as may be necessary to give effect to the rights recognized in the present Covenant."

The right to life of the unborn is also protected by the Convention on the Rights of the Child (1989). Article 6 of the Convention provides that "every child has the inherent right to life."[16] The word "child" is defined in article 1 of the Convention as "every human being below the age of 18 years." Therefore, as human beings below the age of 18, the unborn are "children" within the meaning of the Convention. Language in the preamble supports the conclusion that the Convention applies to unborn human beings as well as to the born. The preamble provides, among other things, that "recognition of the inherent dignity and of the equal . . . rights of *all* members of the human family is the foundation of freedom, justice and peace in the world," and that "the child, by reason of his physical and mental immaturity, needs special safeguards and care, including appropriate legal protection, *before as well as after birth*."

The right to life of the unborn is also protected by at least two human rights treaties adopted by the Organization of American States. Article

1 of the American Declaration of the Rights and Duties of Man (1948) provides, "*Every human being* has the right to life."[17] The American Convention on Human Rights (1969), meanwhile, expressly recognizes the right to life of the unborn. Article 1 states that, for purposes of the Convention, " 'person' means every human being," and article 4 provides, "Every person has the right to have his life respected. This right shall be protected by law and, in general, *from the moment of conception.*"[18] As if anticipating *Roe v. Wade*—which held that the unborn had no right to life under the U.S. Constitution because the framers did not consider them to be "persons"—article 3 of the Convention provides, "Every person has a right to *recognition as a person before the law.*"

III

If the unborn have a right to life, then it follows that whatever rights to reproductive freedom a woman has, the "right" to abort her young is not one of them. We do not recognize rights in dead human beings. The right to life, therefore, is the central right from which all others emanate. Whatever other rights one possesses, those rights are only as secure as his or her right to life. The right to vote, or to free speech, or to freedom of religion, is meaningless if one can be killed before having an opportunity to exercise them.

The alternative to recognizing a right to life in all human beings is to recognize a right to life in just some. Those who concede that the unborn are humans yet insist that they have no right to life necessarily believe that human beings do not have a right to life simply by virtue of being humans; some additional criteria must be met as well. The abortion proponents who fall into this camp, however, do not agree on what these additional criteria are. Some argue that to have a right to life one must possess the "concept of self as a continuing subject of experiences and other mental states, and believe that it is such a continuing entity."[19] Others look for the presence of other factors, like reasoning, the capacity to communicate, a sense of time, concern for others, or idiosyncrasy.[20] The problem with treating any of these alternative criteria as prerequisites for the right to life has to do with how the criteria are derived. How do proponents of these criteria come to the conclusion that their particular criteria determine whether a human being or other organism has a right to life? They typically consider various real or hypothetical living things, separate out those they intuitively feel should have a right to life, and identify one or more common characteristics present in these organisms which distinguish them from the others. Then, reasoning backward, they conclude that these characteristics are required before an individual has a right to life.

This "reasoning backward" approach may be a convenient means of rationalizing our intuitive feelings about who has a right to life, but it is useless for determining whether we recognize a right to life in all those we should. The problem with the approach is that it assumes that our intuitive feelings about who has a right to life are correct. For instance, if I asked a people that practice infanticide to use the same approach to derive the characteristics necessary for the right to life, they would arrive at criteria that exclude newborns. If I made the same request of a people who regard born and unborn human beings as having a right to life, they would arrive at criteria present in both born and unborn human beings. And, if I made the same request of a people who intuitively believed that only human beings of a certain religion had a right to life, they would arrive at criteria that would exclude human beings of other religions.

IV

Ultimately, it is in our own best interest to recognize the right to life of the unborn. If we believe that we can dissociate our fate from that of any class of human beings, we delude ourselves. "Injustice anywhere is a threat to justice everywhere," Martin Luther King wrote. "We are caught up in an inescapable network of mutuality, tied in a single garment of destiny. Whatever affects one affects all indirectly."[21] The relationship between the right to life of the unborn and the right to life of other human beings is a perfect illustration of this "network of mutuality." One cannot deprive any class of human beings—born or unborn—of the right to life without rendering the right to life of the remainder more arbitrary or ephemeral; one cannot deny the unborn a right to life without affecting the right to life of born human beings as well.

Consider, for instance, the difference between recognizing that *every* human being has a right to life and recognizing that only *born* human beings have a right to life. It might seem at first that the right to life of born human beings is as secure under the second standard as the first, but that is not really the case. The problem with recognizing the right to life only of born human beings is that the position is arbitrary—Why should we draw the line at birth? Why not draw it earlier? Or later? Why should a human being's right to life turn solely on *where* it is, as opposed to *what* it is?—and the fact that the position is arbitrary should be disconcerting, for even if the current standard is acceptable, it sets the precedent that the criteria for determining who has a right to life *can* be arbitrary.

Inevitably, some additional criteria must be invoked to justify why born human beings have a right to life but the unborn do not. We have already discussed some examples of these justifications—that the unborn do not have a personality before birth, that a human being is not sufficiently "self-aware" to merit a right to life until after delivery, and so on. Whatever the criteria selected to justify using birth as the threshold, however, the right to life of born human beings is either compromised or becomes more arbitrary, for the particular criteria selected become the real key to the right to life, not whether one is born. For example, if the rationale for choosing birth as the starting point for the right to life is that human beings do not have a personality until after birth, then a society that professes to recognize a right to life of all born human beings either (1) arbitrarily extends the right to born human beings that do not presently manifest a personality (e.g., coma victims, person who are asleep, and perhaps even premature infants and newborns) yet denies the right to the unborn, or (2) does not actually recognize a right to life in all born human beings. In the latter instance, the right to life of born human beings is more ephemeral than in a society that recognizes a right to life in every living human being. Some born human beings would have no right to life.

V

Should one doubt that denying the right to life of the unborn can lead to the erosion of the right to life of born human beings, consider the trend to withhold treatment from "defective" newborns. Typically, the situation involves a newborn with two medical problems: a life-threatening condition that could be corrected (such as intestinal blockage) and another, non-lethal disability which could not be corrected (such as Down's syndrome). In the 1970s and early 1980s, it became common for parents and physicians to agree to withhold or discontinue treatment for these infants simply because the children would remain disabled even if the life-threatening condition were corrected. In 1973, for instance, 43 cases of medical personnel withholding care from disabled newborns were documented at Yale–New Haven Hospital alone.[22] The practice received widespread acceptance in the medical community. A survey of 457 American pediatricians and pediatric surgeons in 1975 revealed that, if the doctors had the sole authority to determine the course of treatment for a Down's syndrome baby with intestinal blockage, a large majority would refuse to authorize the surgery necessary to save the child's life and would withhold all supportive treatment—including tube feedings required to keep the child from starving.[23] At least six of the doctors who responded favored putting the child to death with a lethal injection.[24] In early 1982, a presidential commission on medical ethics submitted a draft report to Surgeon General C. Everett Koop that concluded that some disabled infants were not worth saving.[25]

There can be no question that abortion contributed to the erosion of the right to life of these "defective" infants. Koop observes that, as the medical community grew more receptive to withholding treatment from the infants, there was an increasing tendency among physicians to refer to the disabled child as a "*fetus ex utero.*"[26] And, as in the case of abortion, the "care" prescribed for the children was often rationalized on the basis that they were either not "persons" or not "humanly alive."[27] Some proponents of the active euthanasia of severely disabled newborns even refer to the practice as "postnatal abortion" in an attempt to make the practice more palatable.

In 1984, after a bitter debate, Congress enacted legislation requiring that states implement certain measures to protect disabled children in order to receive Federal grants for child abuse prevention. To receive the grants, states must have programs in place to insure that disabled children are not denied nutrition, appropriate medical treatment, or general care on the basis of their disability, and the state must track and report any instances which do occur.[28] (There is an exception for situations where a child is "chronically and irreversibly comatose" or treatment would merely prolong the dying.[29]) Yet, despite the law, disabled children are still denied necessary medical treatment simply on the basis of their disability. In the first detailed study of the application of the law, Drs. Stephen Wall and John Colin Partridge reviewed the medical records of infants who died over the course of three years in the intensive care nursery at the University of California, San Francisco. They found that, of 121 infants who died following the withholding or withdrawal of medical treatment, doctors had decided to limit the treatment solely for quality-of-life concerns in 23 percent of the deaths.[30]

Indeed, many doctors appear willing to go beyond simply withholding care and are willing to countenance affirmative killing. In June of 1994, for instance, the American Medical Association's Council on Ethical and Judicial Affairs issued a policy statement declaring that it was "ethically acceptable" to remove vital organs from infants with anencephaly while the children were still alive.[31] According to the Council, surveys indicated that two-thirds of leading medical experts in anencephaly and medical ethics also found the practice "intrinsically moral."[32] Although it conceded that opening up living children to cut out vital organs was currently illegal in all 50 states, the Council stated that it issued the policy "in the hope that it will generate a . . . consensus in favor of permitting parental donation of organs from anencephalic neonates before the neonates die."[33]

Not surprisingly, the proponents of killing anencephalic children for their organs point to abortion in support of their position. Jay Friedman defended the removal of anencephalics' organs in a 1992 article in the *Columbia Law Review*. He argued, "The proposals to harvest vital organs from anencephalics are premised on an analysis identical to that used to justify abortion. The moral stricture against harvesting organs applies only to persons. These infants can no more satisfy even minimal criteria of personhood than can fetuses."[34] He explained:

> In common usage, anencephalics might be deemed persons, but that alone bears little weight. In *Roe v. Wade*, the Supreme Court briefly considered the issue of personhood as it relates to fetuses. The conclusion there—that a fetus is not a person for fourteenth amendment purposes—was reached largely on the strength of the finding that abortion statutes existing at the time of the amendment's adoption were liberal, indicating that the framers of the amendment did not intend the term "person" to include the unborn. This interpretive method would probably lead to a similar conclusion about anencephalics. . . . [T]he common law did not view seriously defective infants as full-fledged persons entitled to the protections of the law against homicide.[35]

VI

It may seem at first that our fate is completely removed from that of the unborn or newborns with disabilities, but that is deceptive. All of our fates are intertwined. One cannot deny the right to life of one class of human beings without weakening the right to life of others. Many of us are familiar with Martin Niemöller's haunting warning:

> In Germany the Nazis came for the Communists, and I didn't speak up because I was not a Communist. Then they came for the Jews and I didn't speak up because I was not a Jew. Then they came for the trade unionists and I didn't speak up because I was not a trade unionist. Then they came for the Catholics and I was a Protestant so I did not speak up. Then they came for me. By that time there was no one left to speak for anyone.[36]

Niemöller was not saying that we need only worry if Communists, or union members, or Jews, or Catholics are killed. He was warning that ultimately *it is in our own best interest* to defend the lives and rights of others. Otherwise, there tends to be a domino effect. Killing is messy business. As Lenin—one of the twentieth century's more astute students of human nature—is supposed to have written, "Who says A must say B."[37]

The fact of the matter is that human beings are special *precisely because they are human beings.* In a cynical time such as ours this statement may seem circular, but it is one of the truths the Declaration of Independence concluded was "self-evident" when it stated that all men are endowed with an inalienable right to life. Albert Schweitzer once warned, "Whenever there is lost the consciousness that every man is an object of concern for us just because he is a man, civilization and morals are shaken, and the advance to fully developed inhumanity is only a matter of time."[38]

History provides us with abundant evidence that, when we draw the circle surrounding those whose right to life we will recognize, we tend to draw that circle too narrowly, not too broadly. How often have we recognized a right to life in a class of human beings and concluded later that we were sorry we had? How many horrors could we have averted had we recognized a right to life in those human beings we presumed had none?

There are, of course, those who argue that human beings do not possess an inherent right to life and that the unborn may be killed because they do not presently manifest a personality, or reasoning, or a particular degree of self-awareness, or some other criteria. But whatever criteria they select, they almost invariably recognize exceptions. They argue that whether a human being has a right to life depends on whether it presently manifests a personality, yet they recognize a right to life in those who are asleep. They maintain that a human being has no right to life if it is presently unable to reason, yet they recognize a right to life in those who are unconscious from injury or intoxication. Can we afford to utilize a standard for the right to life which is so narrow that exceptions are necessary to protect those we all agree should be protected? Can we afford to have standards so porous standing as the bulwark between us and murder?

Schweitzer's warning that "fully developed inhumanity" is only a matter of time if we forget that every human being should be an object of concern to us is not mere hyperbole. When the circle surrounding those whose lives society protects is drawn too narrowly, it tends to contract, like a ripple on a pond in reverse. The potential sense of guilt in those who participate or acquiesce in killing is so overwhelming that they cannot objectively re-evaluate their conduct. Instead, they are driven to rationalize the behavior and continue it. Referring to the psychological principle that "atrocity begets atrocity," psychologist Robert Lifton writes, "In psychological terms, we may say that the backed up power so threatening to its possessor is the sense of guilt, which can be fended off only by continuous application of the lethal power."[39] One Holocaust historian has written that, to those who participated in the extermination of the Jews in Nazi Germany, the moral dividing line was a "receding horizon" that they could walk toward but never reach. "[T]here were very few," he writes, "who did not shift the line when they had to cross the threshold."[40] Thus, Dr. Leo Alexander, medical consultant to the Nuremberg war crimes trials, observed, "Whatever proportion these crimes finally assumed, it became evident to all who investigated them that they had started from small beginnings."[41]

We have a choice. Almost two hundred years ago, Thomas Jefferson wrote, "The care of human life and happiness, and not their destruction, is the first and only objective of good government."[42] Clearly, no nation which deems some human beings to have a "fundamental right" to destroy others can be said to place a premium on human life. We must decide whether we subscribe to Jefferson's view or we reject it. And, if we reject it, let's at least be honest with ourselves. Let's dispense with the pretense, the hypocrisy, the prevarication, the empty platitudes. Let's do away with the euphonious rhetoric about the inherent rights of *all* human beings and boldly proclaim what we stand for: that *some* human beings are created equal; that *some* human beings are endowed with an inalienable right to life; that *some* human beings have "human" rights; that *some* human beings have intrinsic worth. "The foundation of morality," T. H. Huxley once observed, "is to have done, once and for all, with all the lying."[43]

NOTES

1. The Declaration of Independence para. 2 (U.S. 1776).

2. *Webster's Third New International Dictionary* (1986).

3. Benjamin Quarles, ed., *Frederick Douglass* (Englewood Cliffs, NJ.: Prentice-Hall, 1968), 67 (emphasis added).

4. From the New Orleans *Bee*, December 14, 1860, quoted in John M. Blum et al., *The National Experience*, 6th ed. (San Diego: Harcourt Brace Jovanovich, 1985), part 1, *A History of the United States to 1877*, 346.

5. *Dred Scott v. Sandford*, 51 U.S. (19 How.) 393, 410.

6. Earl W. Wiley, *Abraham Lincoln: Portrait of a Speaker* (New York: Vantage, 1970), 155.

7. Edward J. Kempf, *Abraham Lincoln's Philosophy of Common Sense: An Analytical Biography of a Great Mind* (New York: New York Academy of Sciences, 1965), part II, 668.

8. Mortimer J. Adler, *We Hold These Truths: Understanding the Ideas and Ideals of the Constitution* (New York: Macmillan, 1987), 45.

9. Adler, *We Hold These Truths*, 42–43.

10. Harry A. Blackmun, foreword, in Adler, *We Hold These Truths*, ix.

11. It is unclear whether Adler himself realized that he and Justice Blackmun differed on this fundamental issue. Adler has written elsewhere, "It must be extremely rare, if it ever happened at all, that anyone would have some doubt about whether a specimen being examined was human or not." Mortimer J. Adler, *Ten Philosophical Mistakes* (New York: Macmillan, 1985), 157. Presumably, then, Adler does not believe that *Roe v. Wade*, or the abortion issue in general, involves serious debate about whether the unborn are human.

12. Quoted in Eugene E. Brussel, ed., *Webster's New World of Quotable Definitions* (Englewood Cliffs, NJ: Prentice-Hall, 1988), 267.

13. Brief Amicus Curiae of Mother Teresa of Calcutta in Support of Petitioners' Petitions for a Writ of Certiorari, *Loce v. New Jersey*, 510 U.S. 948 (1994) (No. 93–1148), *microformed on* U.S. Supreme Court Records and Briefs (Microform, Inc.) 7–8.

14. Universal Declaration of Human Rights, G.A. res. 217A (III), U.N. Doc A/810 at 71 (1948), reprinted in *Encyclopedia of Human Rights*, ed. Edward Lawson (New York: Taylor and Francis Institute, 1991), 1655–1657 (emphasis added).

15. International Covenant on Civil and Political Rights, G.A. res. 2200A (XXI), 21 U.N. GAOR Supp. (No. 16) at 52, U.N. Doc. A/6316 (1966),

999 U.N.T.S. 171, *entered into force* 23 March 1976, reprinted in *Encyclopedia of Human Rights*, 943–950.

16. Convention on the Rights of the Child, G.A. res. 44/25, annex, 44 U.N. GAOR Supp. (No. 49) at 167, U.N. Doc. A/44/49 (1989), *entered into force* Sept. 2, 1990, reprinted in *Encyclopedia of Human Rights*, 287–294.

17. American Declaration of the Rights and Duties of Man, O.A.S. Res. XXX, adopted by the Ninth International Conference of American States (1948), reprinted in *Encyclopedia of Human Rights*, 58–60 (emphasis added).

18. American Convention on Human Rights, O.A.S. Treaty Series No. 36, 1144 U.N.T.S. 123 *entered into force* July 18, 1978, reprinted in *Encyclopedia of Human Rights*, 44–52 (emphasis added).

19. Michael Tooley, "Abortion and Infanticide," in *The Ethics of Abortion*, eds. Robert M. Baird and Stuart Rosenbaum (Buffalo, N.Y.: Prometheus, 1989), 49.

20. See, for example, Mary Anne Warren, "On the Moral and Legal Status of Abortion," *Ethical Issues in Modern Medicine*, eds. John Arras and Robert Hunt (Palo Alto, CA: Mayfield, 1977), 170; and Joseph Fletcher, "Humanness," in *Humanhood: Essays in Biomedical Ethics* (Buffalo, N.Y.: Prometheus, 1979), 12–16.

21. Martin Luther King, Jr., "Letter from Birmingham City Jail," in *The Book of Virtues: A Treasury of Great Moral Stories*, ed. William J. Bennet (New York: Simon & Schuster, 1993), 258.

22. Raymond S. Duff and A.G.M. Campbell, "Moral and Ethical Dilemmas in the Special Care Nursery," *New England Journal of Medicine* 289 (1973): 890.

23. Helga Kuhse and Peter Singer, *Should the Baby Live?: The Problem of Handicapped Infants* (Oxford, England: Oxford University Press, 1985), 77.

24. Kuhse and Singer, 77.

25. Charles Everett Koop, *Koop: The Memoirs of America's Family Doctor* (New York: Random House, 1991), 248–249.

26. Koop, 265.

27. Earl E. Shelp, *Born to Die? Deciding the Fate of Critically Ill Newborns* (New York: Free Press, 1986), 246. See, for example, Duff and Campbell, 892 (where a physician involved in the selective withdrawing or withholding of life support from certain disabled infants explains that the children had little chance of achieving "meaningful humanhood").

28. The Child Abuse Amendments of 1984, Publ. Law 98–457, passed October 9, 1984, 42 U.S.C. § 5106a(b) (1986).

29. 42 U.S.C. § 5106g(10).

30. Stephen N. Wall and John Colin Partridge, "Death in the Intensive Care Nursery: Physician Practice of Withdrawing and Withholding Life Support," *Pediatrics* 99 (1997): 64–70.

31. John Glasson et al., "The Use of Anencephalic Neonates as Organ Donors," *Journal of the American Medical Association* 273 (1995): 1614. Children with anencephaly have incomplete brains, skulls, and scalps. Most are short-lived, but some survive months or even years after birth. (The Council has since reversed its position. See Janet Firshein, "AMA Reinstates Restrictive Infant Donor Policy," *Lancet* 346 (1995): 1618.)

32. Glasson et al., 1614.

33. Glasson et al., 1614.

34. Jay A. Friedman, "Taking the Camel by the Nose: The Anencephalic as a Source for Pediatric Organ Transplants," *Columbia Law Review* 90 (1990): 955.

35. Friedman, 968.

36. Quoted in Lewis D. Eigen and Jonathan P. Seigel, comps., *The Macmillan Dictionary of Political Quotations* (New York: Macmillan, 1993), 130.

37. Quoted in Robert H. Bork, *The Tempting of America: The Political Seduction of the Law* (New York: Free Press, 1990), 32.

38. Quoted in Edward F. Murphy, ed., *The Crown Treasury of Relevant Quotations* (New York: Crown, 1978), 359.

39. Robert J. Lifton, *The Nazi Doctors: Medical Killing and the Psychology of Genocide* (New York: Basic Books, 1986), 433.

40. Raul Hilberg, *The Destruction of the European Jews*, rev. and definitive ed., vol. 3 (New York: Holmes & Meier, 1985), 1028.

41. Leo Alexander, "Medical Science under Dictatorship," in Dennis Horan and David Mall, eds., *Death, Dying and Euthanasia* (Frederick, MD: Alethia Books—University Publications of America, 1980), 584.

42. From a letter to the Republican citizens of Washington County, Maryland, 1809, quoted in *The Morrow Book of Quotations in American History*, ed. Joseph R. Conlin (New York: Morrow, 1984), 159.

43. Quoted in George Seldes, comp., *The Great Thoughts* (New York: Ballantine, 1985), 199.

6

The Objections

[M]an is also unique as a moral beast. Paradoxically, the killing of one man by his fellow men, whether in the case of common murder, or collectively, as in war, is never practiced without a moral justification on the killer's side. It is not far from the point to say that morality is the prerogative of mankilling.

Halldór Laxness

But what is really *original* about it all is that you permit the shedding of blood *in accordance with the dictates of one's conscience.*

Fyodor Dostoyevsky, *Crime and Punishment*

In the previous chapter, we examined the case for recognizing the right to life of the unborn on the basis that they are human beings. Here, we shall turn our attention to the principal reasons offered to support liberal or unrestricted access to abortion. Since we have already addressed many of the arguments on the issues of whether the unborn are living, are human beings, and are persons, we shall devote the bulk of our attention here to arguments which assert that the unborn deserve no protection *even if they are persons.*

Even if the unborn are persons, we should not restrict abortion because doing so would compel pregnant women to act as Good Samaritans, a duty we do not impose on persons in other contexts.[1]

This argument, sometimes called "the Good Samaritan argument," is popular among abortion proponents because it appears straightforward and hints that religion is the real issue behind attempts to restrict abortion. Those who maintain that laws restricting abortion would violate the Equal Protection Clause of the 14th Amendment typically rely on a variation of the same argument: They contend that abortion restrictions would require only women to aid others, thereby denying women equal protection of the laws.[2]

There are a number of problems with the Good Samaritan argument. First, even assuming we imposed no duty upon one person to aid another in other situations, there would be good reason to treat pregnancy differently. A unique affiliation exists between the unborn and the pregnant woman. In other situations, one can leave another alone, conferring no aid but working no injury. Pregnancy is different, however. The destinies of the pregnant woman and the unborn are necessarily intertwined. If a woman decides to abort, the unborn is either killed in the womb or—less frequently—expelled living from the womb into an environment where it is virtually certain to perish.[3] If a woman decides not to abort, her body will continue to provide the unborn with nutrients, protection, and other benefits.

Second, the notion that we do not require one person to aid another in situations other than pregnancy is incorrect. Although the law imposes no *general* duty to render assistance to individuals requiring aid, we *do* have a duty to avoid any affirmative acts which would make their situation worse.[4] Since abortion is an affirmative act which makes the situation worse—infinitely worse—for another person (remember, those who make the "Good Samaritan" argument maintain that abortion is just even if the unborn are persons), it falls within this exception.[5] To maintain that women have a right to abort their young stands for far more than the proposition that one has no duty to *aid* others. It stretches and distorts that principle until one has no duty to *avoid harming* others.

The law also imposes a duty to provide aid on individuals who are responsible for putting others in a position where they require assistance.[6] While pregnancies arising from rape would not fall into this exception, those arising from voluntary intercourse—the overwhelming majority of all pregnancies—would. In pregnancies resulting from voluntary intercourse, the woman is responsible for putting another in a position requiring her assistance: the unborn would not be in the position it is but for her conduct. (This is not to suggest that the mother *alone* owes a duty to the unborn. The father is equally responsible for the situation, and, though he may be physically unable to provide the same sort of biological assistance to the unborn that the mother can, he has no less duty to the child.)

Some, perhaps, will argue that we should treat pregnancy differently from these exceptions to the general rule because the unborn would not exist at all but for the very conduct which put it in a position where it requires the assistance of the woman's body. But why should that dictate a different result? The fact that the unborn was not a human being before conception does not make it any less of a human being afterwards.

There is one other relevant exception to the general rule that one has no duty to aid others. Society has long recognized that parents have a duty to aid their young. A couple cannot simply abandon their newborn child in an apartment while they go to Acapulco. They have a duty to take the baby with them or see that it is cared for in their absence.

The Good Samaritan argument also fails at its most elemental level. The implication behind the argument is that we cannot sacrifice one person on behalf of another. At its best, pregnancy is physically, emotionally, and economically demanding. Can we compel a woman to go through such an ordeal on behalf of another person? The problem with the argument reduced to this level is that it can be turned on its head. If it is wrong to sacrifice one person on behalf of another, then it is also wrong to sacrifice the unborn on behalf of the woman. In either case, one person will be used as a means to benefit the other. The question is, which of the two will be used less—the woman who has to live through the pregnancy, or the unborn *who will not?*

Even if the unborn is a person, a pregnant women should have the option to get an abortion because she gives the unborn no right to the use of her body.

This argument is a close cousin of the Good Samaritan argument but focuses on the rights of the unborn rather than the duties of the woman. Judith Jarvis Thomson uses a version of this argument in her well-known article, "A Defense of Abortion":

I suppose we may take it as datum that in a case of pregnancy due to rape the mother has not given the unborn person a right to the use of her body for food and shelter. Indeed, in what pregnancy can it be supposed that the mother has given the unborn such a right? It is not as if there were unborn persons drifting about the world to whom a woman who wants a child says, "I invite you in."[7]

There are two major problems with the argument that pregnant women give the unborn no right to the use of their bodies. First, like the Good Samaritan argument, this argument can be turned on its head: A woman may not give the unborn a right to the use of her body, but nor has the unborn given the woman a right to sacrifice its life. Assuming both the woman and the unborn are "persons" (as Thomson does for purposes of her article) why should we draw the line in favor of the pregnant woman instead of the unborn? Of the two, the woman is harmed less and is more likely to be responsible for the pregnancy.

Secondly, Thomson's view of the right to life differs markedly from our traditional conception of that right. Historically, we have regarded the right to life as a right human beings possess simply by virtue of being human. Thus, the Declaration of Independence speaks of the "self-evident" truth that "all men" are endowed with an inalienable right to life. Even today, we treat the right as a basic "*human* right" in human rights treaties and other matters of international affairs. Thomson, by contrast, views the right to life as something *conferred* by other human beings: The unborn have no right to life because the pregnant woman "has not given the unborn the right to use her body for food and shelter," and because the woman never says, "I invite you in." Human beings do not have a right to life simply by virtue of being humans, in Thompson's eyes; they must in addition *be wanted*.

Even if the unborn are persons with a right to life, that right is not violated by aborting them.[8]

This argument overlaps to a large extent with the two preceding arguments. Since it is occasionally raised independently, however, I treat it separately here.

Those who admit that the unborn have a right to life but argue that abortion does not violate it ordinarily begin by making a distinction between positive and negative rights. "Positive rights" impose a duty on others *to do something for* the individual with the right; "negative rights" impose a duty on others *to refrain from doing something to* the individual with the right.

Those who argue that abortion does not violate the unborn's right to life start with the premise that the right to life is a negative right. (This is in accord with how the Founding Fathers perceived the right and how it is generally viewed today.) They then reason as follows:

1. Because right to life is a negative right, it does not include the right to have others do something for the individual with the right;
2. Pregnant women's bodies provide nutrients and other aid to the unborn;
3. Given the current state of medicine, abortion is the only means by which pregnant women can discontinue the aid their bodies are providing to the unborn; and,
4. Therefore, women have a right to abort the unborn and can exercise that right without violating the unborn's right to life.

There are a number of problems with this argument, but we shall focus on just two of them here.

As noted in our discussion of the Good Samaritan argument, one cannot validly conclude that, because we have no *duty to aid* others, we have a *right to harm* them. Even assuming the right to life is a negative right and we ordinarily have no duty to aid others, we *do* have a duty to refrain from any action which exacerbates the condition of others who require aid—even if that action is the only way we can discontinue our aid.

Consider, for instance, the situation of Fred, a boat owner, and Emily. Fred would not violate Emily's right to life if he refused to take Emily on a tropical cruise—even if she needs that cruise to cure a life-threatening disease. But if Emily is already aboard the craft—whether by invitation (a planned pregnancy) or stowing away (an unplanned pregnancy)—Fred would violate her right to life if he forced her overboard when the boat was so far offshore that she could not reach land safely. Whether Fred's actions violate Emily's right to life turns, in each instance, on whether he is simply refusing to do something necessary to save Emily or he is engaging in some affirmative conduct which puts her life in greater danger. If he is simply refusing to do something necessary to save Emily, Fred does not violate her right to life. But he does violate her right to life if he deliberately undertakes a course of action that puts Emily's life in danger. The fact that he ordinarily has no duty to aid Emily does not give him the right to force her overboard—*even if forcing her overboard is the only way he can avoid helping her*. Fred's duty to let Emily remain aboard his boat flows not from any duty to affirmatively help Emily, but from his duty to avoid harming her.

Furthermore, even if one accepted the premise that abortion does not violate the unborn's right to life, it would lead to some incongruous results. On the one hand, a pregnant woman could abort her young at any time during pregnancy and for any reason. On the other, she would not have her choice of abortion method: Since her right to abort arises from the fact that her body aids the unborn, she would be entitled to compromise the unborn's right to life only to the extent necessary to discontinue the aid her body provides. Portia reminded Shylock in *The Merchant of Venice*, "This bond doth give thee here no jot of blood;/ The words expressly are 'a pound of flesh.' "[9] Assuming a pregnant woman is entitled to "a pound of flesh" because her body aids the unborn, she has no right to any "jot of blood": all other things being equal, she would have to select the method of abortion most likely to insure the survival of the child.

There is a problem, however, with requiring the use of the method most likely to spare the unborn: ordinarily the abortionist and pregnant woman want nothing *less* than for the child to survive. A live birth is their worst nightmare. In the minds of the abortionist and his patient, the child is a "loose end." Thus, when abortions are performed later in a pregnancy and live birth may be a possibility, many abortionists deliberately select the abortion method most likely to *kill* the unborn, thereby eliminating the live-birth "problem."[10] The destruction of the unborn is one of the objectives of many abortions—not merely an unavoidable consequence of removing the child from the mother's womb. We have come to subscribe to the view expressed by one abortionist when he testified that "the abortion patient has a right not only to be rid of the . . . fetus . . . , but also a right to a dead fetus."[11] Indeed, physicians even disagree as to whether they should try to keep children who survive abortions alive.[12]

Pregnant women have a right to abort—even if the unborn are persons—because the women face a threat analogous to that in situations where we allow one person to kill another in self-defense.

Abortion proponents find this argument, the "self-defense argument," appealing for a number of reasons: it casts the woman as victim; it shifts the focus to the interests of the woman only, rather than balancing her interests against those of the unborn; and it suggests that somehow the unborn is the cause of the pregnancy, as opposed to the mother and father.

Jane English, one of the principal proponents of the self-defense argument, explains it in her article "Abortion and the Concept of a Person." To show that self-defense justifies the killing of even innocent human beings, English starts out by asking the reader to imagine a mad scientist who hypnotizes people to attack strangers with knives. A person attacked by one of these armed hypnotics, she explains, has a right to kill his attacker to prevent serious injury to life or limb. The fact that the hypnotic is himself innocent does not matter, since he is killed in the spirit of self-defense and not retribution.

English then argues that pregnancy is often an analogous situation:

Though the unborn is itself innocent, it may pose a threat to the pregnant woman's well-being, life prospects or health, mental or physical. If the pregnancy presents a slight threat to her interests, it seems self-defense cannot justify abortion. But if the threat is on par with a serious beating or the loss of a finger, she may kill the [unborn] that poses such a threat, even if it is an innocent person.[13]

According to English, the woman's life need not be in danger to justify abortion because our laws and customs regarding self-defense recognize that one may cause an injury "somewhat, but not enormously greater, than the injury to be avoided."[14] Indeed, English argues that the threat need not even be physical:

To consider a somewhat fanciful example, suppose you are a highly trained surgeon when you are kidnapped by a hypnotic attacker. He says he does not intend to harm you but to take you back to the mad scientist who . . . plans to hypnotize you to have a permanent mental block against all your knowledge of medicine. This would automatically destroy your career which would in turn have a serious impact on your family, your personal relationships, and your happiness. It seems to me that if the only way you can avoid this outcome is to shoot the innocent attacker you are justified in so doing. You are defending yourself from a drastic injury to your life prospects. I think it is no exaggeration to claim that unwanted pregnancies . . . often have such adverse life-long consequences as the surgeon's loss of livelihood.[15]

There are a host of problems with the self-defense argument—both generally and as formulated by English. I will confine my attention to three of them. The first pertains to *the way the harm is threatened*, the second pertains to *the extent of the harm threatened*, and the third pertains to *the role of third parties*. After exploring these problems, I shall offer an alternative hypothetical, one that portrays the threat posed by pregnancy more realistically than English's does, and that shows why we cannot justify the destruction of the unborn as "self-defense."

1. The way the harm is threatened. Under traditional notions of self-defense, I may not harm someone simply because doing so would eliminate a threat to my life or limb. For instance, if I discover that I need a heart transplant and no donors are available, I may not steal a heart from someone else and have it put in me. I may inflict harm in self-defense only where (1) a person has engaged in conduct creating a threat, (2) the harm is (or reasonably appears to be) necessary to eliminate the threat, and (3) the harm is directed at the person who created the threat. Thus, if I am in a crowded airport, and an enemy of mine approaches, and points a pistol at me, I may shoot him. But, if I have no gun, I may not grab an innocent bystander and use her as a shield when my enemy starts firing. In the first instance, I imperil the life of the person who engaged in the conduct creating the threat; in the second, I imperil the life of someone else. Even where a person has a gun to his head and kills a third person to save his own life, the courts hold him liable for the killing and guilty of at least manslaughter.[16]

Even assuming pregnancy is a "threat," as advocates of the self-defense argument maintain, a pregnant woman may not take the life of the unborn in "self-defense" because the unborn did not engage in any conduct creating that threat. The unborn did not create the pregnancy; the woman and her partner did. The unborn is not being killed because it has engaged, or will engage, in any harmful conduct; it is being killed simply because it exists. English conveniently sidesteps this problem by posing a hypothetical where the harm used in self-defense is directed at *persons engaged in conduct creating the threat*—the knife-wielding hypnotics. (To show that English's hypothetical breaks down when the harm used in self-defense is directed at someone other than the person engaged in conduct creating the threat, one need only ask, May the person attacked grab an innocent bystander and use her to shield himself from the hypnotized slasher? If not, then the amount of harm one is allowed to do in "self-defense" turns on whether the harm is directed at the person who created the threat, or directed at others.)

English's hypothetical is also severely flawed in the way it treats pregnancy. Women do not become pregnant as the result of anything analogous to the machinations of a "mad scientist." Almost half of all pregnancies are planned,[17] and, even among those that are not, the overwhelming majority result from consensual intercourse. Furthermore, even assuming the unborn are somehow analogous to hypnotized slashers, in the case of voluntary intercourse the woman conspires in the "hypnosis." Pregnancy resulting from voluntary intercourse may be unplanned, but it is *foreseeable*, and we usually hold people liable for the foreseeable consequences of their acts.[18]

For instance, suppose Phil and John secretly slip "angel dust" into Abe's soda, and Abe becomes violent from the drug and attacks Phil. Can Phil use deadly force against Abe if Abe poses a threat to his life and limb and deadly force is necessary to eliminate the threat? According to English's reasoning, Phil can: Abe poses a serious threat to Phil's life, and the harm directed at Abe is necessary to eliminate that threat. The fact that Phil was partly responsible for putting Abe in that situation, and that the threat was foreseeable, is immaterial. But is English's reasoning correct? Phil and John may have only aimed for a little "harmless fun," but it was foreseeable—if unlikely—that their "fun" could result in a situation which presented a threat to them. It may be unfair that Abe attacked Phil instead of John (after all, why should John get off scot-free?) but that does not absolve Phil of his own responsibility. Similarly, it may be unfair that pregnancy affects the mother of the unborn more than the father, but that does not absolve her of her responsibility for the unborn where the pregnancy results from voluntary intercourse. The man and woman may not have planned on a pregnancy, but that result was foreseeable.

2. The extent of the harm threatened. The self-defense arguments also falter in their analysis of the extent of the harm threatened by pregnancy and how that harm should be weighed. In our society, one may use "deadly force"—force likely or calculated to inflict death or serious bodily harm—only where he has reason to believe that he confronts a similar threat and there is no other safe means of defense.[19] Abortion clearly constitutes deadly force, but pregnancy very rarely poses a serious threat to the pregnant woman's life or health.

English and other proponents of the self-defense argument attempt to make up for this shortcoming in the physical threat by pointing to some of the other adverse consequences pregnancy and childbirth can have for the woman. These adverse effects fall into two general categories: the non-physical burdens directly attributable to the pregnancy and delivery (e.g., medical bills and lost wages associated with the delivery and any prenatal care; the emotional burden of carrying the child to term, "looking pregnant," and so on); and the burdens associated with raising a child from birth to maturity (e.g., the change in lifestyle associated with raising a child; the expense of clothing, educating, feeding, and sheltering the child and keeping him or her healthy; and so on).

However, neither category of adverse effects is sufficient to give a pregnant woman the privilege to use deadly force. The burdens related to raising a child after birth cannot be used to invoke the privilege of self-defense because they are *avoidable consequences*: a woman can avoid them without having to harm the unborn. Opponents of abortion do not seek to compel the pregnant woman to actually raise the child herself; they would only have her refrain from aborting it. If the mother decides to keep the child when it is born, that is her prerogative. However, no one is forcing her to do so. She can protect any of her interests which would be jeopardized by raising the child by putting the baby up for adoption or even by leaving it on someone else's doorstep. In our society, one may not use deadly force in self-defense where there is a safe way to defend oneself using non-deadly force.[20] Therefore, a woman cannot justify the use of deadly force against the unborn on the basis of the burdens associated with raising the child. If postnatal consequences of this sort could be used to justify taking the life of an innocent person, infanticide would be permissible as well as abortion.

Nor is it "self-defense" to kill the unborn to avoid the non-physical consequences of pregnancy or childbirth. The privilege of self-defense applies only where there is a *physical* threat: it "extends to the use of all reasonable force to prevent any threatened harmful or offensive *bodily contact*, or any *confinement*."[21] The law recognizes that a person can suffer from non-physical injuries, such as defamation, invasion of privacy, and the intentional infliction of emotional distress. However, one cannot resort to force—much less deadly force—to prevent any of them.

3. The role of third parties. Even assuming abortion could otherwise qualify as "self-defense," the self-defense arguments would collapse on themselves for another reason: their analysis of the role of abortionists. A woman does not ordinarily give herself an abortion; she has an abortionist do the job. But if the woman is the one who is "threatened" by a pregnancy, how does the abortionist acquire the privilege to intervene and harm the unborn on her behalf?

English and other proponents of the self-defense arguments maintain that the abortionist may destroy the unborn on behalf of the woman because third parties have a privilege to intervene in defense of others. Their premise is correct: the law recognizes that third parties have a privilege to defend others, and use such force as the person aided would be entitled to use himself.[22] The problem, however, is that this "defense-of-others" rationale works only if one focuses exclusively on the pregnant woman. If we focus on the unborn, we would reach an entirely different conclusion: that abortion threatens the life of a person—the unborn—and therefore legislators and others should be allowed to intervene on behalf of the unborn to prevent abortions. Indeed, were we to subscribe to English's mistaken reasoning, those seeking to save the lives of the unborn would be entitled to use *deadly force* to do so.

4. An alternative hypothetical. There is a better hypothetical than English's to determine whether abortion falls within the privilege of self-defense. It encompasses pregnancies caused by rape; it does not involve contortions of reality as extreme as mad scientists or knife-wielding hypnotics; and it applies where one person is associated with a threat to others but is not himself responsible for the condition causing the threat.

Suppose a communicable disease appears which causes the same symptoms as those associated with pregnancy and childbirth: "morning sickness," weight gain, "labor" pains, and so on. As in the case of those giving birth, those who come down with the symptoms of the disease typically require a brief hospitalization. The only difference between the illness and pregnancy is that the illness strikes both men and women, and with the illness, there is no child. (By positing that the disease infects both men and women, we eliminate the possibility that our conclusions turn on the sex of those affected.) To show that our hypothetical applies whether or not a pregnancy results from consensual intercourse, we shall also assume that the contagion spreads through the air, and that persons cannot reduce their chances of infection by modifying their behavior.[23] There is no known cure or effective quarantine but, as in the case of pregnancy, there is ordinarily a complete recovery and mortality is very rare. While some infected individuals will manifest the clinical symptoms of the disease, others will simply be "carriers," capable of spreading the disease but not themselves affected by it.

Now, the question: May those who carry the illness be put to death if that is necessary to prevent a like number of persons from coming down with the clinical symptoms of the disease? If one subscribes to the self-defense arguments propounded by abortion proponents, the answer is "yes." The physical threat and cost of treatment are identical. The threat in each case is incidentally associated with an individual who did not himself cause the condition creating the threat. And, in each case, the limited threat to one person can be eliminated only by resorting to the ultimate solution—killing another. For each person spared the symptoms of pregnancy and childbirth another must die.

Personally, I am opposed to abortion, but I am "pro-choice" because I am unwilling to impose my decision on others.

This position—which I shall call the "personally opposed" position—encompasses a wide variety of views, from those opposed to any attempt to influence a woman's position on abortion to those opposed only to actual legislation restricting abortion. It is particularly popular among those who are unwilling to say publicly whether they believe the unborn are human beings, those who regard abortion as strictly a religious issue, and those who wish to distance themselves from abortion without alienating abortion proponents.

The problem with the "personally opposed" position is that it totally avoids the question of whether the unborn are human beings, an issue absolutely central to the abortion controversy. Most opponents of abortion oppose it precisely because they believe it involves killing *human beings*. We have already examined some of the problems inherent in arguing that the unborn are not living or human beings in earlier chapters. But even assuming that those personally opposed to abortion but unwilling to "impose" their decision on others realize the unborn are living human beings, their position is still problematic. Anyone who recognizes that the unborn are human beings yet demands that the law permit others to kill them must believe either: (1) that some human beings have no right to life; or (2) that all human beings have a right to life, but the law should protect only some of them. We have addressed the dangers which follow from accepting the proposition that some human beings have no right to life in the previous chapter. We shall confine our attention here, therefore, to the notion that the unborn are human beings with a right to life yet the law should give others a right to kill them.

Can one sincerely believe that the unborn have a right to life but that the right should not be recognized by law? Certainly, this is a novel conception of what it means to have a right. What significance is there in having a right if the law does not acknowledge it? In any other context, the idea would be dismissed as ludicrous.

Adherents of the position argue that abortion is a special case because many people believe that the unborn are not human beings or are not "persons." But what difference should that make? Would those who insist on subjugating their views about the right to life of the unborn tolerate the murder of Jews or the enslavement of blacks so long as a substantial portion of our society believed those groups were not human? Would they refuse to support legislation protecting the right to life of newborns or women in societies where a significant portion of the population feels either are not "persons"? Would they insist that, even if a majority of the population believed that Jews, blacks, women, or newborns should be protected by law, it was wrong to "impose" that decision on those who did not? Certainly not. Yet this is precisely their position with respect to the unborn. On the one hand, they say they believe the unborn have a right to life. On the other, they support *Roe v. Wade* and insist that states cannot protect the unborn even if that is what a majority of the state's citizens want.

Many of those who profess to be personally opposed to abortion but "pro-choice," of course, do not realize the implications of their position. They do not realize that their position paints them into a corner where they must believe that the unborn are not human beings, or that some human beings have no right to life, or that the law should recognize a right to kill human beings they themselves acknowledge have a right to life. This is the danger of subscribing to an argument that sidesteps the issue of whether the unborn are humans. The failure to consider whether the unborn are human beings is tantamount to saying that it does not matter whether they are humans. But whether the unborn are human beings *does* matter. We accord a wide berth to individuals acting on their personal beliefs only where they will not seriously injure others. We tolerate different faiths, but not wife-beating. We tolerate freedom of speech, but not rape or drunken-driving. To stand on the sidelines when one human being kills another is not "tolerance"; it is an abdication of conscience.

Justice Cardozo once wrote of the "tendency of a principle to expand to the limits of its logic."[24] Once we accept the proposition that we can condone the willful destruction of innocent human beings, there is no logical reason to confine that thinking to just the unborn. One college philosophy professor writes that, while his students acknowledge the reality of the Holocaust, they are increasingly unwilling to condemn it.[25] Personally they deplore the Holocaust and other great evils, he noted, but they are unwilling to "impose their morality" on others. Another college instructor was shocked to discover that, even when pressed, not one of her twenty students would condemn human sacrifice.[26]

This is not "tolerance" or "open-mindedness." It is precisely the type of indifference Holocaust survivor Elie Wiesel warned of when he said, "Indifference, to me, is the epitome of evil. . . . Because of indifference, one dies before one actually dies. To be in the windows and watch people being sent to concentration camps or being attacked in the street and to do nothing, that's being dead."[27]

NOTES

1. See, for example, Judith Jarvis Thomson, "A Defense of Abortion," in *Modern Constitutional Theory: A Reader*, eds. John H. Garvey and T. Alexander Aleinikoff, 2d ed. (St. Paul: West, 1991), 509–516; and Deborah L. Rhode, *Justice and Gender* (Cambridge, MA: Harvard University Press, 1989), 212. (Rhode writes, "Even if the fetus were assumed to be a person, it would not follow that its interests must assume primary importance. Just as we do not compel individuals to serve as Good Samaritans in other contexts, we ought not compel women at all stages of pregnancy to sacrifice their own destiny to embryonic life.")

2. See, for example, Dawn Johnsen and Marcy J. Wilder, "*Webster* and Women's Equality," *American Journal of Law and Medicine* 15 (1989): 178–184.

3. Although abortions do not *ordinarily* result in live births, live births do occur. Some studies have found that live births occur in as many as seven or eight percent of second trimester abortions performed with prostaglandins. Nancy K. Rhoden, "The New Neonatal Dilemma: Live Births from Late Abortions," *Georgetown Law Journal* 72 (1984): 1458. Assuming prostaglandin abortions result in live births only two percent of the time, one study estimated that there were 472 live births from that type of abortion in

1977 alone, and that approximately three percent of those children ultimately survived. Rhoden, 1458.

4. William L. Prosser, *Prosser and Keeton on the Law of Torts*, gen. ed. W. Page Keeton, 5th ed. (St. Paul: West, 1984), 378.

5. Under this rationale, a mother would have no duty to undertake any affirmative action to *benefit* the unborn—whether it is eating, taking vitamins or medicines, undergoing medical treatment, or the like—but she could not engage in any affimative conduct which would *unreasonably harm* the unborn.

6. Prosser, 377.

7. Thomson, 513. (Thomson appears to have overlooked the fact that many women become pregnant because they are actually *trying* to have children. Women who conceive deliberately may opt for abortion because the child is the "wrong" sex or disabled, the relationship with the father has broken off, or for a variety of other reasons.)

8. See, for example, Thomson, 512–513 ("[I]t is by no means enough to show that a fetus is a person, and to remind us that all persons have a right to life—we need to show that killing the fetus violates its right to life.")

9. Shakespeare, *The Merchant of Venice* 4.1.306–307, in *The Unabridged William Shakespeare*, William George Clark and William Aldis Wright, eds. (Philadelphia: Running Press, 1989), 243.

10. Rhoden, 1457 n. 52, 1459–1460.

11. *Planned Parenthood v. Ashcroft*, 462 U.S. 476, 483 (1983).

12. Rhoden, 1472–1473 n. 201.

13. Jane English, "Abortion and the Concept of a Person," *Canadian Journal of Philosophy* 5 (1975): 237.

14. English, 237.

15. English, 238–239.

16. See, for example, *Arp v. State*, 12 So. 301 (Ala. 1893); *People v. Repke*, 61 N.W. 861 (Mich. 1895); *State v. Capaci*, 154 So. 419 (La. 1934); *State v. Fisher*, 59 P. 919 (Mont. 1900); and *Brewer v. State*, 78 S.W. 773 (Ark. 1904).

17. Sally Squires, "Most Pregnancies Unplanned or Unwanted, Study Says," *Washington Post Health*, May 9, 1995: 7.

18. Prosser, 294.

19. Prosser, 127. (After noting that the privilege of self-defense "is limited to the use of force which is, or reasonably appears to be, necessary for protection against the threatened injury," *The Law of Torts* explains, "It is unreasonable to use force which is calculated to inflict death or serious bodily harm . . . unless one has reason to believe that he is in similar serious danger, and that there is no other safe means of defense.")

20. Prosser, 127.

21. Prosser, 124. See also American Law Institute, *Restatement (Second) of Torts* (St. Paul: American Law Institute Pub., 1965–) §§ 64, 66, and 68.

22. Prosser, 130.

23. If one thinks the disease is not comparable to pregnancy because pregnancy sometimes carries with it the stigma of sex outside of marriage, one need only change the hypothetical to make the disease a sexually-transmitted one.

24. Benjamin Cardozo, *The Nature of the Judicial Process* (New Haven: Yale University Press, 1921), 51.

25. Robert L. Simon, "The Paralysis of 'Absolutophobia,' " *Chronicle of Higher Education*, June 27, 1997: B5+.

26. Kay Haugaard, "A Result of Too Much Tolerance," *Chronicle of Higher Education*, June 27, 1997: B4+.

27. Elie Wiesel, "One Must Not Forget," *U.S. News & World Report*, October 27, 1986: 68.

PART II

While Part I of this book was primarily a factual and logical assessment of abortion, Part II is more subjective. It aims to change the way that we *feel* about abortion.

One cannot dismiss the value of an appeal simply because it cannot be reduced to a neat logical syllogism. We are more than mere biological thinking machines; we are creatures of passion. For better or for worse, we have both heart and mind, and our conduct is driven largely by emotion. The tapestry of human history is more a study of the power of fear and courage, hate and love, despair and hope, than an exhibition of applied logic. Photographs attest to the power of emotional appeals. It is one thing to read that many in Somalia are dying of starvation; it is another to confront the blank and dislocated stares in a photo of skeletal Somali villagers mourning their dead. The photograph forces us to be subjective; it draws us in as participants. It communicates to us at a level which transcends simple logic.

At their best, appeals on moral issues resonate in our souls as well as registering in our intellects. Harriet Beecher Stowe did more to change people's attitudes about slavery by penning a sentimental novel than she could have had she written a dispassionate treatise on the ethics of slavery. *Uncle Tom's*

Cabin appealed to people's hearts and souls and consciences, not merely to their sense of *logos*.

Were we to confine our analysis of abortion to a dispassionate analysis of the facts, we would ignore the central role emotion already plays in the abortion debate. Emotion, not logic, is the principal reason we are so reluctant to take a stand against the destruction of the unborn. It would be so much more *convenient* if there were nothing wrong with abortion. We all know people who have had abortions, or performed them, or view any opposition to them as tantamount to misogyny. They are our friends, our partners, our co-workers. Some of us may even fall into one of these categories ourselves. We do not know those whom abortion kills. *We never will.*

A passionless dissection of the issues would belie the fact that abortion takes *human* lives—approximately a million and a half of them each year. The abortion debate is a debate about fundamental human dignity, not how many angels can dance on the head of a pin. At its core is the issue of whether every member of the human family has a right to life or whether it is acceptable to kill those the law deems to be beings of an inferior order. When Frederick Douglass faced another instance in which our country denied part of the human family even the most elemental protection of the law, he raged:

> At a time like this, scorching irony, not convincing argument is needed. O! had I the ability, and could I reach the nation's ear, I would to-day pour out a fiery stream of biting ridicule, blasting reproach, withering sarcasm and stern rebuke. For it is not light that is needed, but fire; it is not the gentle shower, but thunder. We need the storm, the whirlwind and the earthquake. The feeling of the nation must be quickened; the conscience of the nation must be roused; the propriety of the nation must be started; the hypocrisy of the nation must be exposed; and its crimes against God and man must be proclaimed and denounced.[1]

The first chapter in Part II, "It Is Happening Here," examines some of the parallels between the Nazis' killing and abortion in the United States. The second, "Language," explores the role that language plays in the destruction of the unborn. The third, "Arbitrary," explains why the distinctions we draw between abortion and infanticide are arbitrary. The fourth, " 'Hastening Death,' " shows how the reasoning used to devalue the unborn in *Roe v. Wade* is now being extended to the seriously ill. And the last, "The House of Atreus?" suggests why the Greek myth of the House of Atreus may be an appropriate metaphor for abortion in America.

NOTE

1. Frederick Douglass, "What to the Slave Is the Fourth of July," *The Frederick Douglass Papers*, ed. John W. Blassinger, series 1: Speeches, Debates, and Interviews; vol. 2: 1847–1854 (New Haven: Yale University Press, 1982), 371.

7

It Is Happening Here

We are sunk in a barbarism all the deeper because it is tolerated by moral lethargy and covered with a veneer of scientific conveniences.

Winston Churchill

There is a beast in man, and these things could conceivably happen again at any time, anywhere. Whether human beings learn from history, I cannot say. But at least, where we have the facts and where we can put out warning signals, it would be criminal not to do so.

Holocaust expert Gerald Fleming

A little more than sixty years ago, the Nazi leadership in Germany embarked on a revolutionary quest to transform the face of Europe. The end they envisioned was an entirely new social order, a society built upon science and efficiency and free from racial and ethnic strife. No child would be born handicapped. No one would suffer from mental illness. Every person would be "the best and brightest." Twelve million people perished in the concentration camps as part of the quest for this brave new world. Over 100,000 additional men, women, and children were put to death in Germany's hospitals in a crusade to purge the German population of traits resulting in mental or physical disabilities.[1]

How effective we will prove at averting other Holocausts depends on the lessons we draw from our experience with the Nazi death machine. The next Holocaust will not involve Germans murdering Jews or the other groups who met their fate at the Nazis' hands. The specter of the Nazi experience still looms too large for us to tolerate an exact replay of that scenario. But there may well be other Holocausts—Holocausts with different victims and different executioners, different landscapes and different slogans.

We need to decide whether the Nazis' killing was an abomination because they killed *human beings*, or merely because they killed the *wrong* human beings. The racism, anti-Semitism, and other bigotry rampant in the Third Reich were despicable. But the problem with the extermination campaigns is that the Nazis killed innocent human beings—millions of them—not simply that they failed to use a "politically correct" method of deciding who would die. Had the Nazis chosen to exterminate a like number of toddlers, or persons born on a Tuesday, the killing would have been just as wrong. The fact that many today tend to regard the Nazis' extermination of the retarded as somehow less reprehensible, in a qualitative sense, than the annihilation of others shows how far we ourselves have already strayed from the notion that all human beings are created equal.

What makes a society fertile ground for the notions that some human beings are worth more than others or that some are not human at all; that killing can be sanitized with euphemisms and camouflaged with a patina of medicine or science; that one can be an upstanding, moral person and yet acquiesce, or even participate in, the methodical annihilation of fellow human beings? These are disturbing questions—profoundly disturbing—but they are questions we are eminently qualified to answer. *We live in just such a society.*

"Surely," some will say, "abortion in America does not resemble the Holocaust. How could we commit atrocities comparable to those wrought by the Nazis? We are not a nation of savages. We are good people, people with a sense of morality, people who are educated and want the best for their country." No doubt the Germans felt the same way. We have come to view the Holocaust and its origins as something uniquely German, something which could never happen in America or in a democracy. But there is nothing innately different about the German people—or the Cambodians, or the Serbs—that renders them more susceptible to perpetrating atrocities than ourselves. The Holocaust may have had German trappings, but it was not an intrinsically German phenomenon. It could happen here . . . *and it is.*

We are the ones destroying one and a half million human lives each year. We are the ones arguing that some human beings are not "persons" and even that some are not human at all. We are the ones maintaining that some human beings have no right to live. We are the ones who have enshrined a constitutional right to kill.

It is tempting to succumb to the notion that we are somehow incapable of committing atrocities comparable to those of the Nazis, that some unbridgeable chasm separates "normal," educated people like ourselves—people with a sense of right and wrong—from those who could participate in such conduct. Convinced that we *cannot* commit atrocities, we refuse to consider whether we might *already be* committing them.

The flesh and blood of the Nazi death machine, however, was more like us than we wish to believe. The notion that those responsible for the liquidations were uneducated sadists, depraved and altogether repulsive individuals with no respect for human life, is utterly distorted. The majority of SS officers manning the camps came from intellectual professions; their ranks included lawyers, professors, political functionaries and officials, and even an opera singer and protestant minister.[2] In the words of Holocaust expert Raul Hilberg, "[T]he machinery of destruction was a remarkable cross-section of the German population. Every profession, every skill, and every social status was represented."[3] "The bureaucrats who were drawn into the destruction process," he writes, "were not different in their moral makeup from the rest of the population. The German perpetrator was not a special German. What we have to say about his morality applies to him specifically but also to Germany as a whole."[4]

Indeed, the Nazis would never have had the opportunity to commit the horrors they did but for the complicity of a large part of the German population. Hitler and the Nazis did not overthrow the Weimar government; they came to power democratically. And Hitler's willingness to spill innocent blood to achieve his vision of Germany's future was apparent before the Nazis' rise to power. Consider, for instance, Hitler's endorsement of infanticide at the annual party rally at Nuremberg in 1929. There, he urged that Germany emulate the ancient Spartan practice of killing weak newborns, reasoning, "If Germany every year would have one million children and eliminate 700,000–800,000 of the weakest, the end result would probably be an increase in (national) strength."[5] The Nazis received more votes than any other party save one in the elections for the German parliament a year later,[6] and more votes than any other party in the 1932 parliamentary elections.[7] Throughout this period, the party was virtually indistinguishable from its leader. (As recently as 1928, the Nazi ticket had run as the "Hitler Movement."[8]) The fact that the Nazis and their leader could enjoy such success in democratic elections even after Hitler suggested killing hundreds of thousands of *German* infants shows that—even before the Nazis' rise to power—the German people had inured themselves to the idea that some human beings had no right to life.

There is no question that a handful of individuals figured prominently in the nightmare of annihilation the Nazis wrought. But a few men could never have put millions of innocents to death. The network of Nazi death factories required the support of legions of otherwise unexceptional people drawn from the society at large. Hilberg writes:

> [T]he very nature of administrative planning, of the jurisdictional structure, and of the budgetary system precluded the special selection and special training of personnel. Any member of the Order Police could be a guard at a ghetto or on a train. Every lawyer in the Reich Security Main Office was presumed to be suitable for leadership in the mobile killing units; every finance expert to the Economic-Administrative Main Office was considered a natural choice for service in a death camp. In other words, all necessary operations were accomplished with whatever personnel were at hand.[9]

Most of those in the extermination apparatus did not kill for the sake of killing. They regarded themselves as upstanding citizens and beings with a conscience. Referring to the notion that the Nazis' killing was the work of sadistic beasts, Heinz Höhne writes:

> This is too simple a picture. Dr. Ella Lingens-Reiner, who was a prisoner at Auschwitz testified: "I know hardly a single SS man who could not say that he saved someone's life. There were few sadists. . . ."
>
> [T]he really horrifying feature . . . of the annihilation of the Jews was that thousands of respectable fathers of families made murder their official business and yet, when off duty, still regarded themselves as ordinary law-abiding citizens who were incapable of straying from the strict path of virtue. Sadism was only one facet of mass extermination and one disapproved of by SS Headquarters.

Himmler's maxim was that mass murder must be carried out coolly and cleanly; even while obeying the official order to commit murder the SS man had to remain "decent."[10]

Indeed, Hilberg writes that many who participated in the liquidations bore no particular malice toward their victims:

The German bureaucrat made a sharp distinction between duty and personal feelings. He insisted that he did not "hate" Jews, and sometimes he even went out of his way to perform "good deeds" for Jewish friends and acquaintances. . . . While these courtesies pale in comparison with the destructive conceptions that these men were implementing concurrently, the "good deeds" performed an important psychological function. They separated "duty" from personal feelings. They preserved a sense of decency. The destroyer of Jews was no anti-Semite.[11]

Thus, the SS forbade camp staff from tormenting prisoners,[12] and directed that those personnel found to have killed Jews for selfish, sadistic, or sexual motives were to be tried for murder or manslaughter, whichever the facts warranted.[13]

THE ORIGINS OF THE FINAL SOLUTION

Although there is today a tendency to view the Nazi death camps as the almost inevitable result of virulent anti-Semitism, that analysis is far too simplistic. In *The Holocaust and the Crisis of Human Behavior*, George Kren and Leon Rappoport write, "[D]uring the nineteenth century and for several years after World War I, Jews received better treatment in Germany than in Russia, Poland, the Hapsburg Empire and its succession states, Scandinavia, and even France. . . . Consequently, although historical anti-Semitism was clearly relevant to the Holocaust, it cannot be accepted as the primary cause."[14] As Hitler's 1929 endorsement of infanticide shows, the Germans had come to terms with killing their own children before they started killing Jews. Anti-Semitism explains why the Reich targeted the Jews for elimination as opposed to other groups, but it does not explain why the Germans felt the need to exterminate *anyone* en masse, diverting crucial men and materiel from the war effort. Nor does it explain what allowed so many "normal" German citizens to kill without scruple when the government directed them to do so. Racial and religious tensions are common in many societies; institutionalized mass murder is not.

To fully appreciate the parallels between the Holocaust and abortion in America, it is necessary to understand the origins of the Holocaust in its precursor, the so-called "euthanasia" program, and in the eugenics movement.

The Nazis' euthanasia program shows that religious and ethnic bigotry were not the primary motivations behind the extermination campaigns. The first of the Nazis exercises in culling undesirables from the population, the program targeted the disabled for elimination—not religious or ethnic minorities. Numerous authorities on the Holocaust have noted that the euthanasia program was a necessary stepping stone to the Final Solution.[15] The Nazis would use the same techniques to resolve the "Jewish problem" that they used to eliminate the disabled. As J. David Smith writes in *Minds Made Feeble*, "The philosophy, personnel, and equipment—and deadened consciences—required for the Holocaust were developed through the process of killing handicapped people, those who were perceived to be defective, and those who were assumed to be morons."[16]

The euthanasia program, however, cannot be understood except in the context of the eugenics movement. Although the euthanasia program was secret and implemented under Hitler, the philosophical underpinnings of the program were an outgrowth of modern science and existed in German society before the Nazis came to power. As Smith observes, "The mass elimination of handicapped . . . was not a unique Nazi invention. It was the culmination of a eugenic philosophy that had been building in strength for decades. [I]t was not a specific German creation or even a Nazi creation but a phenomenon of Western thought and science."[17] Eugenics laid the foundation for the notion that some human beings were worth less than others and provided a quasi-scientific rationale for killing undesirables. The euthanasia program and the Final Solution were an outgrowth of both principles.

The Development of the Eugenics Movement

"Eugenics" was the name given to the genetic hygiene movement, influential on both sides of the Atlantic during the late nineteenth and early twentieth centuries. Regarded as science at the time, it advocated the selective breeding of men and women to enhance the hereditary traits of the population.

While certain eugenic trends existed beforehand, serious interest in eugenics did not arise until after the publication of Charles Darwin's *The Origin of Species* in 1859. Darwin's theory of natural selection forced many to reassess deeply rooted beliefs about the nature of man and spurred an interest in the application of biological principles to human society. According to the theory of natural selection, competition and reproduction play key roles in the evolution of species. Members of a species that share the same environment compete for limited resources. Even within a species, differences exist between organisms that give some a comparative advantage over others. Those organisms betters uited to an environment—whether because they are faster, stronger, or for some other reason—tend to live longer than their fellows. As a result, they tend to produce more offspring, and their genetic traits tend to become more common in succeeding generations.

Even those who accepted Darwin's theory of evolution tended to find it disconcerting. The theory was new, the concepts complicated, and the implications profound—all of which contributed to the tumult that followed in the wake of the theory's publication. Many mistakenly assumed that natural selection resulted in organisms that were "better" in some abstract sense, rather than simply better suited to their particular environment. Many were also concerned that our tendency to take care of the weak, ill, and impaired was having a deleterious effect on the human race. "With savages," Darwin wrote in *The Descent of Man*, "the weak in body or mind are soon eliminated. . . . We civilized men, on the other hand, do our best to check the process of elimination." This, Darwin felt, "must be highly injurious to the race of man" because "excepting in the case of man himself, hardly anyone is so ignorant as to allow his worst animals to breed."[18]

The eugenicists urged that governments ensure that children have beneficial traits by encouraging individuals with beneficial traits to have more children and those with undesirable traits to have fewer. By the turn of the century, they had proposed measures ranging from monetary incentives for new parents "of civic worth" to sterilization of the mentally-impaired, tuberculosis victims, and bankrupts.[19] Though eugenicists believed that mental and moral characteristics were hereditary, many of the traits they sought to purge from the population were not actually genetically determined. Indeed, support for eugenic measures was often driven less by scientific evidence than by the notion that the "wrong" people were having too many children and the "right" people were having too few. This, supporters of the measures feared, would move society in the "wrong" direction.

Even so, eugenic ideas flourished. They appealed to a world undergoing a scientific awakening and accorded well with trends prominent in Europe and America during the late nineteenth and early twentieth centuries: ethnocentrism, imperialism, romanticism, and religious bigotry. By the early 1920s, groups as diverse as the Ku Klux Klan, progressives, scientists and doctors, early feminists, and aristocrats were endorsing eugenic solutions to a host of social problems.[20] Eugenic principles also underlay much of the early birth-control movement. British scientist and birth-control advocate Marie Stopes advocated the compulsory sterilization of children with disabled relatives—even if the children themselves had no disability.[21] Havelock Ellis, Emma Goldman, and Planned Parenthood founder Margaret Sanger, among others, lent considerable support to the eugenics movement.[22] Sanger explained that she promoted birth control "to stop the multiplication of the unfit"—a quest she described as "the most important and greatest step toward race betterment."[23]

The Eugenics Movement in Germany

Eugenic ideas found particular favor in Germany. They fit in neatly with the views of the Volkists, a group who believed that an immutable bond exists between man and nature and that the "blood and purity" of the German people surpassed that of others. Perhaps most important, eugenics in Germany enjoyed the support of a particularly gifted proponent: Ernst Haeckel, an eminent biologist, influential philosopher, and Darwin's greatest champion on the Continent.

Today, Haeckel is perhaps best known as the scientist who coined the word "ecology."[24] But his support for eugenic principles was very influential in Germany at the turn of the century. Because he had been an early and enthusiastic advocate of the theory of natural selection, Haeckel's views carried a great deal of clout—with his fellow scientists and in the intellectual community at large. The first issue of the German eugenics journal *Archiv*, published in 1904, was dedicated to him.[25] He also founded the Monist League, a group devoted to advancing eugenic principles and that included many prominent intellectuals.[26] Many Germans were familiar with Darwin's theory of evolution only because they had been introduced to it by Haeckel. In *The Scientific Origins of National Socialism*, Daniel Gasman writes, "[S]ince the publication in 1866 of Haeckel's *Natürliche Schöpfungsgeschicte*, the Germans understood Darwin and Darwinism through the distorted lens of Haeckel."[27] *Weltsrätsel*, Haeckel's 1899 book about man and his place in nature, was one of the most read and popular books in Germany in the decade following its release.[28] Half a million copies were sold in Germany by the time the Nazis came to power.[29]

The Monists and other German eugenicists urged the government to provide incentives to couples with desirable traits to have more children. They also argued that, to prevent "suffering" in generation after generation, the sick and feeble should be denied health care and discouraged from reproducing.[30] A national board would screen prospective parents in order to eliminate disabled infants.[31] By the 1920s, eugenics enjoyed widespread support among the German medical establishment.[32] The Germans also became increasingly receptive to eugenic solutions involving the elimination of the "unfit." In 1920, Karl Binding, one of Germany's leading specialists in constitutional and criminal law, and Alfred Hoche, a physician, wrote *Permission for the Destruction of Life Unworthy of Life*, an influential book advocating the destruction of individuals afflicted with certain disabilities.[33] Years before Hitler came to power, many doctors called for the euthanasia of "incurables."[34] Haeckel himself endorsed the destruction of disabled newborns, calling it "a practice of advantage to the infants themselves and to the community."[35]

Despite increasing popular support for eugenic measures, Germany did not seriously attempt to implement them until after the ascent of the Nazis in 1933. Nazi ideology had been strongly influenced by the Volkist movement and placed a premium on technology, triumph through struggle, and the innate superiority of the German people. The party rose to prominence by promising to restore Germany from the political, economic, and social dislocation that befell the country following its defeat in World War I. To resurrect the nation, the Nazis argued, Germany would have to reorder its society in accord with eugenic principles; the country could not fulfill its full potential if the feeble and indolent continued to pass along their traits at a greater rate than productive citizens.

The Nazi commitment to eugenics was not mere window dressing. Gasman notes that "Naziism completely assimilated the fundamental ideas of Haeckel and the Monists" and that, among Monists, "National Socialism was openly and enthusiastically welcomed as the ideology which they had been espousing for years."[36] Persons of "good worth" were told they had a patriotic duty to have as many children as possible, and all public officials were required to marry.[37] The government coaxed couples to have children with loans, debt forgiveness, and tax penalties.[38] Maternal communities, called *Lebensborn*, were set up to tend to and guard the secrecy of unwed mothers during the period of their confinement—provided that both mother and father were of "good blood."[39] Men in the SS—all ostensibly screened for genetic purity—were encouraged not to let the proprieties of marriage stand in the way of supplying the country with "superior" offspring.[40]

The measures taken to reduce the number of "undesirable" members of the German population were more sinister. A Law for the Genetic Health of the German People required couples to undergo a medical exam before marrying; only those free from venereal disease and certain other diseases believed to be hereditary were allowed to wed.[41] A Law for the Protection of Genetically Diseased Offspring established a network of genetic health courts that had the power to order the sterilization of those deemed to suffer from "genetically determined" diseases, like feeble-mindedness, schizophrenia, manic-depressive psychosis, genetic epilepsy, deafness, and even "serious alcoholism." In 1934 alone, the Reich's genetic health courts ordered more than 60,000 sterilizations.[42]

The Nazis had another means of eliminating threats to the genetic hygiene of the German people. Hitler had confided as early as 1935 that he supported the "euthanasia" of "defectives," but he believed that the political opposition was too great to implement the measure at that time.[43] As war began to seem increasingly imminent, however, killing became a more enticing option than sterilization—maintaining the "useless eaters" would divert resources crucial for the impending war effort.[44]

In 1937, Hitler gave certain official physicians the authority to exterminate children with physical handicaps at a hospital near Wurthemberg. "The children were killed with overdoses of drugs mixed in their food. Those who would not eat were killed with injections or suppositories. Soon, questionnaires were sent to all institutions that housed children. On the basis of the questionnaire results, children who were deemed incurable or genetically defective were picked for *'besondere Heilvesfahren'* (special healing procedures)."[45]

Initially, only children up to the age of three were put to death.[46] Within two years, however, the program was expanded to cover children up to the age of twelve.[47] And, in late 1939, the program was expanded yet again to include another class of "beings unworthy of life" (*lebensunwertes Leben*): adults with physical or mental disabilities.[48]

At first, there was a selection procedure. Institutions treating the physically, mentally, and emotionally disabled had to fill out patient questionnaires, and doctors and medical students evaluated the responses, identifying those patients they felt were incurable or genetically tainted.[49] Soon, however, the selection procedure became a token gesture. According to one physician who worked in the program: "Most institutions did not have enough physicians, and what physicians there were were either too busy or did not care, and they delegated the selection to the nurses and attendants. Whoever looked sick or was otherwise a problem patient from the nurses' or attendants' point of view was put on a list and was transported to the killing center."[50]

The euthanasia personnel turned their attention next to the tuberculosis hospitals and workhouses.[51] By the summer of 1940, disconcerting rumors had started to circulate, and many elderly refused to go to retirement homes.[52] The architects of the euthanasia program had initially anticipated that the entire project would involve taking the lives of 65,000–70,000 individuals.[53] By August 28, 1941, when public outcry finally forced the Chancellery to end the program, over 90,000 men, women, and children had been put to death.[54] The Nazis did not halt the euthanasia program entirely, however. While adults were spared, the Nazis continued to put disabled children and adolescents to death until the end of the war.[55]

When they discontinued killing adult "defectives," the Nazis turned their attention to eliminating "sick" inmates at the concentration camps.[56] Shortly thereafter, they expanded the killing to include criminals, political prisoners, and one of the other classes of subordinate beings they felt presented a threat to the gene pool: Jews.[57]

Jews, it is important to note, were considered a threat because of their biology, not their theology. Individuals with Jewish ancestors were considered tainted regardless of their own religious beliefs.[58] The Nazis perceived the Jews as an ethnic group, or "race," rather than as members of varied ethnic groups who happened to share the same religion. Because the Nazi leadership had become convinced that Jews were inferior to other Germans, it felt that interbreeding between the two groups threatened the genetic health of the German population. Although certain eugenicists had always subscribed to the idea that some individuals were less fit than others simply by virtue of their race, the eugenics movement in Germany did not become fundamentally racist in nature until after the Nazis came to power.[59] Even then, not all elements of the party agreed that Jews were inferior. Dr. Leonardo Conti, one of the heads of the program to annihilate Germany's disabled adults, had declared that the new Germany should be adverse to any form of racial hatred and that the Jews were not an inferior race.[60]

As in the case of the disabled, the scope of Jews targeted for elimination was narrow in the beginning, then increased incrementally until it included the entire class. The circle spread from Jewish 'Bolshevist leaders' to political officers, to intellectuals, to public officials, to persons suspected of aiding partisans—until, ultimately, it included every Jew.

As the number targeted for elimination grew, the SS—the order charged with implementing the "Final Solution"—searched for a quicker and more efficient means of execution. They settled upon the technique that had already become the method of choice in the euthanasia program: poison gas. Using gas allowed personnel at the killing centers to minimize their contact with their victims. Furthermore, thanks to the euthanasia program, gas chambers were ready and waiting at psychiatric hospitals, and SS personnel loaned to the program were already accomplished at killing with gas.[61] The SS drafted Christian Wirth, the head executioner in the euthanasia program, to devise the means to gas one million Polish Jews.[62] To test the efficacy of his plan, Wirth had several hundred concentration camp prisoners transported to the gas chambers at mental hospitals.[63]

The Final Solution to the "Jewish question" began where the solution to the "defectives" question left off.

The Parallels Between the Eugenics Movements in Germany and in the United States

The development of the American eugenics movement closely paralleled the development of the movement in Germany during much of the 1920s and 1930s. As defendants in the Nuremberg war crimes trials pointed out after the war, the idea of putting the useless and incurable to death had been suggested in the United States as well as in Germany.[64] And compulsory sterilization was commonplace. Authorized by some states since 1907, over 27,000 individuals were forcibly sterilized in the United States by 1938.[65] Thirty states had statutes authorizing the procedure.[66] In Virginia, whole families of mountaineers were rounded up and sterilized in the 1930s.[67] When German proponents of compulsory sterilization urged their government to authorize the practice, they pointed to the United States as a model.[68] Indeed, after the Germans adopted and enthusiastically implemented their sterilization program, one prominent American eugenicist complained, "The Germans are beating us at our own game."[69]

The U.S. Supreme Court even upheld the constitutionality of compulsory sterilization. In *Buck v. Bell*,[70] decided in 1927, the Court ruled that Virginia could, consistent with the Constitution, compel the sterilization of Carrie Buck, an 18–year-old single mother who had been diagnosed with "a failure of mental development."[71] Justice Holmes' opinion for the Court reflects the eugenic sentiment prevalent at the time:

> It would be strange if [the public welfare] could not call upon those who already sap the strength of the state for these lesser sacrifices . . . in order to prevent our being swamped with incompetence. It is better for all the world if instead of waiting to execute degenerate offspring for crime, or to let them starve for their imbecility, society can prevent those who are manifestly unfit from continuing their kind. . . . Three generations of imbeciles are enough.[72]

(Decades after Buck was sterilized, it was discovered that she had been misdiagnosed.[73])

Planned Parenthood founder Margaret Sanger—now revered as an icon of modern feminism—resorted to even stronger language in support of eugenic measures. "[I]t is a curious but neglected fact," she wrote, "that the very types which in all kindness should be obliterated for the human stock, have been permitted to reproduce themselves and to perpetuate their group, succored by the policy of indiscriminate charity or warm thoughts uncontrolled by cool heads."[74] Elsewhere, Sanger wrote of the "meaningless, aimless lives which cram this world": "hordes of people . . . who have done absolutely nothing to advance the race. . . . Their lives are hopeless repetitions. . . . Such human weeds clog up the path, drain the energies and the resources of this little earth. We must clear the way for a better world; we must cultivate our garden."[75]

But perhaps the best example of the symmetry between the eugenics movements in Germany and the United States is Harry Laughlin, a biologist and—in the 1920s and 1930s—one of America's foremost proponents of compulsory sterilization. Laughlin urged state and foreign governments to adopt legislation requiring the sterilization of individuals deemed to be genetically defective—a category Laughlin believed included alcoholics, criminals, and the blind and deaf, among others.[76] His views won wide acceptance in the United States and, after he appeared before the House Committee on Immigration and Naturalization, the Committee appointed Laughlin its "expert eugenics agent."[77]

Yet the measures Laughlin advocated did not differ greatly from those proposed by German eugenicists—a fact Laughlin himself acknowledged in a 1936 letter thanking the dean of the University of Heidelberg after the school awarded him an honorary degree. In that letter, Laughlin wrote:

> I consider the conferring of this high degree upon me not only as a personal honor, but also as evidence of a common understanding of German and American scientists on the nature of eugenics as research in and the practical application of those fundamental biological and social principles which determine the racial endowments and the racial health . . . of future generations.[78]

The United States, of course, did not embark on a campaign to liquidate undesirables from its population. But, as in Germany, eugenics combined with bigotry to provide fertile soil for the notion that some human beings were more "human" than others and some not human at all. For instance, dehumanization and ideas of differential human worth figured prominently in the War in the Pacific. "In Europe we felt that our enemies, horrible and deadly as they were, were still people," Ernie Pyle wrote shortly after being transferred to the Pacific Theater. "But out here I soon gathered that the Japanese were looked upon as something subhuman and repulsive; the way some people feel about cockroaches and mice."[79]

The military, media, and public at large routinely referred to the Japanese with sub-human metaphors.[80] Admiral Halsey often called them "monkeymen" and "stupid animals," and, at a news conference in early 1945, stated that he believed the "Chinese proverb" that "the Japanese were the product of mating between female apes and the worst Chinese criminals who had been banished from China by a benevolent emperor."[81] Cartoons routinely depicted the Japanese as apes or the "missing link." In *War without Mercy*, historian John Dower writes, "Even when one reviews the political cartoons of wartime

America with foreknowledge of the fondness for apish imagery in depicting the Japanese enemy, the extensiveness of such representations is startling. . . . The simian image was ubiquitous in the American . . . media, appearing in publications both conservative and liberal, popular and high-brow."[82]

Since they were so often denied even the vocabulary of human beings, it should come as no surprise that the usual rules did not apply when fighting the Japanese. Public opinion polls in the United States during World War II showed that between 10 and 13 percent of Americans consistently supported the "annihilation" or "extermination" of the Japanese as a people.[83] Edgar Jones, a former war correspondent, wrote in the *Atlantic Monthly* of soldiers who deliberately adjusted their flame-throwers so that their Japanese targets would have an opportunity to suffer before they died.[84]

American servicemen regularly stripped the Japanese fallen of their skulls, ears, bones, scalps, and teeth—all regarded as battle trophies. The practice was so widespread that customs officials in Hawaii routinely asked U.S. troops returning from the South Pacific whether they had any bones in their luggage.[85] Astonishingly, many soldiers and civilians seemed to find nothing unusual about the practice. One soldier sent President Roosevelt a letter opener carved from a bone from a Japanese corpse; another attempted to bribe a chaplain by promising him the third pair of ears he collected.[86] The *Baltimore Sun* detailed the saga of an indignant local mother whose plans to nail a Japanese ear to her door were frustrated when authorities would not allow her son to mail his prize back from the South Pacific.[87] Then there are two telltale photographs Dower describes from *Life* magazine: "*Life* published a full-page photograph of an attractive blonde posing with a Japanese skull she had been sent by her fiancé in the Pacific. *Life* treated this as a human-interest story. . . . Another well-known *Life* photograph revealed the practice of using Japanese skulls as ornaments on American military vehicles."[88]

If a scientific rationale were necessary to explain why the Japanese had to be treated differently, there were plenty forthcoming—many with eugenic overtones. The *New York Times Magazine*, for instance, informed its readers that anthropologists had determined that the Japanese soldier was a "truculent and vengeful bully" because Japanese mothers lost interest in one child as soon as they gave birth to another. The *Magazine* concluded, "If birth control were practiced in Japan he might grow up to be a gentleman. Better yet, he might not be born at all."[89] After a curator at the Division of Physical Anthropology at the Smithsonian informed President Roosevelt that the Japanese were "as bad as they were" because they had skulls "some 2,000 years less developed than ours," Roosevelt suggested that, after the Allies won the war, they should do their best to encourage the Japanese to intermarry with other races.[90]

These incidents pale in comparison to what unfolded in Nazi Germany, but they do, at least, suggest what we Americans are capable of when we succumb to pseudo-science, dehumanization, and ideas of differential human worth.

THE PARALLELS

On a number of occasions in recent years, prominent opponents of abortion have compared the Holocaust to the destruction of the unborn. Abortion proponents, predictably, see no comparison. Nor do some members of groups the Nazis victimized. Individuals from both camps have argued that to suggest that any similarity exists between the unborn and those who perished at the Nazis' hands is gravely offensive and diminishes the memory of the Nazis' victims.

Abortion in America is by no means *identical* to the extermination campaigns waged by the Nazis. But extensive parallels do exist between the two that make comparisons inevitable. One is the prominent role of language: in both cases, those involved in the killing go to extreme lengths to ensure that the destruction process is sanitized with language in which human beings are no longer "human," and killing is no longer "killing." (We shall examine the role of language in the destruction of the unborn in more detail in the next chapter.) Another is the sheer scale of the devastation. Between their various extermination campaigns and the concentration camps, the Nazis killed approximately 12 million human beings.[91] Abortionists in the United States have killed well over that number in the last decade alone.[92]

These are just two of a host of parallels between the destruction of the unborn and the destruction of the Nazis' victims. Some distinguish the two from other enterprises of widespread killing; others are common to virtually all such enterprises. We shall examine some of the more prominent parallels in detail.

Living Human Beings

We have noted in earlier chapters that many Americans support abortion only because they believe that it does not involve killing human beings. The unborn, in their view, are either not alive or not human. Yet if individuals cannot be morally culpable for "terminating" those they believe are not alive or not human, then many of those in the Nazi extermination machine are not culpable for the murders they perpetrated. Like many involved in the destruction of the unborn, many of those involved in the Nazis' killing believed their victims were not human or not alive.

"The Nazis did not treat the Jews as humans," historian Yehuda Bauer writes, "because they did not see them as humans."[93] Time and time again, prominent Nazis explained that Jews were not human beings. Chief Judge Walter Busch declared that "National Socialism has recognized that the Jew is not a human being."[94] Heinrich Himmler called the campaign against the Jews "a struggle between humans and sub-humans"[95] and urged German soldiers to discard the "long-outmoded conception . . . that even a Jew was a human being and that, as such, he could not be harmed."[96] Propaganda Minister Joseph Goebbels railed against the "stupid, absurd statements of middle-class intellectuals to the effect that the Jew is a human being."[97] Hitler expressed the view that the "difference which exists between the lowest so-called men and the other highest races is greater than that between the lowest men and the highest apes."[98] He clearly felt that Jews fell on the lower, non-human end of this ladder. Referring to the Jews in Linz, he wrote in *Mein Kampf,* "In the course of the centuries, their outward appearance had become Europeanized and had taken on a *human* look."[99]

Even German scientists succumbed to the notion that Jews were not human. Professor Hirt, director of anatomy at the Reich University at Strasbourg submitted a report to Himmler in which he referred to "Jewish-Bolshevist commissars" as a "repulsive but characteristic sub-humanity."[100]

Jews were not the only people the Nazis regarded as non-human. Virtually all of the groups they exterminated fell into that category. Nazi documents frequently referred to Gypsies, Poles, and Russians as belonging to subhuman species—primates somewhere between humans and chimpanzees.[101] A pamphlet called "The Sub-Human" *(Der Untermensch)*, produced by the Main Administrative Office of the SS, explained that Slavs were beings of an inferior order as well: "To the outward eye the sub-human is biologically an entirely similar creation of nature; he has hands, feet and a sort of brain with eyes and a mouth. In fact, however, he is a totally different and frightful creature, a caricature of a man with features similar to a human being but intellectually and morally lower than any animal."[102]

Predictably, those put to death in the Nazis' euthanasia program were not human either. They were "creatures": "travesties of human form" that existed on "the lowest animal level."[103] Following a visit to an insane asylum, a German journalist described the patients as "grinning grotesques who bear scarcely any relationship to human beings."[104] At the Nuremberg doctors' trial, one of the physicians on trial explained that he decided to help kill the disabled only after visiting an asylum firsthand and seeing a certain little three or four-year-old girl there. He testified, "It was simply a torso. It had no arms, no legs, a big head, albino, red inflamed eyes. And at that age, it was not able to speak a single word yet. It was a terrible sight—simply a body with a head and no possibility that a human being could develop from this creature."[105]

One cannot overestimate the role that dehumanization of this sort played in the Nazis' killing. When German General Erich von dem Bach-Zelewski was asked at the International War Crimes Trial how his peer, General Otto Ohlendorf, could admit murdering 90,000 people, Bach-Zelewski replied, "I am of the opinion that when, for years, for decades, the doctrine is preached that the Slav race is an inferior race, and Jews not even human, then such an outcome is inevitable."[106]

Experts in the field have pointed to dehumanization as one of the distinguishing features of the Holocaust. Kren and Rapport write, "If the qualitative difference between the Holocaust and prior acts of mass murder can be named at all, the only appropriate term for it is *dehumanization*."[107] It is no coincidence that dehumanization figured prominently in the Holocaust and continues to play a major role in the destruction of the unborn. Dehumanization facilitates the participation of "normal" people in the killing process: Even individuals who believe that every human being has rights can kill without scruple once they convince themselves that their victims are not human.

The Nazis also sought solace in the notion that those they eliminated were not "living." When the Chancellery prepared a film about the euthanasia program to show to trusted insiders, for instance, it bore the title *Existence Without Life (Dasein ohne Leben)*.[108] The German journalist who wrote of mental patients as "grinning grotesques" entitled the article about his visit to the asylum "Alive Yet Dead."[109]

The idea that the disabled are not alive is patently ridiculous, of course—but so is the notion that a living baby arises spontaneously from inanimate matter. Those who referred to the disabled in this way did not *really* mean to assert that the disabled were not living. Rather, they used the words "living," "life," and "alive" in much the same way some abortion proponents do today: to distinguish between those human beings who possess a right to life and those who do not. Those human beings who they feel have no right to life are not "alive."

Differential Worth of Human Beings

Some of those associated with the Nazis' killing, however, *did* realize that their victims were alive and human. Like those abortion proponents who admit that the unborn are human but insist their lives cannot be compared to the life of the mother (or even to the inconvenience of carrying a child to term), the Nazis felt that some human beings are inherently worth more than others, that some have no right to life, and that some are not "persons."

The idea that some human beings are worth less than others played a key role in the Nazis' killing. Even relatively early in the eugenics movement, Ernst Haeckel argued that, because the "lower races" were "psychologically nearer to the mammals (apes and dogs) than to civilized Europeans, [one] must . . . assign a *totally different value to their lives*."[110] The Nazis routinely characterized the Jews as "worthless life" (*unwertes Leben*). Speaking to a Nazi party meeting in the occupied Ukraine, Erich Koch, the Commissar of the Ukraine, reminded his audience, "We . . . must remember that the lowliest German worker is racially and biologically a thousand times more valuable than the population here."[111] The euthanasia program encountered little resistance among the directors of the institutions which housed the disabled because, even before the program was implemented, the directors had come to regard the disabled as "life of lesser value."[112]

Like many abortion proponents, those associated with the Nazis' killing did not consider all human beings "persons." The individuals who laid the intellectual foundation for the extermination campaigns went to considerable lengths to explain why those destined for elimination were not "persons."[113] Some of these efforts were outright, but others were more subtle. Consider the film *I Accuse (J'accuse)*—a drama contrived by high-ranking euthanasia personnel to make the public more receptive to the elimination of the unfit. The heroine in the film, recently diagnosed with multiple sclerosis, warns that she will soon no longer be "a person any more" but "just a lump of flesh."[114] She begs her husband to "deliver" her before that happens. Others rationalized the killing by explaining that those targeted for elimination had no right to life for the same reasons abortion proponents now argue that the unborn are not "persons." According to Karl Brandt, for instance, the insane given "relief through death" in the euthanasia program were individuals who "could no longer take any conscious part in life."[115] Theologians sympathetic to euthanizing the mentally disabled rationalized the practice by arguing that those killed lacked a personality and were, therefore, simply lumps of flesh.[116]

How curious that we find the Nuremberg Laws despicable but hail *Roe v. Wade*. What the Nuremberg Laws did to one class of human beings, *Roe* has done to another. The Nuremberg Laws *figuratively* reduced the Jews to the status of non-persons, declaring that they could not be citizens of the Reich and banning them from marrying or having sexual relations with "citizens of German or cognate blood."[117] *Roe literally* held that the unborn were not persons, denying them a right to life.

The Role of the Tools of "Advanced Culture"

Another distinctive feature common to both the destruction of the unborn and the Nazis' victims is the role played by tools of "advanced culture." Those sympathetic to the abortion movement typically cast the battle over abortion as a struggle between two conflicting cultures, one "progressive" and one "reactionary." The proponents of abortion are the progressives—more enlightened, more compassionate, more modern. They recognize that the freedom to "terminate" the unborn is essential for a new, better social order—one where women are regarded as truly equal, where children need not be born with birth defects, where fewer people will tax the earth's limited resources. In the mantra of former Surgeon General Joycelyn Elders, "every child" will be "a planned and a wanted child."

The foes of abortion, however, are viewed as reactionaries. They want to move society backward. Their opposition to abortion stems not from any genuine concern for the unborn but from antiquated ideas about sex, science, the role of women, or the proper place of religion in a free society.

The tendency to equate progress with what seems to be "progressive" can be dangerous, however. Eugenics was regarded in its day as modern, progressive and scientific.[118] Those opposed to it—like conservative fundamentalists who challenged the forced sterilization of Carrie Buck in *Buck v. Bell*—were dismissed as reactionary and behind the times.[119] The Nazis also saw themselves as in the vanguard of progress. When German Alfred Hoche co-wrote a text endorsing the destruction of the severely disabled in 1920, he warned that future generations would regard the "over-exaggerated notions of humanity" present at the time as barbaric.[120] Years later, when the Nazis came to power, Himmler spoke of the pivotal role that the Final Solution and the SS would play in Europe's history.[121] Hitler, meanwhile, forecast that, by implementing the Final Solution, "we shall have accomplished for mankind a deed whose significance cannot be imagined yet."[122] Indeed, the Nazis' ability to cast themselves as visionaries and agents of progress accounted for much of their appeal. Kren and Rapport write that "most serious students of the Holocaust know that what it reveals is the *fragility of nature* in the face of human agents operating with the technical and conceptual tools of 'advanced culture.' "[123]

Seemingly laudable objectives are an indispensable element in modern, institutionalized killing. The killing is not an end in itself. The victims are destroyed in the name of the future. As Zygmunt Bauman explains in *Modernity and the Holocaust*:

Murderous motives in general, and motives for mass murder in particular, have been many and varied. . . .

Truly modern genocide is different. Modern genocide is genocide with a purpose. Getting rid of the adversary is not an end in itself. It is a means to an end: a necessity that stems from the ultimate objective, a step that one has to take if one wants ever to reach the end of the road. *The end itself is a grand vision of a better, and radically different society.* Modern genocide is an element of social engineering, meant to bring about a social order conforming to the design of the perfect society. . . .

Stalin's and Hitler's victims were not killed in order to capture and colonize the territory they occupied. Often they were killed in a dull, mechanical fashion with no human emotions—hatred included—to enliven it. They were killed because they did not fit, for one reason or another, the scheme of a perfect society. Their killing was not the work of destruction but of creation. They were eliminated so that an objectively better human world—more efficient, more moral, more beautiful—could be established.[124]

Thus, Ernst Wenzler, a German pediatrician, would testify after the war that his involvement with the euthanasia program—where he helped select which disabled would be terminated—was "something positive" and that he had "made a small contribution to human progress."[125] Referring to the elimination of the Jews in an October 1943 speech to top commanders implementing the Final Solution, Heinrich Himmler said, "To have gone through this and—apart from the exceptions caused by human weakness—to have remained decent, that has hardened us. That is a page of glory in our history."[126] Thomas Mann would write after the war, "[I]f it did not sound like detestable condonation, one might say that the Nazis committed their crimes for dreamy idealism."[127]

"Idealism" also figures prominently in the destruction of the unborn. We are told that abortion will help combat population growth, poverty and child-abuse; that it will reduce the incidence of children with Down's syndrome and other disabilities; and that children are better off aborted than given up for adoption. Seattle abortionist Suzanne Poppema has said, "Every day I feel I've made a small difference in the world."[128] Warren Hern, a Colorado abortionist, feels that, by performing abortions, he is "doing something very important for the cause of freedom."[129] Elizabeth Karlin, another abortionist, writes, "As a feminist physician, . . . I can think of no greater, more interesting, or more challenging work than providing . . . abortions." [130]

Feminist leaders since the 1960s have argued that abortion on demand is absolutely essential to women's equality—so much so, in fact, that abortion has become the *sacrament* of modern feminism. Karlin argues, "By definition, all abortion provision is a feminist endeavor."[131] Laura Kaplan, a member of a group of feminist non-physicians who banded together in the late 1960s to perform abortions in their apartments, explains, "We saw abortion as a potential catalyst for personal growth . . . ," and, "Because our work was based on a feminist political perspective, we attempted to use our service to raise women's consciousness, to turn an illegal abortion into a transformative experience. . . ."[132]

Others take these sentiments one step further. In a 1994 issue of *Mother Jones*, D. Redman writes that she felt "almost heroic" after obtaining a chemical abortion because the procedure was experimental and she would be a pioneer for other women.[133] When the blood from the abortion first appears, at a Woman's Day march, Redman slips into a state of bliss: "At last, the blood I've been praying for. I look at the other women around me and think how glorious we are in our rebellion. . . . My life feels luxuriant with possibility. For one precious moment, I believe that we have the power to dismantle this system. I finish the march, borne along by the women."[134]

In 1985, a convention of nearly 3,000 feminists in Barcelona decided to do something "decisively courageous" to protest abortion restrictions in Spain. The feminists' leaders arranged to have two young pregnant women aborted in a room next door.[135] When the bottled remains of their offspring were presented to the convention, "the hall rocked with cheers."[136] The organizers played a videotape of one of the abortions so all the conventioneers could share in the event more intimately. Virtually all of those present signed "confessions of responsibility" for the abortions, hoping to prompt a showdown with Spanish authorities.

The more extreme elements of the feminist movement have compared abortion to a sacrament itself. In her book *The Sacrament of Abortion*, Ginette Paris calls abortion "a sacred act" and makes the perverse argument that treating it as a sacrament would foster increased respect for the sanctity of life.[137] Similarly, in a 1993 article written for the *New Age Journal*, Brenda Peterson refers to abortion as a "sacrament" and "sacred act of compassion."[138]

But even feminists who are not particularly "militant" on the issue tend to treat abortion as a sacrament. In a 1995 article in *The New Republic*, Naomi Wolf, a prominent feminist author and opponent of abortion restrictions, decries the "hardness of heart" evident in incidents like those I have just described. But, in the same article, after acknowledging that abortion is an act of killing and that the unborn are fully human, Wolf refers to their destruction as "heroic" and speaks of it in terms that are nothing short of sacramental. By failing to come to terms with the moral gravity of abortion, Wolf argues, the "pro-choice" movement has left the abortionists "with blood on their hands," the blood of every abortion they perform.[139] But she adds, "*This is the blood that the doctors and clinic workers often see clearly, and that they heroically rinse and cause to flow and rinse again. And they take all of our sins, the pro-choice as well as the pro-life among us, upon themselves.*"[140] The abortionists and their staff, engaged in the willful destruction of innocent human beings, are not "killers." They are the *Agnus Dei*: the Lamb of God taking away the sins of the world.

The Role of "Science"

Of the "tools of advanced culture" which play a crucial role in the destruction of the unborn and figured prominently in the Holocaust, "science" is perhaps the most important. We are told that science has not yet determined whether the unborn are alive or human, that concepts of natural law and "souls" are obsolete in an era of test-tube babies and genetic engineering, and that the propriety of experimenting on the unborn and parceling out their organs are issues best resolved by scientists.

Yet "science" also played a central role in the destruction of the Nazis' victims. According to Kren and Rappoport, "The science and technology which had been increasingly celebrated for almost a century as the bastion of Western rationality and had become synonymous with liberal-progressive thought turned out to be a major factor contributing to the feasibility of the Holocaust."[141] They note, "[F]rom its dim origins in the euthanasia program to its final large-scale industrial actualization at Auschwitz, the scientific mode of thought and methodology attached to it were intrinsic to mass killings."[142]

Indeed, the Third Reich regarded itself as thoroughly grounded in science. Gasman writes, "The entire literature of National Socialism was suffused with veneration of nature and adherence to the dictates of science. . . . In innumerable scholarly journals and books the biological basis of the new state was stressed and the re-birth of the German people linked to the laws of biology."[143] The Reich promoted National Socialism as "the biological will of the German people," "political biology," and "the expression of our biological knowledge."[144] Doctors, biologists, and "racial anthropologists" played key roles in the formulation and administration of Nazi policy. Eugenic scientists decided who was or was not a Jew and used the organs from those killed in the camps for research.[145] Years before Hitler became a force in German politics, Haeckel—Germany's most prominent biologist—urged the nation to practice selective infanticide and destroy the ill and deformed.[146]

Even the very highest levels of the Third Reich's leadership tended to view National Socialism as the extension of science. Gasman writes that, from the content of Hitler's conversations, "it is patently clear that he thought of himself as rooted in the rational and scientific tradition of modern European civilization and that he was certain that there was a basis in science for all of the beliefs and policies which he espoused."[147] He regarded even the "Jewish Question" as fundamentally a biological problem.[148] Heinrich Himmler, head of the SS, had a background in agricultural genetics and saw much of what the SS did—from the selection of recruits to the extermination campaigns—as biological in nature.[149] Gasman notes, "He thought of himself as operating completely within the framework of science."[150]

The fact that science played a central role in the Nazis' extermination campaign and now occupies a central role in abortion is no coincidence. Because most people associate science with truth and objectivity, any movement that emphasizes the "scientific" basis of its belief tends to give itself the veneer of credibility. Furthermore, scientific thinking is a virtually essential component in large-scale routinized killing. In their study of the Holocaust, Kren and Rappoport observe that massive killing requires "detached technical expertise grounded on a scientific rationale of *logos*, and in only a small degree supported by emotionality or passion."[151] They explain:

> It should be clear that the mental splitting which separates emotionality from rationality is deliberately inculcated into science-oriented Western culture in order that people may repress or suspend reflexive emotions that might block achievement of abstract, distant goals. The ability to categorize objects, then to perform mental (imaginary) operations upon these objects and thus transform the meaning of the objects into something other than what we started is fundamental of all science. . . . Yet this capacity for scientific-intellectual functioning in Western culture is what can make extraordinary horrors possible. *By exercising this capacity, we can make judgments that some people are better than others, and ultimately, that some are not people at all.*[152]

The Suppression of Criticism

Those involved in the destruction of the Jews and the Nazis' other victims used a variety of techniques to minimize the guilt associated with their actions. Some are common to many instances of killing; others are more distinctive. One feature common in instances where seemingly "normal" people engage in extensive killing is the suppression of criticism.

We have already noted that most of those involved in the Nazis' killing retained a sense of conscience. Even in the midst of their killing, they regarded themselves as thoroughly moral. The same is true of those associated with killing the unborn. The average person involved with abortion has not forsaken right and wrong. The killing of the unborn simply does not offend their sense of conscience.

The suppression of criticism is absolutely essential where "normal" people like these are associated with killing. Criticism threatens the killing enterprise because it challenges the killers' perception of themselves as "decent." Referring to the Nazi death camps, Hilberg writes, "There was nothing so irksome as the realization that someone was watching who was not involved."[153] To counter this threat, the Nazis insisted that the killing be kept secret and that, among those who did know, everyone possible should participate in the killing operations—from staff officers to clerks to office chiefs from Berlin—so that all would share in the collective guilt.[154] Involvement in the destruction process acted as *blutkitt* ("blood cement") and reduced resistance to the killing.

Abortion proponents are unable to coerce others to participate in the actual act of killing the unborn, but they do consistently support measures that would force others to become more involved. Consider, for instance, their recent attempts to force obstetrics and gynecology residency programs to require residents to receive abortion training and perform abortions. Abortion defenders were concerned about surveys which showed that, while abortion training remained available in 70 percent of residency programs—the same proportion as ten years before—far fewer of the programs *required* the training, and far fewer residents were choosing to perform abortions.[155] The "pro-choice" groups' solution was to try to take the choice away from the residency programs and doctors. The National Abortion Federation, Planned Parenthood, and other abortion proponents successfully lobbied the Accreditation Council for Graduate Medical Education to add a standard that residency programs must require that residents have "experience with induced abortion" for the program to receive accreditation.[156]

Other prominent examples of the push to increase the involvement of others in abortion include the Clinton administration's efforts to provide taxpayer-funded abortions as part of its national health care plan and the administration's aggressive efforts to "export" abortion—by promoting it as part of international "family planning" strategies, for instance, and by insisting that other countries recognize that women have a "fundamental right" to rid themselves of their unborn young.

The abortion movement has been largely successful in its attempt to squelch criticism of the destruction of the unborn. Politicians and other leaders frequently point to activities that they do not think should be outlawed but are willing to call "wrong," or "immoral," or even "evil." Examples include flag burning, pornography, gambling, adultery, and certain types of substance abuse. But abortion is an entirely different matter. Even among those people who consider themselves "pro-choice" but are "personally opposed" to abortion, very few are willing to publicly condemn abortion (even in simply moral terms) and fewer still are willing to try to persuade women not to get them. They understand that being "pro-choice" not only means that you oppose legislation which would prevent women from getting abortions, but also that you will not try to dissuade them from making that decision.

The lengths to which the Supreme Court has been willing to go to protect abortionists and women seeking abortions from criticism is best illustrated by *Akron v. Akron Center for Reproductive Health*.[157] There, the Court held that the Constitution prohibited a City of Akron ordinance that required that women seeking abortions must be informed that the unborn is alive, human, and a child. All of this information is true, of course,[158] and the Court did not attempt to refute any of it when it ruled on the ordinance. Nevertheless, the Court ruled that the ordinance was "designed to influence the woman's informed choice between abortion and childbirth" and struck it down.[159]

Killing in "Self-Defense"

Another technique sometimes used to minimize the guilt associated with killing is to cast the victims as a threat. Killing done to defend oneself or others does not carry the same stigma as the willful destruction of innocent human beings. Thus, where people who regard themselves as "decent" kill, they tend to try to rationalize the killing in terms of self-defense or defense of others. Such rationalizations played an important part in the elimination of the Nazis' victims and continue to play a prominent role in the destruction of the unborn today.

Carrying the unborn to term can occasionally pose a serious threat to the life or health of the pregnant woman. Such instances are rare given the current state of medicine, but they do occur. However, the so-called "self-defense" arguments used by numerous abortion proponents do not apply just to this small group of pregnancies. Instead, abortion proponents tend to argue that, even if the unborn are "persons," pregnant women kill them in "self-defense" in any instance where giving birth would impair the women's livelihood or lifestyle. Jane English, for instance, argues that one has a right to kill persons—even innocent ones—if that is necessary to avoid "drastic injury" to the killer's "life prospects."[160] English starts matter-of-factly with the assertion that a surgeon has a right to kill if that is necessary to preserve his career, and then argues by analogy that a pregnant woman can abort the unborn because "pregnancies (most obviously among teenagers) often have such adverse consequences as a surgeon's loss of livelihood."[161]

The Nazis also massaged their consciences by justifying their killing in terms of "self-defense." Two of the most common excuses used to justify mass killings were fear of epidemics and fear of collaboration with the enemy.[162] Himmler told his SS generals, "We had the moral right vis-à-vis *our* people to annihilate *this* people which wanted to annihilate us."[163] SS units received a standard lecture warning them, "From the earliest times to our own day the Jew has quite literally killed and exterminated the peoples upon whom he has battened insofar as he has been able to do so. Elimination of the Jew from our community is to be regarded as an emergency defence measure."[164] Hitler ordered that "Communists, . . . Jews, gypsies, saboteurs, and agents must basically be regarded as persons who, by their very existence, endanger the security of the troops and are therefore to be executed without further ado."[165] Elsewhere he argued that Jews had to be treated as "tuberculosis bacilli" that could infect a healthy body.[166] This was not cruel, he explained, because sometimes even innocent creatures, like rabbits and deer, had to be killed to prevent harm.[167]

We believe—and rightly so—that it was wrong for personnel at the concentration camps to have killed their prisoners. Yet in the best of circumstances, the consequences of disobeying orders would have jeopardized these individuals' "life prospects" far more than a pregnant woman's life prospects would be harmed by carrying a child to term. Concentration camp personnel were officially members of the Waffen-SS.[168] During the war, release was impossible; the most camp personnel could hope for was a transfer to another unit—most likely one where they stood a much slimmer chance of surviving to the end of the war.[169]

Those inclined to take that chance and request a transfer might ponder Himmler's warning in an October 1943 speech to SS officers: "If anyone you know should be disloyal to the Führer or the Reich, even if only in thought, it is your duty to ensure that this man leaves our Order and we will ensure that he leaves this life."[170]

A number of Nazis raised the "self-defense" argument at the war-crimes trials after the war. Those who performed involuntary experiments on concentration camp prisoners, for instance, argued that they had no choice. Shortly after the trials, one of the American medical experts who assisted in the prosecution of the their crimes responded to the argument that those on trial did what they did because they "had a gun at their head":

> That is true in many cases. They had a gun at their head. But from the standpoint of the law if someone has a gun at my head and puts a gun in my hand and tells me he will shoot me unless I shoot a certain individual, I am a murderer under mitigation. I have no right to murder under the law even though I might be killed if I did not commit the murder.[171]

Superior Orders versus "Choice"

The destruction of the unborn and those associated with the destruction of the unborn and the Nazis' victims share another common feature: in each case, those associated with the killing attempt to minimize their guilt by insisting that it is not their *choice*. Many prominent Nazis tried to use the "superior orders" argument to disavow responsibility for their role in the killing. The concentration camp personnel and their superiors argued that they had simply followed orders, and therefore, were in no way morally culpable for the killing themselves. In the minds of the concentration camp personnel, Raul Hilberg writes, "a clear order was like absolution."[172]

Yet, despite the fact that the Nazis' "superior orders" argument is well known and widely condemned, we approach the issue of "choice" in much the same way. We destroy over 4,000 of our unborn young *each* day, yet no one will accept responsibility for it. The "pro-choice" politicians are not responsible; they are simply "empowering women to make their *own* moral decisions." The fathers of the unborn are not responsible; they know that whether pregnant women choose to abort is exclusively "the woman's decision." The abortionists are not responsible; they are simply using their expertise to allow pregnant women a "meaningful opportunity" to make "their own life choices." And, of course, the women aborting their young are not responsible either. Women do not choose to become pregnant, abortion proponents argue, and, even if they did, they do not choose to have a child which is male instead of female, disabled rather than "normal," etc. If a woman decides to abort, her choice is a choice which is no choice at all: "terminating the pregnancy" is the only way that she can avoid giving the child up for adoption or making the emotional and economic sacrifices entailed in raising the child herself. Naomi Wolf has gone so far as to write that, where pregnancy would interfere with a woman finishing her higher education, the woman may even have an *obligation* to abort.[173]

Many of us know that the unborn are living human beings, and we say we believe that no human life is worthless. Yet we still argue that a woman should be free to kill the unborn if she so chooses. Somehow, we believe we can remain morally insulated from the killing so long as we are not actually doing it ourselves. That argument is no more persuasive now than it was at the Nuremberg trial of the major Nazi war criminals. In the final phrase of his opening argument for the prosecution in that trial, Justice Robert Jackson accused the defendants of "an abdication of personal intelligence and moral responsibility."[174] The defendants continually argued that they did not issue the orders or commit the misdeeds themselves. Nevertheless, they had deliberately closed their eyes to what was going on around them, and as far as the War Crimes Tribunal was concerned, that was enough.

One cannot condone or acquiesce in the willful destruction of innocent human beings and remain blameless. There are times when one has a moral obligation to get off the sidelines. As Holocaust survivor Elie Wiesel has observed, "[T]he opposite of love is not hate; it is indifference."[175]

Accelerating the Inevitable

Those involved in the destruction of the Nazis' victims and the unborn also attempt to minimize their feelings of guilt with another technique: they insist that they are not actually responsible for *killing* their victims, but only for accelerating the inevitable. For instance, abortion proponents are fond of pointing out that abortions performed before viability kill unborn who could not survive outside the womb. But what difference does that make? The unborn are inside the womb, not outside of it. Furthermore, the same abortion proponents who argue that many of the unborn are not viable are often unwilling to restrict the destruction of the unborn even *after* viability. The viability of the unborn is not a real distinction to these abortion proponents, therefore, so much as a convenient rationalization. By focusing on the idea that the unborn would not survive long outside the womb, they dissociate themselves from the result of abortion: the deliberate destruction of the unborn *inside* the womb. The fact that the unborn would not be dead but for the abortion is pushed aside; the fact that abortionists routinely kill even viable young is ignored. Similarly, those who advocate removing the organs from living anencephalic infants defend the practice by pointing out that anencephalic children are typically short-lived.

The Nazis employed similar ruses. The disabled were—in the words of one official Nazi publication—"completely unsuited for living."[176] Those put to death in the euthanasia program were deemed "incurably ill."[177]

Similar rationalizations figured prominently in the atrocities perpetrated at the death camps. The first wave of killing at the camps themselves, "Aktion 14f13," targeted "sick" prisoners.[178] (The designation "14f13" was taken from the abbreviation used for the Inspectorate of Concentration Camps followed by the code used to denote the death of a sick inmate.[179]) Referring to the annihilation of the Jews, Hitler once remarked, "One must not have mercy with people who are determined by fate to perish."[180] When Nazi doctors were tried for performing experiments on the prisoners at the concentration camps without the prisoners' consent, the doctors argued that they had done nothing wrong because their subjects had already been sentenced to die by the Nazi-SS leadership.[181] The doctors also argued that if it was permissible to take the lives of the incurable and the useless—an idea popular in the United States and Britain before the war—then it was permissible to take the lives of those destined to die for political reasons.[182]

"Humane" Killing

Perhaps the most striking feature which distinguishes the destruction of the unborn and the Nazis' victims from widespread killing is the notion of "humane" killing. Abortion proponents frequently contend that some children are better off aborted than born. They maintain that a "termination of pregnancy" is in the best interests of the child when the mother or father cannot provide a loving home, where the child is disabled, or for a variety of other reasons. Indeed, in a recent "Hers" column in *The New York Times Magazine*, abortionist Elizabeth Karlin went so far as to write, "There is only one reason I've ever heard for having an abortion: the desire to be a good mother."[183] Brenda Peterson refers to abortion as "a sacred act of compassion."[184] Ginette Paris, meanwhile, insists that abortion is "an expression of maternal responsibility," and that women must sometimes "sacrifice" the unborn "to a higher cause, namely, the love of children and the refusal to see them suffer."[185]

Those in the Nazi extermination apparatus also took solace in the notion that their actions were "humane." When laborers at the camps became ill or incapacitated, they were "mercifully killed."[186] When Hitler pointed to Spartan practice of selective infanticide as a model for the new Germany, he hailed the practice as "more decent and in truth *a thousand times more humane* than the wretched insanity of our day which preserves the most pathological subject."[187] Later, in his political testament, he would refer to the "humane" means by which he resolved the Jewish Question.[188]

The idea of "humane" killing was especially significant in the euthanasia program. The destruction of the disabled was described as a "humane act"—not "murder."[189] When one of the heads of the program asked Hitler whether the disabled should be killed with gas or overdoses of narcotics, Hitler responded by asking, "Which is more humane?"[190] When actual footage of the gassing of mentally ill patients is shown in the Nazi propaganda film *Mentally Ill*, the narrator explains that the procedure is an act of kindness: "the tortured face and distorted inhuman form of the unfortunate suffering . . . is smoothed into repose through the peace of a gentle death which finally brings the salvation of deliverance."[191] Nurses responsible for the disabled found their role in the killing troubling, but, according to historian Michael Burleigh, "they also regarded it as necessary to 'release' the 'regrettable creatures' in their care from their suffering."[192]

Time and time again after the war, those involved in the euthanasia program would protest that they had acted in the best interests of their victims. At his trial, Karl Brandt—one of the architects of the program—testified that he had not acted against his conscience and had been "motivated by absolutely humane feelings."[193] "Valentin" Faltlhauser, implicated in the killing of hundreds of the disabled, explained that for him "the decisive motive was compassion."[194] Hermann

Pfanmüller—who ran one of the hospitals involved in liquidating the disabled—declared that when he decided which of his patients would die, he "worked . . . solely in the interests of the patients in [his] care."[195]

The families of these patients, incidentally, did not necessarily mind that their relatives had been killed: Pfanmüller pointed to letters he received from parents thanking him for dispatching their handicapped children.[196] Other personnel in the program referred to parents who brought their disabled children to the institutions and asked that they be "put to sleep."[197]

The concept of "humane" killing played an essential role in the Nazis' extermination campaigns. "The 'humaneness' of the destruction process was an important factor in its success," Raul Hilberg writes.[198] But he adds, "[T]his humaneness was evolved not for the benefit of the victims but for the welfare of the perpetrators."[199] The myth that the killing was humane allowed the killers to kill yet still regard themselves as "decent": as individuals who retained their compassion and sense of conscience even in the midst of their killing.

Although the Nazis' capacity for rationalizing their killing as "humane" may seem odd at first, it does account for much of the Nazis' conduct which would otherwise seem inexplicable. It explains how Dr. Wilhelm Pfannenstiel, an SS officer and professor of hygiene, could say that he traveled to a death camp to see whether the extermination process "was accompanied by any acts of cruelty."[200] It explains how Heinrich Himmler could orchestrate the destruction of millions yet denounce hunting for sport.[201] It explains how Hitler could order that German servicemen crippled with physical or psychological injuries be put to death,[202] yet state that he could never harm a little deer and denounce hunters who wounded animals without killing them.[203] Hitler even justified his prosecution of the war in terms of "humaneness": the most drastic methods of warfare were the most humane, he argued, because by shortening war they curtailed its misery.[204]

The Expanding Circle

The most insidious aspect of the idea of "humane" killing is that, by destigmatizing killing, it fosters the proliferation of still more killing. The Nazis' extermination campaigns are a case in point. Hitler's 1929 statement about culling the German population concerned only newborns. In 1937, when he instituted the "euthanasia" program, only children three or younger were targeted. Several years later, the program was expanded to include children up to the age of twelve, and then expanded again to include adults as well.

Why were the young designated for elimination first? And why did the Nazis continue the "children's euthanasia" program when they discontinued the killing of disabled adults? Children did not pose the greatest threat to the German gene pool, obviously; they could not pass on their traits until they were sexually mature. But it was easier to kill the young. It was easier to invoke the "humane" motivations ostensibly behind the killing, it was harder for the killers to put themselves in their victims' shoes, and it was less likely that their victims would apprehend what lay in store for them. The more the killers killed, the more threatening it became for them to reassess their conduct, as opposed to rationalizing it. There was no going back. And, because there was no going back, there was only going forward.

The same phenomenon accounts for the erosion of the selection criteria used to determine which of the disabled and which of the Jews would die. At first, only narrow classes of each group were designated for elimination, but as the scope of the killing progressed, so did the scope of those to be killed.

This same tendency for the scope of killing to expand is already apparent with respect to abortion. The psychological barriers we once had to killing are eroding. When the abortion issue first came to the fore, abortion proponents went to great lengths to distinguish between abortions based on the stage of pregnancy and the reasons for aborting. They tended to condone abortions performed early in pregnancy for compelling reasons but condemn those done later for trivial reasons.[205] But, as we have become accustomed to the destruction of the unborn, abortion proponents have expanded the scope of abortion they find acceptable. Increasingly, they defend a woman's decision to abort her young *whatever* the stage of pregnancy and *whatever* her reasons for wanting to rid herself of the unborn. She should have the unfettered discretion to eliminate her young even if she is making her decision because she wants a son instead of a daughter, a child with blue eyes instead of brown, or because a baby would interfere with her summer vacation to Europe.

The acceptance of abortion has also led to the erosion of the psychological barriers to killing the *born*. We have, in earlier chapters, noted the willingness—in the medical community and the population at large—to withhold treatment from certain disabled infants and even to kill them. As noted there, those sympathetic to such practices tend to borrow the language and rationalizations legitimized in the abortion movement. The newborn which will die is not a "baby"; it is a *fetus ex utero.* The euthanasia of the child is not "killing"; it is a "postnatal abortion." And, of course, the children born with these defects are—like the unborn—not "technically alive," not "human beings," and not "persons."

Nowhere is the connection clearer than in a brief submitted by the American Civil Liberties Union in the Baby Theresa case in Florida several years ago. Arguing in support of those who wanted to remove the organs of an infant with anencephaly while the child lived, the ACLU wrote that "there is absolutely no morally significant change in the fetus between the moments immediately preceding and following birth."[206] The ACLU's brief pointed out "the inconsistency of permitting the termination of pregnancies up to the moment of birth" but "prohibiting the donation of organs just after birth."[207] In other words, if the unborn have no right to life, then it follows that newborns like Baby Theresa have no right to life either. Parties in the same case argued that, under *Roe v. Wade,* parents had a privacy right to remove the organs from their living children if the children were born with anencephaly and the organs would be transplanted.[208]

Killing anencephalic infants and parceling out their organs may strike many of us as obscene, but that idea—like abortion—already enjoys considerable support in the medical community. Although illegal in all 50 states, it has been advocated in numerous articles in medical journals and was deemed "ethically acceptable" in a June 1994 policy statement issued by the American Medical Association's Council on Ethical and Judicial Affairs.[209] Indeed, the Council noted that surveys showed that two-thirds of leading experts in anencephaly and medical ethics regarded the practice as "intrinsically moral."[210]

Those inclined to think that killing in America could never expand beyond the unborn or newborns with serious birth defects would do well to consider a recent incident, described in the *Los Angeles Times* and the *St. Louis Post-Dispatch,* involving the Los Angeles chapter of the high-IQ society Mensa.[211] In November 1994, the chapter's monthly newsletter published two articles from Mensa members advocating the extermination of certain groups of people.[212] In one article, a lawyer argued that society must kill off those who are elderly, sickly, stupid, or unproductive. "We better face that we have to kill people," he explained. "There are not unlimited amount [*sic*] of resources."[213] In the other article, a Ph.D advocated killing the homeless. Some of the homeless, he wrote, are simply victims of circumstance, but the vast majority should be "humanely done away with, like abandoned kittens."[214] He also argued that people with mental disabilities which prevent them from living in normal society should be put to death—again "humanely"—once they are recognized as "defective."[215] Such killing is not wrong, the author explained, because one must distinguish between a "human being" and what is simply "[a] piece of meat in the shape of a man."[216]

Note that the authors of the newsletter articles stress that the killing would be "humane," that it is necessary as a population control measure, and that the victims were not "humans"—all rationalizations which play a prominent role in the destruction of the unborn. (Even the reference to human beings as pieces of meat is familiar. A number of abortion proponents have referred to the unborn as just that.[217]) Equally revealing is a comment made by the newsletter's editor, Nikki Frey, who was surprised that the articles had caused a stir. "I don't think it was harmful," she said. "I don't even think it was that offensive—nobody wants to have a deformed child."[218] The implication behind the last phrase—"*nobody wants to have a deformed child*"—is clear: outrageous as the measures described in the articles are, they might be justified if necessary to avoid having to raise a deformed child.

The Role of the Medical Community

The destruction of the unborn and of the Nazis' victims also differs from other instances of routinized killing because of the extensive involvement of health care personnel. Many in the medical community refuse to take part in abortion, but there is no denying that doctors, nurses, hospitals, and clinics play a central role in the destruction of the unborn. Physicians take the lives of approximately a million and a half of the unborn each year. Indeed, abortion—once condemned by the American Medical Association as the "unwarrantable destruction of human life"[219]—has now become one of the most commonly performed "medical procedures" in the nation. Most obstetrician/gynecologists have done them. And doctors are also at the forefront of related issues, such as experimentation on the aborted remains of the unborn and the push to allow research on living human embryos.

The medical community also played a prominent role in the crimes of the Third Reich. Of all professions, doctors had the greatest involvement in the Nazi party: over 45 percent of physicians were party members.[220] They actively participated in the development and use of torture equipment. They figured prominently in both the leadership and the day-to-day killing of the euthanasia program.[221] They played key roles in selecting which of the disabled and which concentration camp prisoners would die—selections frequently conducted at hospitals.[222] And they killed approximately 100,000 camp prisoners in medical "experiments."[223] As in the case of the doctors currently eager to perform research on the unborn and human embryos, the Nazi doctors were anxious to perform cutting-edge research in an unexplored area.[224] Many of the atrocities perpetrated by these health care personnel were well known and tolerated within the German medical community.[225]

As in the case of the atrocities perpetrated by doctors under the Third Reich, the extensive involvement of medical personnel in the destruction of the unborn has led to the erosion of some of our most fundamental canons of medical ethics. Consider, for instance, the Declaration of Geneva, adopted by the World Medical Association. Under the Declaration, physicians pledge, "I will maintain the utmost respect for human life *from its beginnings*, even under threat, and I will not use my medical knowledge contrary to the laws of humanity."[226] Can a doctor maintain the "utmost respect" for human life while snuffing it out?

Abortion is also irreconcilable with the time-honored physicians' maxim *primum non nocere*—"above all do no harm." In abortion, doctors do more than harm, they kill. And in those instances where the abortion is "unsuccessful," the surviving child is often mutilated or otherwise disabled as a result of the abortionist's handiwork.

And abortion is proscribed—expressly—by the most famous of all ethical standards in medicine: the Hippocratic Oath. The Supreme Court conceded as much in *Roe v. Wade*.[227] The Court concluded, however, that the Oath was simply a "Pythagorean manifesto and not an absolute standard of medical conduct."[228]

The Nazis also found the Hippocratic Oath a stumbling block. Time and time again they tried to dismiss it with approaches strikingly similar to those used by the Supreme Court in *Roe*. In Binding and Hoche's influential 1920 book advocating the destruction of the "unfit," Hoche argued that there had to be exceptions to the Hippocratic Oath and pointed specifically to the Oath's prohibitions on doctors performing abortions.[229] Standards of medical ethics, Hoche wrote, "are not to be regarded as something which remains the same for all eternity."[230] Karl Brandt, who played an instrumental role in the euthanasia program, saw the Oath in similar terms. "One may hang a copy of the Oath of Hippocrates in one's office," he testified at his trial after the war, "but nobody pays any attention to it."[231]

Like the Supreme Court, the Nazis pointed to ancient Greece and Rome as precedent for their views on medical ethics. To increase public support for euthanasia in Germany, Nazi propaganda films noted the Greeks and Romans permitted it.[232] One doctor who selected who would die in the children's euthanasia program explained that the Hippocratic Oath was immaterial because it predated the Stoic concept of euthanasia.[233]

The Nazis' references to Greece and Rome were not mere coincidence. In his study of the German euthanasia program, historian Michael Burleigh writes that those who laid the intellectual foundation for the Nazis' killing attempted to reduce public resistance by pointing to similar practices in ancient society and by manufacturing new definitions of "person" designed to exclude those human beings they intended to kill.[234] The Supreme Court would do much the same thing in *Roe*—on the one hand pointing to free abortion practices in Greece and Rome to undercut the application of the Hippocratic Oath, and on the other, defining "person" so as to exclude those human beings it deemed to have no right to life.

The *Roe* Court's casual dismissal of the Hippocratic Oath stands in stark contrast to the view of the Oath enunciated by Dr. Andrew Ivy. Ivy, one of the medical experts who assisted in the prosecution in the Nuremberg doctors' trial, referred to the Oath in an article he wrote shortly after the trial, analyzing the role played by the medical community in the Nazis' crimes. There, Ivy explained that the medical atrocities perpetrated by the Third Reich were possible only because the doctors involved had forsaken the Hippocratic Oath. After noting that the Oath "has served as the ethical guide for the medical profession for twenty-two centuries,"[235] he wrote, "This Oath pledges us to . . . demonstrate a reverence for life. In the interpretation of biology, there is one important thread that runs throughout and that is, as Schopenhauer pointed out, 'the will-to-live'. If we apply the golden rule to the will to live, we derive therefrom a reverence for life. The Oath of Hippocrates is the golden rule of the physician."[236]

On the basis of his analysis of the Nazi medical crimes, Ivy concluded, "[I]t is dangerous to stray from the ethical code of Hippocrates."[237] "The weakening of one moral principle favors the weakening of others," he warned, "until the individual or profession becomes immoral or amoral."[238]

GERMANY'S HIGH COURT DECISION

Abortion proponents typically dismiss comparisons between the killing of the unborn and the "Final Solution" as the ravings of pro-life extremists. But even those outside the pro-life movement have recognized parallels between the destruction of the unborn and the destruction of the Nazis' victims. The similarities between the two did not escape West Germany's highest court, for instance, when it confronted the abortion question. In *Judgment of February 25, 1975,* a decision reaffirmed by the high court in unified Germany in 1993, the Federal Constitutional Court ruled that under West Germany's Constitution, called the "Basic Law," the state not only had the *right* to protect the lives of the unborn, but the *duty* to do so.[239] In other words, the court held that legalized abortion was unconstitutional in Germany.

The court's decision turned on two provisions in the Basic Law adopted to prevent crimes against humanity like those perpetrated under the Third Reich. The first, at Article 2, Paragraph 2, Sentence 1 of the Basic Law, provides, "Everyone has a right to life." The Constitutional Court held that abortion violates this provision because the word "everyone" applies to every human being—born and unborn. "The right to life," the court wrote, "is guaranteed to everyone who 'lives'; no distinction can be made here between various stages of the life developing itself before birth, or between unborn and born life. 'Everyone' . . . includes the yet unborn human being."[240] The German Constitution, therefore, recognizes a right to life in human beings that we are told the U.S. Constitution gives us a right to kill.

The fact that the Federal Constitutional Court recognized that the unborn are "living" is significant. The U.S. Supreme Court's decisions gloss over the fact that the right to abort is tantamount to a right to kill by stating that science has not yet resolved the question of whether the unborn are living.[241] Germany's high court, however, was under no delusions about whether the unborn are alive. It wrote, "The task of the penal law from the beginning has been to protect the elementary values of community life. . . . [T]he life of every human being is among the most important legal values. . . . The interruption of pregnancy irrevocably destroys an existing human life. Abortion is an act of killing. . . .

The description, now common, 'interruption of pregnancy,' cannot camouflage this fact."[242]

The Constitutional Court also expressly renounced the notion, advanced by certain German abortion proponents, that whether human beings have a right to life turns on their state of development. It wrote:

> The process of development . . . is a continuing process which exhibits no sharp demarcation and does not allow a precise division of the various steps of development of the human life. The process does not end even with birth; the phenomena of consciousness which are specific to the human personality, for example, appear for the first time a rather long time after birth. Therefore, the protection of . . . the Basic Law cannot be limited either to the "completed" human being after birth or to the child about to be born which is independently capable of living. . . .
>
> The sense and purpose of the Basic Law require that the protection of life should also be extended to the life developing itself. The security of human existence against encroachments by the state would be incomplete if it did not also embrace the prior step of "completed life," unborn life.[243]

In addition to holding that the "right to life" provision in the Basic Law protects the unborn, the Constitutional Court also held that the unborn were protected under Article 2, Paragraph 1, of the Basic Law, which protects human dignity.[244] "Where human life exists," the court wrote, "human dignity is present to it; it is not decisive that the bearer of this dignity himself be conscious of it and know personally how to preserve it. The potential faculties present in the human being from the beginning suffice to establish human dignity."[245]

The Constitutional Court recognized that, because life is the fundamental right from which all other human rights emanate, the right to life must be treated with special deference, and not simply relegated to the status of one right among many. "Human life," it explained, "represents, within the order of the Basic Law, an ultimate value, the particulars of which need not be established; it is the living foundation of human dignity and the prerequisite for all other fundamental rights."[246] While the court acknowledged that women have a right under German law not to become parents, the court also noted that that right had limits—"the rights of others, the constitutional order, and the moral law"—and that it could never "include the authorization to intrude upon the protected sphere of right of another without a justifying reason much less to destroy that sphere along with the life itself."[247]

In support of its construction of the Basic Law, the Constitutional Court explained that the protections the Basic Law extended to human life and dignity had to be read in light of Germany's experience under the Nazis:

> Underlying the Basic Law are principles for the structuring of the state that may be understood only in light of the historical experience and the spiritual-moral confrontation with the previous system of National Socialism. In opposition to the totalitarian state which claimed for itself limitless dominion over all areas of social life and in which, in the prosecution of goals of state, consideration for the life of an individual meant nothing, the Basic Law . . . has erected an order bound together by values which places the individual human being at the focal point of all its ordinances. At its basis lies the concept . . . that human beings possess an inherent worth as individuals in order of creation which uncompromisingly demands unconditional respect for the life of every human being, even for the apparently socially "worthless," and which, therefore excludes the destruction of such life without legally justifiable grounds.[248]

"The express incorporation into the Basic Law of the self-evident right to life," the Constitutional Court wrote, "may be explained principally as reaction to the 'destruction of life unworthy of life' [and] to the 'final solution' and 'liquidations,' which were carried out by the National Socialistic Regime as measures of state."[249]

CONCLUSION

The preceding discussion outlines just some of the similarities between abortion in America and the Nazis' killing. The two are *not* identical. But I do not think that I debase the memory of the approximately 12 million individuals who perished in the Nazis' death camps and asylums by suggesting the two are comparable. We have killed well over that number of our unborn—deliberately and dispassionately—since 1985 alone. To say that the two are not comparable one must believe that the unborn are not human beings or that not all human beings are created equal. I reject both propositions.

But even those not concerned about the actual destruction of the unborn have good reason to find the proliferation of abortion disturbing. The ramifications of our accommodation of abortion stretch far beyond the effect on the unborn themselves. As abortion has become accepted as part of the fabric of American culture, the corrosive thinking underlying it has also taken root. Directly and indirectly, abortion proponents tell us that some of our species are not human beings and that some human beings have no right to live. We are told that one may kill so long as the killing is "humane," or the end is a "better" society, or the killing is necessary to preserve one's "life prospects." We are told that it is permissible to kill those who will soon be dead anyway, and that the Hippocratic Oath and other long-held medical standards can be dispensed with if they become inconvenient or unfashionable. We are told that whether individuals are human beings is a "subjective question" and that we have no duty to prevent the destruction of the innocent so long as those doing the killing regard their victims as subhuman.

These notions, obviously, have consequences that reach far beyond abortion. Some may be content to limit their application to the unborn, but others will follow them through to their logical conclusion—and logically there is no reason to distinguish between the child before it passes through its mother's birth canal and afterward.

After World War II, Werner Catel—a German professor who helped decide who would die in the euthanasia program—managed to avoid prosecution, secure a position teaching pediatric medicine, and publish a book advocating the "mercy killing" of certain infants with birth defects.[250] In a 1964 interview in *Der Spiegel*, Catel defended his position by arguing that the disabled newborns were "not people, but simply beings produced by people."[251] "Believe me," he explained, "in every case it is possible to distinguish these creatures without a soul from those who will become human."[252] Catel urged physicians to tell parents that these children were "beyond help, that they will never become a person."[253] The same rationales Catel used to defend infanticide over thirty years ago are prominent in the abortion movement today. And, increasingly, the same arguments are used to justify the destruction of disabled newborns.

Deep down, all of us would like to deny the nightmare of large-scale atrocities. It is easier to take solace in a comfortable myth than to confront the terrible truth. How else can one explain the substantial portion of the population which persists in the denying that the Holocaust occurred—even in the face of mountains of evidence to the contrary? Yet we have seen in Nazi Germany the perils that can follow from dehumanization and the abdication of conscience. We have seen that Americans too can perpetrate atrocities. We have seen that people with a sense of right and wrong can kill.

In this country, conceived in the notion that all human beings are created equal and that each has an inherent right to life, we cannot afford to countenance the destruction of the unborn—or any other innocent human beings. The nation has not always lived up to the high ideals it set for itself in 1776, but never have we looked back and decided that we erred by concluding that *too many* human beings were equal or that *too many* had a right to life. The idea that some members of the human family have no intrinsic worth, that they can be snuffed out without consequence, is not only wrong, it challenges the very philosophical core of who we are as a people.

The inherent rights of all human beings seemed obvious to us after World War II. We prosecuted the Nazis for "crimes against humanity"; we signed human rights treaties in which we declared that "recognition of the inherent dignity and . . . equal and inalienable rights of all members of the human family is the foundation of freedom, justice and peace throughout the world."[254] These expressions of noble sentiment are rank hypocrisy unless we are prepared to live by them.

NOTES

1. Heinz Höhne, *The Order of the Death's Head: The Story of Hitler's SS*, trans. Richard Barry (New York: Ballantine, 1969), 425.

2. Höhne, 404–405.

3. Raul Hilberg, *The Destruction of the European Jews*, rev. and definitive ed. (New York: Holmes & Meiers, 1985), vol. 1, 410.

4. Hilberg, *The Destruction*, vol.3, 1010.

5. *Volkischer Beobachter*, no. 131, August 7, 1929, quoted in Donald J. Deitrich, *Catholic Citizens in the Third Reich: Psycho-Social Principles and Moral Reasoning* (New Brunswick, NJ: Transaction Books, 1988), 217.

6. Eliot Barculo Wheaton, *Prelude to Calamity: The Nazi Revolution 1933–35* (Garden City, NY: Doubleday, 1968), 94.

7. J. M. Roberts, *The Penguin History of the World* (New York: Penguin, 1987) 870.

8. Wheaton, 90.

9. Hilberg, *The Destruction*, vol. 3, 1010.

10. Höhne, 432–433.

11. Hilberg, *The Destruction*, vol. 3, 1025.

12. Höhne, 432–433.

13. Hilberg, *The Destruction*, vol. 3, 1009.

14. George Kren and Leon Rappoport, *The Holocaust and the Crisis of Human Behavior*, rev. ed. (New York: Holmes & Meiers, 1994), 15.

15. See, for example, Hilberg, *The Destruction*, vol. 3, 873 (" 'Euthanasia' was a conceptual as well as technological and administrative prefiguration of the 'Final Solution' in the death camps."); Kren and Rappoport, 23 ("[T]he euthanasia program could not have failed to serve as a model for the later Holocaust."); Gerald Fleming, *Hitler and the Final Solution* (Berkeley, CA: University of California Press, 1984), 24 ("A straight path leads from the built-in gas chambers of the euthanasia institutes in Brandenburg, Bensburg, Grafeneck, Hartheim, Hadamar, Sonnenstein, and Eichberg to the extermination camp in Sobibor."); David Weinberg and Bryan L. Sherwin, "The Holocaust: A Historical Overview," in *Encountering the Holocaust: An Interdisciplinary Survey*, eds. Bryan L. Sherwin and Susan G. Ament (Chicago: Impact Press, 1979), 17: "The Euthanasia Program, in a sense, was a 'dry run' for the extermination of Jews a few years later."

16. J. David Smith, *Minds Made Feeble: The Myth and Legacy of the Kallikaks* (Rockville, MD: Aspen, 1985), 166.

17. Smith, 165.

18. Charles Darwin, *The Descent of Man*, in *The World's Greatest Classic Books*, CD-ROM (Ottawa: Fulcrum, 1995).

19. James Burke, *The Day the Universe Changed* (Boston: Little, Brown, 1985), 261.

20. The solutions advanced by eugenicists included euthanizing degenerates and allowing mothers to smother disabled children. Curiously, however, the eugenicists generally rejected abortion. "[T]he American Eugenic Society regarded it as murder, unless performed on strict medical grounds." Daniel J. Kevles, *In the Name of Eugenics* (New York: Knopf, 1985), 92.

21. "The SS—Blood and Soil," *The War File*, PBS, WITF, Harrisburg, PA, April 20, 1991.

22. Kevles, 90. For a detailed discussion of Sanger's connection to the eugenics movement, see Angela Franz, "Margaret Sanger & PPFA: The Eugenics Connection," *National Right to Life News*, September 30, 1997: 10+ (Part I) and October 21, 1997: 10+ (Part II).

23. Margaret Sanger, *My Fight for Birth Control*, quoted in Donald K. Pickens, *Eugenics and the Progressives* (Nashville: Vanderbilt University Press, 1968), 83.

24. Gould, "Racism and Recapitulation," in his *Ever Since Darwin: Reflections in Natural History* (New York: W. W. Norton, 1977), 217.

25. Daniel Gasman, *The Scientific Origins of National Socialism: Social Darwinism in Ernst Haeckel and the German Monist League* (New York: American Elsevier, 1971), 150.

26. Gasman, 150.

27. Gasman, 161.

28. Gasman, 8, 14, 61.

29. Gasman, 14.

30. Gasman, 95.

31. Gasman, 150.

32. "The SS—Blood and Soil."

33. Michael Burleigh, *Death and Deliverance: Euthanasia in Germany 1900–1945* (New York: Cambridge University Press, 1994), 15–18.

34. Burleigh, 3.

35. Gasman, 165.

36. Gasman, 172–173.

37. "Himmler the Mystic," *The War File*, PBS, WITF, Harrisburg, PA, November 30, 1991.

38. "The SS—Blood and Soil."

39. Höhne, 179.

40. Höhne, 177, 179.

41. Sheila Faith Weiss, *Race Hygiene and National Efficiency: The Eugenics of Wilhelm Schallmeyer* (Berkeley: University of California Press, 1987), 155.

42. Henry Friedlander, *The Origins of Nazi Genocide: From Euthanasia to the Final Solution* (Chapel Hill: University of North Carolina Press, 1995), 26.

43. Richard Breitman, *The Architect of Genocide: Himmler and the Final Solution* (New York: Knopf, 1991), 90.

44. Breitman, 90.

45. Smith, 164.

46. "Adolf Hitler," *The War File*, PBS, WITF, Harrisburg, PA, May 5, 1991.

47. "Adolf Hitler."

48. "Adolf Hitler."

49. Smith, 164.

50. Smith, 164.

51. "Adolf Hitler."

52. "Adolf Hitler."

53. "Adolf Hitler."

54. Fleming, 23.

55. Burleigh, 180, 238.

56. Burleigh, 180, 238.

57. Burleigh, 221.

58. "Adolf Hitler."

59. Weiss, 2; Kevles, 117.

60. Höhne, 373.

61. Höhne, 425.

62. Höhne, 425.

63. "Adolf Hitler."

64. Andrew C. Ivy, "Nazi War Crimes of a Medical Nature," in *Ethics in Medicine: Historical Perspectives and Contemporary Concerns*, eds. Stanley Joel Reiser, Arthur J. Dyck, and William J. Curran (Cambridge, MA: MIT Press, 1977), 270.

65. Smith, 139.

66. Smith, 139.

67. Kevles, 116.

68. Burleigh, 36–37.

69. Kevles, 116.

70. 274 U.S. 200.

71. Smith, 139.

72. 274 U.S. at 207.

73. See Paul A. Lombardo, "Three Generations, No Imbeciles: New Light on Buck v. Bell," *New York University Law Review* 60 (1985): 30.

74. Those associated with the Nazis' euthanasia campaign sometimes sought solace in a Nietzsche maxim that is strikingly similar: "What causes more suffering than the stupidity of the compassionate?" Burleigh, 202.

75. Margaret Sanger, "The Need for Birth Control in America," in *Birth Control: Facts and Responsibilities*, ed. Adolf Meyer (Baltimore: Williams and Wilkins, 1925), 47–48, quoted in Franz, "Margaret Sanger & the PPFA" (Part I).

76. Smith, 138.

77. Smith, 138.

78. Smith, 158.

79. Ernie Pyle, *Last Chapter* (New York: Henry Holt, 1945), 5, quoted in John W. Dower, *War without Mercy: Race and Power in the Pacific War* (New York: Pantheon, 1986), 78.

80. Dower, 77–93.

81. Dower, 85.

82. Dower, 86–87.

83. Dower, 53.

84. Dower, 64.

85. Dower, 71.

86. Dower, 65.

87. Dower, 65.

88. Dower, 65.

89. Dower, 129.

90. Dower, 108.

91. "Germany," *Encyclopaedia Britannica: Macropedia*, 15th ed. (1995).

92. Currently, there are approximately 1.4 million abortions in the United States each year. Steven Waldman, Elise Ackerman, and Rita Rubin, "Abortions in America," *U.S. News and World Report*, January 19, 1998: 22. The number has dropped somewhat from the 1.6 million abortions reported in 1990. *Statistical Abstract of the United States, 1997* (Washington: Government Printing Office, 1997), 83.

93. Yehuda Bauer, *The Holocaust in Historical Perspective* (Seattle: University of Washington Press, 1978), 9.

94. Helmut Krausnick, "The Persecution of the Jews," trans. Dorothy Long, Institute für Zeitgeschicte (Munich, Germany), in *Anatomy of the SS State*, trans. Richard H. Barry, Marian Jackson, and Dorothy Long (London: Collins, 1968), 22.

95. Höhne, 370.

96. Fleming, 41.

97. Press report, *New York Post*, November 16, 1938, quoted in George Seldes, comp., *The Great Thoughts* (New York: Ballantine, 1985), 163.

98. Gasman, 164.

99. Adolf Hitler, *Mein Kampf*, trans. Ralf Manheim (London: Hutchinson, 1969) 47 ff, quoted in Werner Maser, *Hitler: Legend, Myth and Reality*, trans. Peter Ross and Betty Ross (New York: Harper, 1971), 164 (emphasis added).

100. Hilberg, *The Destruction*, vol. 3, 946. (Hirt's report noted that scientists had few skulls from Jews and certain other peoples to study. He requested, therefore, that doctors in the concentration camps select specimens from each group, record their vital statistics, and then kill them and retrieve their skulls. Fifteen people—Jews, Central Asians, and Poles—were killed to this end. The incident has a morbid parallel in the abortion movement. In Finland in 1974, American researcher Peter Adam used a grant from the National Institutes of Health to cut the heads off living aborted children and study their brain metabolism. Peter Adam et al., "Cerebral Oxidation of Glucose and D-beta-Hydroxy Butyrate in the Isolated Perfused Human Head," *Transactions of the American Pediatrics Society* 309 (1973): 81; Richard Doerflinger, "The U.S. Government and Fetal Research: A Record of Shame," *National Right to Life News*, March 16, 1994: 10+. While Hirt may have regarded the subjects of his research as non-human or "subhuman," the title of Adam's article shows that Adam knew his own subjects were "human.")

101. Ivy, 267–268.

102. Höhne, 567–568.

103. Burleigh, 45, 52, 98.

104. Burleigh, 44.

105. Burleigh, 274.

106. "Judgment of the International Military Tribunal Against Major Nazi War Criminals and Criminal Organizations," *Temple Law Quarterly* 20 (1946): 236.

107. Kren and Rappoport, 20.

108. Robert J. Lifton, *The Nazi Doctors: Medical Killing and the Psychology of Genocide* (New York: Basic Books, 1986), 76.

109. Burleigh, 44.

110. Gasman, 40 (emphasis added).

111. John Tusa and Ann Tusa, *The Nuremberg Trial* (New York: Atheneum, 1984), 166.

112. Burleigh, 37.

113. Burleigh, 298.

114. Burleigh, 212.

115. Burleigh, 97.

116. Burleigh, 25.

117. "Nuremberg Laws," *Encyclopaedia Britannica: Micropedia*, 15th ed. (1995).

118. Burleigh, 3.

119. Stephen Jay Gould, "Carrie Buck's Daughter," in *The Flamingo's Smile: Reflections in Natural History* (New York: Norton, 1985), 310.

120. Quoted in Burleigh, 19.

121. Höhne, 414.

122. Fleming, 2.

123. Kren and Rappoport, 138.

124. Zygmunt Bauman, *Modernity and the Holocaust* (Ithaca, NY: Cornell University Press, 1989), 91–92.

125. Burleigh, 100.

126. Hilberg, *The Destruction*, vol. 3, 1010.

127. Thomas Mann, "Germany and the Germans," *Yale Review*, Winter 1946: 235, quoted in Wheaton, 489 n. 233.

128. Carroll Bogert, "Abortion and the Fight for God," *Newsweek*, October 17, 1994: 40.

129. Bogert, 40.

130. Elizabeth Karlin, " 'We Call It Kindness': Establishing a Feminist Abortion Practice," in *Abortion Wars: A Half Century of Struggle, 1950–2000*, ed. Rickie Solinger (Berkeley: University of California Press, 1998), 274.

131. Karlin, 279.

132. Laura Kaplan, "Beyond Safe and Legal: The Lessons of Jane," in *Abortion Wars: A Half Century of Struggle, 1950–2000*, ed. Rickie Solinger (Berkeley: University of California Press, 1998), 33, 35.

133. D. Redman, "The Choices," *Mother Jones*, January/February 1994: 32.

134. Redman, 35.

135. Edward Schumacher, "Feminists Stage Abortions," *New York Times*, November 10, 1985, sec. I: 7.

136. Schumacher.

137. Ginette Paris, *The Sacrament of Abortion*, trans. Joanna Mott (Dallas: Spring, 1992) 57, 107.

138. Brenda Peterson, "Sister Against Sister," *New Age Journal*, September/October 1993: 143, 144.

139. Naomi Wolf, "Our Bodies, Our Souls: Re-thinking Abortion Rhetoric," *New Republic*, October 16, 1995: 35.

140. Wolf, 35 (emphasis added).

141. Kren and Rappoport, 145.

142. Kren and Rappoport, 145.

143. Gasman, 172.

144. Gasman, 172; and "Himmler the Mystic."

145. "Adolf Hitler"; and Weiss, 158.

146. Gasman, 91, 95.

147. Gasman, 162.

148. Gasman, 164.

149. Gasman, 172.

150. Gasman, 172.

151. Kren and Rappoport, 147.

152. Kren and Rappoport, 147 (emphasis added).

153. Hilberg, *The Destruction*, vol. 3, 1013.

154. Hilberg, *The Destruction*, vol. 3, 1013; and Höhne, 415.

155. H. Trent MacKay and Andrea Phillips MacKay, "Abortion Training in Obstetrics and Gynecology Residency Programs in the United States, 1991–1992," *Family Planning Perspectives* 27.3 (1995): 112–115.

156. Julie Rovner, "Congress Votes to Block Abortion Training Requirements," *Lancet* 347 (1996): 894; and David Andrusko, "ACGME Requires Mandatory Abortion Training for Obstetricians," *National Right to Life News*, February 22, 1995: 8.

157. *Akron v. Akron Center for Reproductive Health*, 462 U.S. 416.

158. I have explained why the unborn are living and human beings in Chapters 2 and 3. I explain why they are "children" in the next chapter.

159. 462 U.S. 416, 443–444.

160. Jane English, "Abortion and the Concept of a Person," *Canadian Journal of Philosophy* 5 (1975): 238.

161. English, 238–239.

162. Höhne, 415–416.

163. Hilberg, *The Destruction*, vol. 3, 1009.

164. Höhne, 371.

165. Höhne, 406.

166. Fleming, 156.

167. Fleming, 156.

168. Hans Buchheim, "Command and Compliance," trans. Richard Barry, Institute für Zeitgeschichte, 395.

169. Buchheim, 395.

170. Buchheim, 373–374.

171. Ivy, 270.

172. Hilberg, *The Destruction*, vol. 3, 1024.

173. Wolf, 33.

174. Tusa, 407.

175. Elie Wiesel, "One Must Not Forget," *U.S. News & World Report*, October 27, 1986: 68.

176. Smith, 165–166.

177. Maser, 245.

178. Burleigh, 220.

179. Burleigh, 220.

180. Hilberg, *The Destruction*, vol. 3, 1029.

181. Ivy, 270.

182. Ivy, 270.

183. Elizabeth Karlin, "An Abortionist's Credo," *New York Times Magazine*, March 19, 1995: 32.

184. Peterson, 143.

185. Paris, 8, 107.

186. Ivy, 267.

187. Gasman, 165 (emphasis added).

188. Hilberg, *The Destruction*, vol. 3, 1009.

189. "Life Support/Conceiving the Future," *Medicine at the Crossroads*, PBS, WITF, Harrisburg, PA, April 12, 1993.

190. Lifton, 72.

191. Burleigh, 202.

192. Burleigh, 105.

193. Burleigh, 277

194. Burleigh, 227.

195. Burleigh, 129.

196. Burleigh, 143.

197. Burleigh, 96.

198. Hilberg, *The Destruction*, vol. 3, 1009.

199. Hilberg, *The Destruction*, vol. 3, 1009.

200. Kren and Rappoport, 73.

201. Wheaton, 351.

202. Maser, 171.

203. Wheaton, 351.

204. Maser, 159.

205. See, for example, Judith Jarvis Thomson, "A Defense of Abortion," in *Modern Constitutional Theory: A Reader*, eds. John H. Garvey and T. Alexander Aleinikoff, 2d ed. (St. Paul: West, 1991), 513; and English, 242–243.

206. Quoted in Paul Greenberg, "The Power of a Cartoon," *National Right to Life News*, December 13, 1994: 18.

207. Quoted in Greenberg.

208. *In re T.A.C.P.*, 609 So.2d 588, 593 n. 9 (Fla. 1992).

209. John Glasson et al., "The Use of Anencephalic Neonates as Organ Donors," *Journal of the American Medical Association* 273 (1995): 1614.

210. Glasson et al., 1614.

211. See Nora Zamichow, "Newsletter Articles Stir Furor in High-IQ Group," *Los Angeles Times*, January 10, 1995: B1+; and Elaine Viets, "Something Scary about These 'Smart' Writers," *St. Louis Post-Dispatch Everyday Magazine*, November 9, 1994: 3F.

212. Both the Greater Los Angeles Area Mensa chapter and American Mensa, Ltd. point out that the newsletter articles represented the individual members' opinions and neither Mensa nor its membership endorsed the newsletter's contents. Zamichow.

213. Zamichow.

214. Zamichow.

215. Zamichow; and Viets.

216. Zamichow.

217. James Tunstead Burtchaell, *Rachel Weeping and Other Essays* (Kansas City: Andrews & McMeel, 1982), 196.

218. Zamichow.

219. *Roe v. Wade*, 410 U.S. 113, 142 (quoting the report of the American Medical Association's Committee on Criminal Abortion in *Transactions of the American Medical Association* 12 [1859]: 28, 78).

220. Annette Tufts, "Apologies for Nazi Crimes," *Lancet* 344 (September 17, 1994): 808.

221. For instance, Dr. Leonardo Conti, Reich Minister for Health, and Dr. Karl Brandt, one of Hitler's personal physicians, performed the first killing in the adult euthanasia program to emphasize that the very highest medical authorities were involved. Burleigh, 134.

222. Smith, 164; Burleigh, 220–221; and Hilberg, *The Destruction*, vol. 3, 973.

223. Tufts, "Apologies for Nazi Crimes," 808.

224. Hilberg, *The Destruction*, vol. 3, 940.

225. Albert R. Jonsen and Leonard A. Sagan, "Torture and the Ethics of Medicine," in *The Breaking of Bodies and Minds: Torture, Psychiatric Abuse and the Health Professions*, ed. Eric Stover and Elena O. Nightingale (New York: W. H. Freeman, 1985), 30.

226. "The Declaration of Geneva," reprinted in Jonsen and Sagan, 268.

227. 410 U.S. 113, 131.

228. 410 U.S. at 132.

229. Burleigh, 18.

230. Burleigh, 18.

231. Burleigh, 275.

232. Burleigh, 213.

233. Burleigh, 100.

234. Burleigh, 298.

235. Ivy, 270.

236. Ivy, 270.

237. Ivy, 271–272.

238. Ivy, 271.

239. Robert E. Jonas and John D. Gorby, "West German Abortion Decision: A Contrast to *Roe v. Wade*," *John Marshall Journal of Practice and Procedure* 9 (1976): 605; and Stephen Kinzer, "German Court Restricts Abortion, Angering Feminists and the East," *New York Times*, May 29, 1993: 1. In its 1993 decision, the Constitutional Court held that abortion is illegal, but Parliament could pass legislation exempting the abortionist and woman from prosecution where the abortion occurs within the first trimester and the woman has undergone counseling directed toward saving the unborn at least three days beforehand. Annette Tufts, "Germany: Illegality of Abortion," *Lancet* 341 (1993): 1467.

240. Jonas and Gorby, 638.

241. See, e.g., *Roe v. Wade*, 410 U.S. 113, 159. (The Supreme Court has reinforced this misconception by referring to the "difficult" or "unanswerable" question of whether the unborn are living and by routinely referring to the unborn as "potential life." Examples of these references can be found in Chapter 2.)

242. Jonas and Gorby, 645.

243. Jonas and Gorby, 638.

244. Jonas and Gorby, 641.

245. Jonas and Gorby, 641.

246. Jonas and Gorby, 642.

247. Jonas and Gorby, 642.

248. Jonas and Gorby, 662.

249. Jonas and Gorby, 637–638.

250. Burleigh, 284.

251. Quoted in Burleigh, 284.

252. Quoted in Burleigh, 284.

253. Quoted in Burleigh, 284.

254. Universal Declaration of Human Rights, G.A. res. 217A (III), U.N. Doc A/810 at 71 (1948), reprinted in *Encyclopedia of Human Rights*, ed. Edward Lawson (New York: Taylor and Francis Institute, 1991), 1655–1657.

8

Language

"But I only killed a louse, Sonia. A useless, nasty, harmful louse."
"A human being—a louse?"
Fyodor Dostoyevsky, *Crime and Punishment*

Most of the occasions for the troubles of this world are grammatical.
Michel Eyquen Montaigne, *Essays*

Anyone familiar with the abortion debate knows language plays a central role in it. Both camps have their own lexicons. Those opposed to abortion call themselves "pro-life." They refer to the unborn as a "child," a "baby," a "human being," and a "person"; they regard abortion as "killing" and even "murder"; they tend to view abortion as a "human rights" issue; and they refer to their opposition as "pro-abortion." Abortion proponents, however, refer to themselves as "pro-choice." They call the unborn a "clump of cells," a "blob," "tissue," and "part of the mother"; they regard abortion as a routine but sometimes essential "medical procedure"; they perceive abortion as a "women's issue" and as necessary for women to have full equality in society; and they refer to their opposition as "anti-choice." Both camps seem to regard the battle over language to be as crucial to the outcome as securing the high ground in a military campaign.

Why do both sides expend so much energy arguing over the labels that will be used in the abortion debate? Whatever their differences on the issue of abortion itself, pro-life and pro-choice leaders realize that the language we use affects our attitudes about abortion. We condone the destruction of the unborn, in large part, because the language we use with respect to abortion disguises the fact that the unborn are humans and that they are children, and that abortion involves killing them.

I

Sometimes our dehumanization of the unborn through language is obvious. We refer to the unborn as a "pre-human," "a chunk of tissue," "the pregnancy," "the conception," "a gobbet of meat protruding from a human womb," "cell matter," "part of the mother's body," "potential life," and "sub-human non-personhood."[1] Certainly these are not terms one uses to refer to human beings. Indeed, there is even a tendency to use language that suggests that the unborn is somehow malignant, in addition to non-human. Betty Friedan has compared abortion to a mastectomy, for instance.[2] Others have referred to the unborn as "growths" and compared them to tumors and parasites.[3] In his book *Abortion Practice*, for instance, the nation's most widely used textbook on abortion methods and procedures, Dr. Warren Hern writes, "The relationship between the gravid [pregnant] female and the fetoplacental unit can best be understood as one of host and parasite."[4]

Persons who defend abortion also tend to dehumanize the unborn by denying that they are "children." No child is a "child," in their view, until after birth. The Supreme Court of Tennessee put the matter bluntly in a recent case involving the fate of frozen embryos. There, the court said that "'child' means something other than 'fetus.'"[5] Garret Hardin, a biologist and staunch abortion proponent, refers to the unborn as an "embryo" or a "fetus" but not as a "child" because he feels calling the unborn a "child" is "a sneaky way of implying that the powers, privileges, and rights of a later stage belong also to an earlier one. . . . We give a child the right to life. Until we have decided that we want also to give the embryo the very same right, unconditionally, we should not call it an *unborn child*, for that would prejudice inquiry."[6]

There are a number of problems with Hardin's argument. First, he assumes that children do not have a right to life simply by virtue of being human. Born children have a right to life, he says, because we *"give"* them one, and the unborn have no right to life unless we decide to *give* them one also. Second, to Hardin, the word "child" has no independent ontological significance: It is simply a means of distinguishing which of our young may be killed. Those with a recognized right to life are "children"; those who do not are something else. Using Hardin's logic, a people that routinely practices infanticide is not killing "children" because the victims do not have a recognized right to life.

While Hardin's argument has its own peculiar weaknesses, his reasoning is representative of that of most abortion proponents who argue that the unborn are not "children." They have not come to terms with the fact that abortion kills children. They defend abortion and realize that abortion kills the unborn. But, because they cannot imagine they could ever defend the killing of children, they reason backward and assume that the unborn cannot be children.

While abortion proponents are understandably uncomfortable with the notion, the fact of the matter is the unborn *are* children. *Webster's Third New International Dictionary* defines "child" in part as "an unborn or recently born person: FETUS, INFANT, BABY."[7] The *American Heritage Dictionary* attributes a similar definition to the word: "an unborn infant; fetus."[8] So does *The Oxford English Dictionary*. The definitions of "child" there include "the unborn or newly born human being; foetus, infant."[9] Furthermore, as I explained in Chapter 5, the unborn are protected as "children" under the UN Convention on the Rights of the Child (1989).

In other cases, the dehumanization is more insidious. Consider, for instance, the terminology used to refer to the unborn in *The New York Times*, a paper regarded as solidly pro-abortion. James Burtchaell has observed:

When the *Times* is either editorializing on behalf of abortion freedom, or presenting new stories in furtherance of that end, there is talk only of "the fetus," "the unborn," "the embryo," and other terms which consistently avoid any acknowledgment of human peerage in the womb. But when the *Times* is reporting or opining on medical efforts to rescue the unborn from various misfortunes, its vocabulary enlarges to speak of "the endangered baby," "the baby still residing in the womb," or, simply, "the baby." The clear inference from this language is that when a child is welcomed, he or she is a baby from the start.[10]

Many of the other "mainstream" news media do the same thing.

Sometimes the dehumanizing aspect of the language we use to refer to the unborn is entirely unintentional; the unborn are relegated to the status of non-humans because of our lack of information about them, or shortcomings in the English language. Consider, for instance, the words "embryo" and "fetus." Both terms can properly be applied to human unborn under particular circumstances.[11] But neither word necessarily refers to human beings. The term "embryo" can refer to any animal in its early stages of growth and differentiation.[12] The same word used to describe the developing human being also refers to the developing sea urchin. The term "fetus," meanwhile, can refer to *any* unborn or unhatched young vertebrate, especially once it begins to re-semble the adult animal in structure.[13] A "fetus" can be a human being within the womb or a young lizard within its leathery shell.

Ordinarily, of course, people do not characterize the unborn as "em-bryos" or "fetuses" in a deliberate attempt to dehumanize them. But the habitual use of the terms can, nevertheless, have a dehumanizing ef-fect. Referring to the unborn as a "fetus" or "embryo" is akin to refer-ring to Scots or Hindus as "animals." Technically, the term may be correct, since human beings are animals, but it tends to obscure the fact that we are referring to a very special type of animal: *a human being.*

The pronoun we use most often to refer to the unborn—"it"—is also problematic. Intentionally or not, the word reinforces the idea that the unborn are not human beings. Generally, of course, we do not use the word "it" to refer to human beings; we use "him" or "her." "It" is reserved for things which are sub-human: animals, plants, and non-living things. But, because we do not know whether the unborn is a "he" or a "she" in many instances, and because English does not afford us with another alternative, we resort to "it" to refer to our young—in-advertently lumping them together with the other, sub-human "its."

II

The language that we use to refer to the actual *act* of abortion is also problematic. It obscures just what abortion involves. We are reluctant to admit that abortion is an act of killing, one which results in the de-struction of a human being. Instead, we camouflage the deed with euphemisms to make what should disturb us less disturbing. Through language abortion is transformed from an act of killing to a sterile medi-cal procedure—a "termination of pregnancy" or a "reproductive health service." Or it is transformed into a political act: those who abort are not destroying their young, they are simply making a "choice" or exercising their "reproductive freedom." George Will writes:

> Abortion advocates have speech quirks which may betray qualms. Homeowners kill crabgrass. Abortionists kill fetuses. Homeowners do not speak of "terminating" crabgrass. But Planned Parenthood of New York City . . . has published an abortion guide that uses the word "kill" only twice, once to say what some women did to themselves before legalized abortion, and once to describe what some contraceptives do to sperm. But when referring to the killing of fetuses, the book, like abortion advocates generally, uses only euphemisms, like "termination of potential life."[14]

The manipulation of language so permeates the abortion movement that many abortion proponents are reluctant even to characterize abortion as "abortion." Glanville Williams, a leading advocate for abortion on demand in Britain, concedes that "many doctors attempt to avoid what they consider to be the unsavory connotations of the word 'abortion' by speaking instead in terms of 'termination of pregnancy.' "[15] Warren Hern, who has claimed that he is "internationally known as specializing in late abortion," vehemently objected to a columnist's characterization of him as an "abortionist." According to Hern, "abortionist" is a "demeaning, degrading term that conveys evil and disgrace," and the columnist's reference to someone who performs abortions as an "abortionist" was "a deliberate insult that reveals his antipathy toward me, toward the cause I serve, and toward women."[16]

Henry P. David would do away with the word "abortion" entirely. He suggests:

> I wish to make a plea for aborting the word "abortion." For far too long and for too many people its image has been associated with misguided ideas about sin and murder. Birth planning has become a social necessity, whether through foresight or hindsight procedures. Just as the term "family planning" overcame the negative connotations of "birth control," an acceptable substitute for "abortion" is needed. With the new prostaglandins we may begin talking about "postconception planning" or "pregterm suppositories."[17]

Why do we cloak the unborn and abortion with the language that we use? As Americans, it is ingrained in us that it is gravely wrong to kill innocent human beings, especially children. We believe that no man is worthless and that every one has certain rights—including a right to life—simply by virtue of being human. Yet we kill innocent human beings through abortion—approximately a million and a half of them every year. Language affords us the means to reconcile these two irreconcilable positions, for words, as Joseph Conrad once observed, "are the great foes of reality."[18] We feel every "person" and "child" has a right to life, so we invent new definitions of "person" and "child" to exclude those whose right to life we wish to ignore. We believe that it is wrong to take the life of another "human being," so we fashion new definitions of "human being" to exclude those whose lives we would snuff out. We believe that it is wrong to "kill," so we refer to the unborn as only "potential life"—one cannot kill what is not alive.

Of course, we are not the first to resort to such wordplay to loose the strictures of conscience. It is a virtually indispensable component in any enterprise which involves routinized killing. The Nazis did what they did while bewitched by language. Their victims were not "human beings": the disabled were "lumps of flesh," "travesties of human form," "mere existences," and "creatures"; those who perished in the concentration camps were *untermensch*—sub-humans. Referring to the Nazis' use of language, Heinz Höhne observes, "In the murderer's vocabulary, the word murder did not appear; instead he used a picturesque selection of ostensibly innocent code words."[19] The Nazis did not "kill" in their hospitals or death camps. The disabled were "given relief through death."[20] Their elimination was a "release," a "deliverance," a "liberation," or an "act of healing" or "kindness."[21] The "Jewish problem" was resolved with "special actions," "cleansings," "resettlement," and "special treatments."[22] Even in their secret correspondence referring to the "final solution," the Nazis never referred to "killing."[23] One Holocaust scholar has observed that, after poring through thousands of Nazi documents, he happened upon the word "killing" only once—in an edict concerning dogs.[24] In his book about the role of Nazi doctors at the camps, psychologist Robert Lifton writes, "[T]he language used gave Nazi doctors a discourse in which killing is no longer killing; and need not be experienced, or even perceived as killing."[25]

Others have made similar use of language to sedate their consciences. As noted in the previous chapter, dehumanization played a significant role in atrocities perpetrated against the Japanese during the War in the Pacific. According to historian John Dower, the "dehumanization of the Other contributed immeasurably to the psychological distancing that facilitates killing."[26] In *War without Mercy*, Dower notes that language played a primary role in that dehumanization:

> A characteristic feature of this level of anti-Japanese sentiment was to resort to nonhuman or subhuman representation, in which the Japanese were perceived as animals, reptiles, or insects. . . . The variety of such metaphors was so great that they sometimes seemed casual and almost original. On the contrary, they were well routinized as idioms of everyday discourse, and immensely consequential in their ultimate functions. At the simplest level, they dehumanized the Japanese and enlarged the chasm between "us" and "them" to the point where it was perceived to be virtually unbridgeable. . . . [T]he enemy in Europe "were still people." The Japanese were not, and in good part they were not because they were denied even the ordinary vocabulary of "being human."[27]

As is the case with the unborn, there was a tendency among the Nazis and some Americans to refer to Jews and the Japanese, respectively, in terms of parasites or a disease—at once reinforcing the notion that the subjects were not human and hinting that they posed a threat that justified their eradication. The Nazis referred to Jews as "parasites,"[28] "lice,"[29] "bacilli,"[30] "vermin,"[31] "disseminators of disease,"[32] and similar terms. The Japanese were dehumanized with similar metaphors. In cartoons and in speech, they were routinely called "vermin," "insects," "rats," and "a pestilence."[33]

The perils of thinking of our fellow human beings as parasites or a disease should, by now, be obvious. But what about the subtle, and in many instances unintended, dehumanization which can result from habitually referring to the unborn as a "fetus" or an "embryo"? Can words as seemingly innocuous as these really render killing less objectionable? We need not speculate. There is at least one example outside the context of abortion where the word "fetus" has been used to do just that.

As techniques in pediatric surgery have grown more sophisticated, physicians have acquired the capacity to save children born with birth defects that, without surgical intervention, would kill the child in a matter of weeks or even days. During the 1970s and 1980s many in the medical community concluded that some infants born with these defects were not worth saving—particularly where the child with the defect was also mentally impaired. Doctors and nurses refused to treat the children, often withholding intravenous feedings if the children could not eat themselves. C. Everett Koop, a pioneer in pediatric surgery and former U.S. Surgeon General, notes that as this attitude became more prevalent, physicians increasingly tended to refer to the disabled newborn as a *"fetus ex utero."*[34] "It was," Koop writes in his autobiography, "a strange way to refer to a baby. The Supreme Court had denied human rights to a fetus, so branding a defective newborn as a *fetus ex utero* served to deny human rights to a newborn human."[35]

Nor is "fetus" the only word borrowed from the "pro-choice" lexicon to make culling defective infants seem more appealing. Some of those who believe that severely disabled infants should be subjected to active euthanasia—given lethal drugs or denied ordinary medical care—refer to the practice as "postnatal abortion" and characterize the children as "sub-human" life.

III

One of the most noteworthy recent discussions of the role of language in the abortion debate appears in Naomi Wolf's October 1995 article in *The New Republic*, "Our Bodies, Our Souls."[36] In the article, Wolf, an influential feminist and *supporter* of abortion rights, decries the rhetoric habitually used by the "pro-choice" movement to obscure the fact that the unborn are human and alive and that abortion is an act of killing. Noting with concern that many feminists tend to use language which portrays the unborn as "at best valueless; at worst an adversary, a 'mass of dependent protoplasm,' " Wolf warns her fellow defenders of abortion, "Clinging to a rhetoric . . . in which there is no life and no death, we entangle our beliefs in a series of self-delusions, fibs and evasions."[37] She explains that relying on this rhetoric leads to "hardness of heart, lying, and political failure" and that, by resorting to it, those who defend abortion risk becoming "callous, selfish and casually destructive [individuals] who share a cheapened view of human life."[38] Wolf argues that the "pro-choice" movement must "admit that the death of the fetus is a real death"[39] and "act[ ] with moral accountability and without euphemism."[40] And she predicts that a "more honest and moral rhetoric" about abortion will only increase support for the movement.[41]

Wolf should be commended for her courage and intellectual honesty. Though she leaves no doubt in her piece that she supports abortion on demand, Wolf was at least willing to take a hard look at an issue treated as sacrosanct by her colleagues in the feminist movement, and she was willing to admit what abortion is. For more than a generation, the defenders of abortion have equated the unborn with a "blob of cells," a "tissue," a "gobbet of meat"—perhaps living, perhaps not. But Wolf concedes that abortion involves the deliberate destruction of a *human* life. In her article she acknowledges the "humanity of the fetus" and the "moral gravity" of killing it.[42] She simply errs when she concludes that "*the mother must be able to decide that the fetus, in its full humanity, must die.*"[43] The fact that abortion involves killing human beings may not be dispositive to Wolf, but it will be to many others.

Wolf believes that "a more honest and moral rhetoric" about abortion will only increase support for abortion rights. Actually, however, just the opposite is true. The more honest and moral the language used, the more difficult it becomes to defend abortion. Thus Ron Fitzsimmons, the executive director of the National Coalition of Abortion Providers, admitted that he "lied through [his] teeth" in a November 1995 *Nightline* interview on partial birth abortion because he feared that the truth hurt the "pro-choice" movement.[44] Indeed, Wolf's article itself is an excellent case in point. Wolf writes poignantly about the need for honest discourse, the importance of fully acknowledging the humanity of the unborn, and the fact that abortion results in "a real death." But in the very same article, while trying to make the case for allowing the destruction of the unborn, she inadvertently resorts to the same slippery euphemisms she condemns among her fellow defenders of abortion.

Wolf may believe that she has come to terms with the fact that abortion involves killing human beings, but her language clearly shows that she has not. Time and time again she bends over backward to avoid saying that the unborn are "human" and that abortion involves "killing" them. Though she vigorously denounces the "dehumanization" of the unborn, Wolf herself never refers to them as "human," "human beings," "children," or any other term that might acknowledge their humanity. Instead, she characterizes them in terms carefully tailored to avoid any hint that the unborn are human. "Fetus" is her favorite—it appears roughly thirty times during the course of her seven-page article—but she resorts to others as well. The unborn are "life," "manifestations of life," "beings," and "being[s] that might have been," among others.[45] Shortly after warning of the dangers of using dehumanizing language to refer to the unborn, Wolf writes, "Second Wave feminists reacted to the dehumanization of women by dehumanizing the *creatures* inside of them."[46] And this in the same article where she argues, "Free women must be strong women, too; and strong women do not seek to cloak their most important decisions in euphemism."[47]

Wolf argues that it is always wrong to minimize "the lives" destroyed by abortion.[48] But she does just that by refusing to really acknowledge the humanity of the unborn. Human lives are worth more than other lives. A human being is not simply a "manifestation of life," like an eel, a termite, or a fungus. A human being has special worth simply by virtue of being human. The language Wolf uses is important because, as she herself admits, "The language we use . . . limits the way we let ourselves think about abortion."[49]

Wolf runs into similar problems with respect to acknowledging that abortion "kills" the unborn. She refers numerous times in her article to the "death" of the unborn, and even argues that those who defend abortion must admit that "the death of a fetus is a real death."[50] But she refers to "killing" only once, when she suggests that a person who "believes that abortion is killing" but is still "pro-choice" could always use contraception.[51] (Note that, even here, Wolf is careful not to say that abortion is "killing"; she simply addresses those abortion proponents who might regard it as such.) The distinction between the "death" of a human being and "killing" one is significant. Death is a fact of life. No one is necessarily to blame. But "killing" is another matter. There, one human being deliberately snuffs out the life of another. The unborn does not simply *die* during an abortion; it is *killed*.

Unfortunately, Wolf is true to her feminist roots when she passes out the blame for the abortion movement's rhetoric. Who is responsible? Our sexist society. After expressing her desire for a world which has long since discarded the notion of gender as a barrier (a world which, in her view, necessarily includes free contraceptives in every public health building), Wolf writes, "In that world we might well describe the unborn and the never-to-be born with the honest words of life."[52] The unborn are more than simply "life," of course. But what Wolf should ask herself is, Why must we wait for a society where sexism is a distant memory before we use honest words to describe the unborn? The unborn are not sexists, and their lives should not be forfeit for the misdeeds of others. Why can't we use honest words to describe them *now*?

IV

We have avoided the truth about abortion for too long. Rather than honestly confronting the facts, we have become enmeshed in a tangle of hypocrisy, self-deception, and lies. When it comes to abortion, our language and our attitudes are thoroughly Orwellian. The destruction of the unborn is fraught with doublethink and sanitized with antiseptic language.

In June of 1973, months after the Supreme Court announced its decision in *Roe v. Wade,* Nobel prize winning biologist James Watson declared that, "If a child was not *declared to be alive* until three days after birth, then all parents would be allowed the choice that only a few are given under the present system [that is, to have their "defective" children killed]. The doctor could allow the child to die if the parents so chose and save a lot of misery and suffering."[53] A little more than four years later, fellow scientist and Nobel prize winner Dr. Francis Crick argued that "no newborn infant should be *declared human* until it has passed certain tests regarding its genetic endowment . . . if it fails those tests it forfeits its right to live."[54]

Does either of these prominent scientists really believe that these newborns are not "human" or "alive." Certainly not. Both are careful to say only that the infants should not be "*declared*" human or alive.[55] They are trying to make an end run around the consciences of those with antiquated notions about "killing" and the inherent right to life of all "human beings." Acknowledging the newborns for what they are is an impediment to eliminating them.

Orwell warned of language "designed to make lies sound truthful and murder respectable, and to give an appearance of solidity to pure wind."[56] Watson and Crick's comments fall squarely within that definition, but so does much of our rhetoric condoning abortion. Indeed, Watson and Crick's statements are simply an extension of the logic we use with respect to the unborn. I have, in previous chapters, pointed to countless instances where the destruction of the unborn is rationalized by saying that the victims of abortion are not alive or not human. So long as we refuse to refer to the unborn as "living," abortion is not an act of killing; so long as we refuse to call them "human," the unborn have no right to life. There is no real difference between our views and those of Watson and Crick. The difference is simply a matter of days. We draw the line at birth; they draw it a few days afterwards. We both try to mask our views with language: Only some living beings are "living"; only some human beings are "human"; only some killing is "killing."

We condone the destruction of the unborn because they are not "persons." But Orwell's Big Brother did not kill persons either: those destined for elimination were deemed "unpersons" beforehand.[57]

Our attitudes concerning the destruction of the unborn are classic "doublethink." "*Doublethink,*" Orwell wrote in *1984,* "means the power of holding two contradictory beliefs in one's mind simultaneously and accepting both of them."[58] We reject spontaneous generation, but believe that our young arise from inanimate matter. We believe that every human being is a person but that the unborn are not. We believe that all human beings have a right to life but that the unborn have none. We believe that all human beings are equal but that some are more equal than others.[59]

We believe that so long as we kill our young before they are born, we are not actually killing "*beings*" but merely—to use the words of some abortion proponents—"potential life" or "*beings that might have been.*" Orwell's description of the elimination of "unpersons" in *1984* accords perfectly with our view of the destruction of the unborn: "You will be lifted clean out of the stream of history.... Nothing will remain of you: not a name in a register, not a memory in a living brain. You will be annihilated in the past as well as in the future. *You will never have existed.*"[60]

NOTES

1. Celeste Michelle Condit, *Decoding Abortion Rhetoric: Communicating Social Change* (Urbana: University of Illinois Press, 1990), 213; and James Tunstead Burtchaell, *Rachel Weeping and Other Essays* (Kansas City: Andrews & McMeel, 1982), 196.

2. Betty Friedan, "Feminism's Next Step," *New York Times Magazine,* July 5, 1981: 15.

3. *Planned Parenthood v. Ashcroft,* 462 U.S. 480, 483 n.7 (1983); and Burtchaell, 196–198.

4. Quoted in Dave Shiflett, "Dr. Hern and Mr. Clinton," *Weekly Standard,* November 11, 1996: 15.

5. *Davis v. Davis,* 842 S.W.2d 588 (Tenn. 1992), *cert. denied sub nom. Stowe v. Davis,* 507 U.S. 911 (1993).

6. Garret Hardin, *Mandatory Motherhood: The True Meaning of "Right to Life"* (Boston: Beacon Press, 1974), 16–17.

7. *Webster's Third New International Dictionary* (1986).

8. *The American Heritage Dictionary,* 2d College ed. (1985).

9. *The Oxford English Dictionary* (1986). *The Oxford English Dictionary* notes that the word "child" was originally always used in this sense—in relation to the mother as the "fruit of the womb"—and that only by gradual ex-

tension did the word come to mean "young person of either sex below the age of puberty" as well.

10. James Tunstead Burtchaell, *Rachel Weeping and Other Essays* (Kansas City: Andrews & McMeel, 1982), 201–202.

11. Both "embryo" and "fetus" have specific scientific meanings when used to refer to human unborn. "Embryo" refers to the unborn from the time of implantation in the uterus to the end of the eighth week after conception. "Fetus," meanwhile, refers to the unborn from eight weeks after conception until birth. See, for example, "embryo" and "fetus" in *The American Heritage Dictionary.*

12. *The American Heritage Dictionary.*

13. See, for example, *Webster's Third New International Dictionary.*

14. George Will, "Discretionary Killing," *Newsweek*, September 20, 1976: 96. (Before Planned Parenthood came to be so pro-abortion, it was more forthright. A 1961 Planned Parenthood brochure entitled "Plan Your Children for Health and Happiness" distinguished abortion from birth control by explaining, "An abortion kills the life of a baby after it has begun.")

15. Glanville Williams, *The Sanctity of Life and the Criminal Law*, The 1956 James S. Carpenter Lectures at Columbia Law School (New York: Knopf, 1957), 147, quoted in Burtchaell, 202.

16. Shiflett, 15.

17. Henry P. David, "Abortion: Public Health Concerns and Needed Psychosocial Research," *American Journal of Public Health* 61 (1971): 515, quoted in Burtchaell, 197.

18. Joseph Conrad, *Under Western Eyes* (1911; London: Nelson, n.d.), 1.

19. Heinz Höhne, *The Order of the Death's Head: The Story of Hitler's SS*, trans. Richard Barry (New York: Ballantine, 1969), 415.

20. Michael Burleigh, *Death and Deliverance: Euthanasia in Germany 1900–1945* (New York: Cambridge University Press, 1994), 17.

21. Burleigh, 17, 23, 100, 199.

22. Höhne, 402–403, 415, 420.

23. Raul Hilberg, *The Destruction of the European Jews*, rev. and definitive ed., vol. 3 (New York: Holmes & Meiers, 1985), vol. 3, 1016.

24. Raul Hilberg, "Confronting the Moral Implications of the Holocaust," *Social Education* 42 (1978): 275.

25. Robert J. Lifton, *The Nazi Doctors: Medical Killing and the Psychology of Genocide* (New York: Basic Books, 1986), 445.

26. John W. Dower, *War without Mercy: Race and Power in the Pacific War* (New York: Pantheon, 1986), 11.

27. Dower, 81–82.

28. Höhne, 282.

29. Hilberg, *The Destruction*, vol. 1, 20–21.

30. Gerald Fleming, *Hitler and the Final Solution* (Berkeley: University of California Press, 1984), 156.

31. Höhne, 426.

32. Höhne, 282.

33. Dower, 89–92.

34. Charles Everett Koop, *Koop: The Memoirs of America's Family Doctor* (New York: Random House, 1991), 265.

35. Koop, 265.

36. Naomi Wolf, "Our Bodies, Our Souls: Re-thinking Abortion Rhetoric," *New Republic*, October 16, 1995: 26.

37. Wolf, 26, 28.

38. Wolf, 26, 28.

39. Wolf, 26.

40. Wolf, 28.

41. Wolf, 33.

42. Wolf, 33.

43. Wolf, 33 (emphasis added).

44. David Stout, "An Abortion Rights Advocate Says He Lied about Procedure," *New York Times*, February 26, 1997: A-12.

45. Wolf, 33, 32, 35.

46. Wolf, 28 (emphasis added).

47. Wolf, 32.

48. Wolf, 33.

49. Wolf, 34.

50. Wolf, 26.

51. Wolf, 35.

52. Wolf, 35.

53. Quoted in James Manney and John C. Blattner, *Death in the Nursery: The Secret Crime of Infanticide* (Ann Arbor, MI: Servant Books, 1984), 117 (emphasis added).

54. Quoted in Manney and Blattner, 118 (emphasis added).

55. Note that both Watson and Crick believe that we do not necessarily intuitively recognize whether a being is human or alive. (If we did, we would not have to be told, as they suggest.) I address the issue of whether we intuitively recognize who is human in more detail in the next chapter.

56. George Orwell, "Politics and the English Language," *The Collected Essays, Journalism, and Letters of George Orwell*, eds. Sonia Orwell and Ian Angus, vol. 4, *In Front of Your Nose* (New York: Harcourt, 1968), 139.

57. George Orwell, *1984* (New York: Penguin, 1981), 40–41, 130.

58. Orwell, *1984*, 176.

59. "All animals are equal, but some animals are more equal than others." George Orwell, *Animal Farm* (New York: Harcourt, 1946), 112.

60. Orwell, *1984*, 210 (emphasis added).

9

Arbitrary

Every morn and every night
Some are born to sweet delight.
Some are born to sweet delight,
Some are born to endless night.

William Blake, "Auguries of Innocence"

Theft, incest, infanticide, parricide, have all had a place among vir-
tuous actions.

Blaise Pascal, *Pensées*

When the Supreme Court announced its decision in *Roe v. Wade*, the
Court went to great lengths to downplay the fact that the Hippocratic
Oath enjoined abortion. How the Oath treated abortion had nothing
to do with the legal question before the Court, of course: women either
had a constitutionally-protected right to rid themselves of their unborn
young or they did not. The fact that doctors swore not to engage in
abortion could not take away the right if it were conferred by the Constitution. But the Court was uncomfortable sanctioning conduct expressly proscribed by what the Court itself described as "a long
accepted and revered statement of medical ethics."[1] To pass abortion
off as "just another medical procedure," the Court would have to explain away the Oath's prohibition of it.

The Court attempted to do this, in part, by pointing to attitudes concerning abortion among ancient Greek philosophers. In one of the most telling lines of its opinion, the Court wrote, "The Oath was not uncontested even in Hippocrates' day; only the Pythagorean school of philosophers frowned upon the related act of suicide. Most Greek thinkers, on the other hand, commended abortion, at least prior to viability. See Plato, Republic, V, 461; Aristotle, Politics, VII, 1335b 25."[2]

The fact that two Greek philosophers embraced abortion, of course, does not mean that "most" did. But the real significance of the Court's statement lies in the passages the Court cited in support of its position: the Aristotle and Plato passages both "commend" the destruction of newborns in addition to the unborn.

In the same passage the Court cites from *Politics,* Aristotle endorses infanticide as well as abortion:

As to the exposure and rearing of children, let there be a law that no *deformed* child shall live, but that on the ground of an *excess* in the number of children, if the established custom of the state forbid this (for in our state population has a limit), no child is to be exposed, but when couples have children in excess, let abortion be procured before life and sense have begun; what may or may not be lawfully done in these cases depends on the question of life and sensation.[3]

The citation to Plato's *Republic* is even more revealing. Immediately prior to the passage the Court cites, Plato endorses the infanticide of children with disabilities or inferior parents: "The children of the good, then, they will take . . . into the fold, and hand them over to certain nurses who will live in some place apart in the city; those of the inferior sort, and any one of the others who may be born defective, they will be put away as is proper in some mysterious, unknown place."[4] And in the same passage the Court cites, Plato endorses the elimination of children born of older parents. After noting that, in the ideal state, individuals beyond their prime should be free to consort with whomever they please, Plato writes, "However . . . we must warn them to be as careful as possible not to bring any of such conceptions into the light, not even one; but if a child is born, if one forces his way through, they must dispose of it on the understanding that there is no food or nurture for such a one."[5]

Clearly, the Court did not mean to condone infanticide by referring to these passages. Yet it is curious that, cognizant of the fact that the passages advocated snuffing out the lives of born and unborn alike, the Court would use them to try to destigmatize abortion. Presumably, the Court would have preferred that the passages not mention infanticide, but the references to infanticide do not seem to have bothered the Court either.

The fact that the Court would cite these passages is appropriate, however, even if coincidental. The passages show what even individuals of good will and high intellect—individuals like Aristotle and Plato—can embrace once they decide some members of the human family have no right to live. And they also show that there is a tendency to extend the reasoning applied to the unborn to newborns as well.

Many abortion proponents recoil at the notion that abortion and infanticide are comparable. In reality, however, they are two sides of the same coin. The distinction we draw between killing inside the womb and killing after birth has little to do with any intrinsic change in our young as they are born: The fetus undergoes no metamorphosis as it passes through the mother's birth canal. Rather, birth is simply an arbitrary criterion which we have chosen to distinguish those human beings whose right to life we recognize from those whose right to life we prefer to ignore. We not only treat our unborn young as though they were less than human; we treat them as though they were less than other animals as well.

I

One can illustrate just how tenuous the distinction is between infanticide and abortion easily. Consider, for instance, the Supreme Court's opinion in *Planned Parenthood v. Ashcroft*.[6] The Court referred to the testimony of two abortionists called as witnesses for abortion proponents at trial. One testified that he performed D&E abortions—abortions which involve dismembering the unborn—through the 26th week of pregnancy; the other testified that he performed them through the 28th week.[7] Currently, however, *more than three quarters* of all children actually born during the *25th* week of pregnancy survive the first, most perilous six months of their lives, and most of these will go on to live healthy, happy lives.[8] Occasionally, children will survive birth after only 22 weeks of pregnancy.[9] The same child doctors would be struggling to save if born premature, an abortionist can dismember if it remains in the womb.

And sometimes the child need not even remain in the womb. Consider the "D&X" or "partial-birth" abortion method accurately described in a November 20, 1995, article in *American Medical News*: "The procedure usually involves the extraction of an intact fetus, feet first, through the birth canal, with all but the head delivered. The surgeon forces scissors into the base of the fetus' skull, spreads them to enlarge the opening, and uses suction to remove the brain."[10] One of the abortionists who developed the procedure performs them on children through the 26th week of pregnancy—and still later if the mother is depressed or the child has a cleft lip.[11] The tenuous distinction between abortion and infanticide was vividly illustrated on June 30, 1998, when a Phoenix doctor started to perform a partial birth abortion on what he thought was a 23-week-old fetus, and ended up delivering a 6-pound, 2-ounce full term baby girl—a girl who entered the world with a factured skull and facial cuts thanks to his handiwork.[12]

The irony of our situation did not escape former Surgeon General C. Everett Koop, who made his initial reputation on the basis of his pioneering surgery on newborns. In his autobiography, Koop writes:

> It all crystallized for me one Saturday in 1976. My residents and I had spent the day operating on three newborn babies with defects that were incompatible with life, but were nevertheless amenable to surgical correction. Surgery on the newborns is time-consuming, and although we started at 8:00 a.m., we did not get the third youngster safely in his incubator with his immediate future assured until early evening. . . . I said to my two colleagues: "You know, we have given over two hundred years of life to three individuals who together barely weighed ten pounds."
>
> One of my residents answered, "And while we were doing that, right next door in the university hospital they were cutting up perfectly formed babies of the same size just because their mother didn't want them." I knew then that as a surgeon of the newborn, I had to do something about the slaughter of the unborn.[13]

Even many prominent abortion *proponents* have recognized the arbitrariness of the distinction between abortion and infanticide. They condone the killing of the born in addition to the unborn. Mary Anne Warren concedes that infanticide is wrong but argues that it is wrong not because infants have a right to life, but "for reasons analogous to those which make it wrong to wantonly destroy natural resources or great works of art."[14] Others are willing to go still further. Philosopher Peter Singer maintains that there is no logical reason to treat newborns differently from the unborn and that one can kill newborns without violating the principle of respect for persons.[15] Indeed, he argues that where a baby has Down's syndrome, and in other instances of "life that has begun very badly," parents should be free to kill the child within 28 days of birth.[16] Michael Tooley writes, "New-born humans are neither persons nor quasi-persons, and their destruction is in no way intrinsically wrong."[17] In his view, killing infants becomes wrong when the child acquires "morally significant properties"—an event he feels occurs about three months after the child is born.[18] "As they develop further," Tooley explains, "their destruction becomes more and more seriously wrong, until eventually it is comparable in seriousness to the destruction of a normal adult human being."[19] Biomedical ethicist and abortion proponent Joseph Fletcher sums up his position in a sentence which is at once strikingly candid and rife with euphemism: "*It is ridiculous to give ethical approval to the positive ending of subhuman life*, in utero . . . *but to refuse to approve of positively ending a subhuman life* in extremis."[20]

II

If many abortion foes and a significant number of abortion proponents recognize the arbitrariness of distinguishing between abortion and infanticide, why do we as a society treat the two so differently? Why do we draw a distinction between the person who snuffs out a premature infant in a hospital nursery and one who destroys the same child in the womb?

Logically there may be little reason to distinguish between the two, but logic is only part of the equation here. In emotionally charged issues like abortion and infanticide, people tend to derive their positions based on their intuitive sense of right and wrong: they have a visceral reaction to the issue which they then seek to support intellectually. Glanville Williams, a leading abortion proponent in Britain, argues, "Infanticide has been all but suppressed while abortion is still rampant. The reason for the difference is not far to seek. The infant child is felt as a human being, so that protective feelings are easy to arouse; but the embryo is not."[21]

The difference between our intuitive reactions to the destruction of the unborn and the destruction of newborns is important. Most abortion proponents are not going against their intuitive sense of right and wrong when they defend abortion. They simply assume that, if the unborn really were comparable to newborns and other human beings, abortion would offend their intuitive sense of right and wrong in the same way infanticide does. The fact that abortion is widely accepted by others in society validates their own intuitive feelings.

There are a number of problems with this line of thinking, however. First, the fact that many condone abortion does not show that abortion *should be* condoned. Slavery, torture, attempts to eradicate rival peoples, and even human sacrifice have been accepted in many cultures through the ages; nevertheless, all are wrong.

Second, the very fact that we live in a society where abortion is pervasive but infanticide is rare colors our intuitive attitudes about each. Human societies tend to exhibit a sort of cultural inertia. Since our notions of right and wrong are, to a large extent, learned from others, individuals in any society tend to regard what is accepted by their fellows as "ethical" and what is condemned by them as "wrong." We know of friends, siblings, children, and peers who have had abortions—or perform them, or defend them—but few of us have any experience with infanticide. As a result, abortion and infanticide have different connotations. Abortion, in our minds, is modern necessity: sterile gowns, working mothers, hospitals, and fluorescent lighting. But infanticide is *primitive*. It is "savages" and caves, torchlight and pagan cruelty.

Abortion proponents suggest that the low incidence of infanticide shows that we intuitively recognize when our young have worth. But actually, our experience with infanticide should show us that just the opposite is true: our intuitive feelings regarding the value of our children's lives are highly suspect.

The destruction of newborns has been widely accepted in many cultures throughout history. Studies of prehistoric human burial sites indicate that between 15 and 20 percent of children born alive fell victim to infanticide.[22] Cemeteries from ancient Carthage contain the remains of thousands of children offered as sacrifices in religious rituals.[23] Greek law and public opinion accepted infanticide,[24] and, as noted earlier, even Plato and Aristotle endorsed the practice. The Spartan constitution, meanwhile, required the destruction of weak or deformed newborns.[25]

Infanticide also enjoyed wide acceptance in Rome, where such luminaries as Seneca, Pliny the Elder, and Justinian endorsed it.[26] The Romans routinely drowned newborns in the Tiber and later, under the famous Code of Justinian, fathers had a duty to destroy disabled children.[27] Up until 374 A.D. infanticide was entirely legal.[28] Even afterwards, only direct killing was outlawed: exposure and other indirect means of doing away with newborns were still permitted.[29]

Public acceptance of infanticide waned in Europe with the advent of Christianity, but the practice persisted in private. Many medieval mothers rid themselves of unwanted babies by "overlaying"—"accidentally" smothering the child after rolling over in bed.[30] Parents frequently retained wet nurses for the express purpose of discreetly doing away with unwanted newborns.[31]

The level of infanticide has fluctuated somewhat since then, but the current low rates are a relatively recent phenomenon. Even in the eighteenth and nineteenth centuries, infanticide was rife in England and France.[32] Jeff Lyon writes, "During the 1860s some 150 dead infants were found in London each year floating in the Thames, or lying in the streets, ditches, and parks. The sewers of Paris were full of tiny corpses."[33]

Infanticide was also well accepted among non-western cultures. It was endemic among many tribal peoples—from Bushmen to Inuits.[34] And, as in the western cultures, "civilized" peoples also freely exterminated their young. Lyon writes that the Japanese "subscribed so openly to infanticide that they even had a special word for it, *mabiki*, whose collateral meaning was 'weeding' or 'thinning rice seedlings.' "[35] In China, meanwhile, Jesuit missionaries of the last century were aghast to find girl babies dumped on the street like refuse, to be collected each morning by sanitation workers.[36] Even today, as the recent documentary *Secret Asia—The Dying Rooms* attests, infanticide continues to be a major problem there—particularly with respect to female or disabled newborns.[37]

How could these people remorselessly exterminate their own children? Perhaps they realized that infanticide is an abomination but were willing to forsake their consciences. This explanation seems improbable, however, given the pervasiveness of infanticide. The practice could never have become so well accepted in so many cultures if only those dead to right and wrong would tolerate it. Plato, Aristotle, and Seneca—and no doubt many of the other individuals who endorsed the destruction of infants throughout the ages—were not evil people. They were individuals of conscience. They did not promote infanticide because they were immoral; they did so because—for one reason or another—the destruction of newborns did not offend their intuitive sense of right and wrong. The same is probably true for most of those who did the actual killing.

It might be comforting to believe that we cannot engage in barbarous conduct without tripping some innate sense of right and wrong in us: that we cannot perpetrate atrocities without consciously choosing to do wrong. The facts, however, prove otherwise.

Some abortion proponents try to get around these difficulties by suggesting that we can intuitively recognize who is *human*—as opposed to intuitively recognizing what is right or wrong. But a careful examination of the evidence shows that we do not necessarily recognize who is human. Jean-Jacques Rousseau was just one of the eighteenth-century intellectuals who thought that orangutans were human beings.[38] Spanish and Portuguese adventurers in the New World exploited the indigenous peoples because they did not regard Native Americans as human.[39] Alfred Wallace and Louis Agassiz—two of the most prominent biologists in the nineteenth century—were, like many scientists of the time, convinced that blacks and whites were separate species.[40] And, as we have seen previously, many prominent Nazi leaders believed that Jews, the disabled, and many of the Nazis' other victims were not human. Either our intuitive sense of who is human is not very reliable or it is plastic enough to allow us to redefine who is "human" when it becomes convenient to do so.

Agassiz's experience is in some respects the most revealing. The nation's foremost biologist in the mid-1800s, he initially assumed that blacks and whites had common ancestors and were not simply look-alikes.[41] But he changed his mind when he actually encountered blacks, working as waiters in a Philadelphia hotel, in 1846. He recounted the experience to his mother in terms which cannot help but make modern readers wince:

> I can scarcely express to you the painful impression that I received, especially since the sentiment that they inspired in me is contrary to all our ideas about the confraternity of the human type and the unique origin of our species. . . . I experienced pity at the sight of this degraded and degenerate race, and their lot inspired compassion in me thinking that they are really men. Nonetheless, it is impossible for me to repress the feeling that they are not the same blood as us. In seeing their black faces with their thick lips and grimacing teeth, the wool on their head, their bent knees, their

elongated hands, their large curved nails, and especially the livid color of the palms of their hands, I could not take my eyes off their faces in order to tell them to stay far away. And when they advanced that hideous hand towards my plate in order to serve me, I wished I were able to depart to eat a piece of bread elsewhere, rather than to dine with such service.[42]

Although he opposed slavery, Agassiz continued to believe that blacks and whites were separate species until his death in 1873.[43] Given his feelings about slavery, his demonstrated expertise in classifying organisms, and his initial assumption that blacks and whites were related, it seems inconceivable that Agassiz could conclude that blacks were the product of a separate creation if we really do intuitively recognize who is human.

III

Why then do we tolerate the killing of unborn children that we would insist doctors save if the children were born premature? Eugene Quay once wrote that the distinction abortion proponents draw between infanticide and abortion has to do with the difference between what they must see and what they can avoid seeing.[44] Quay put his finger on something here. Much of the reason our ideas about abortion and infanticide differ results from the fact that we see newborns but not the unborn. We can have the unborn killed without having to see them dispatched or even to look upon them beforehand. It is more difficult with born children.

In his influential article "Part and Parcel in Animal and Human Societies," zoologist Konrad Lorenz, one of the pioneers in the study of animal behavior, argued that infants tend to evoke feelings of nurturing and affection in us, at least in part, because of their physical appearance. According to Lorenz, the features we associate with juvenility—a bulging forehead, large eyes and cheeks, a retreating chin, short and thick extremities, clumsy movements, and so on—act as important behavioral cues, stirring feelings of tenderness in us.[45] The response that these features evoke makes good biological sense: juveniles that elicit feelings of tenderness and caring are more likely to be cared for and—all other things being equal—are more likely to live to pass their traits on to the next generation. Since Lorenz believed our response to such juvenile traits is innate, he referred to the traits as "innate releasing mechanisms."

Whether the feelings of nurturing and affection we feel for individuals with juvenile traits are innate or learned, or whether they are simply a response we have learned to associate with those traits, there is no denying that juvenile traits can influence us in subtle yet powerful ways. Lorenz noted that the abstract features that we associate with human young tend to evoke strong feelings of affection in us even when they appear in non-humans.[46] He pointed out, for instance, that we tend to feel affection for animals with large eyes, bulging foreheads, and retreating chins, but not for their small-eyed, long-snouted cousins.[47] (Compare the shape of a Boston terrier's head, or that of a cocker spaniel, with the head of a wolf or dingo.) The same phenomenon accounts for our tendency to respond to the young of certain animals with more tenderness than the adults: a kitten or a puppy has juvenile traits that we associate with our own young, and therefore they tend to evoke more tender feelings in us than the adult cat or dog. Lorenz even noticed that in his native German, the names of animals with juvenile features tend to end in the diminutive suffix "-chen"—even when those animals are larger than closely-related species without juvenile features.[48]

In the early stages of development, obviously, the unborn do not possess features we would recognize as juvenile—even if we could see them outside the womb. But the unborn do exhibit these traits later in pregnancy. As a result, we can kill a child eight months after conception more easily if the child remains in the womb than if it lies in a crib or incubator.

In a 1995 article in *Reader's Digest*, for instance, a young Chinese doctor describes her experience with a child aborted eight months into pregnancy.[49] After hearing the cries of a newborn, a midwife informed the doctor that there had been a complication with an abortion: the child had been born alive. This posed a problem for the young doctor. "As the obstetrician in charge," she writes, "I had the duty of ensuring that there were no abortion survivors. That meant an injection of 20 milliliters of iodine or alcohol into the soft spot on the infant's head. It brings death within minutes."[50]

Although she had performed first-trimester abortions before, she had never before had to kill outside the womb—somehow, there had always been a more senior physician present to perform that task. Nevertheless, syringe in hand, she went to find the child and do her duty.

Next to a garbage pail with the words DEAD INFANTS scrawled on the lid was a black plastic garbage bag. It was moving, and cries were coming from the inside. . . .

I had imagined a premature newborn, hovering between life and death. Instead I found a perfect 4½-pound baby boy, flailing his tiny fists and kicking his feet. His lips were purple from lack of oxygen.

Gently, I cradled his head in one hand and placed the fingertips of the other on the soft spot. The skin there felt wonderfully warm, and it pulsed each time he wailed. My heart leapt. *This is a life, a person*, I thought.[51]

The doctor changed her mind and resolved to save the baby boy. Two hours later, he was sleeping peacefully in the delivery room. But the doctor's superiors at the hospital continued to insist that she terminate the infant. While the doctor was busy arguing with them on the baby's behalf, one of the other staff finished the abortion and killed the child.

The Chinese doctor's experience shows the powerful emotional impact of actually seeing the unborn. As an obstetrician, she knew what a child should look like at eight months after conception. But she did not decide to save the child when she heard how old it was, or even when she heard it cry. It was only when she actually saw and felt the child that she realized she could not kill it: "*This is a life, a person*," she recognized. Horrific as the incident she relates is, however, it is no worse than what presently goes on in our own country. We kill children of the same age here on a regular basis; we are just so proficient at it that they rarely remain alive when they are removed from their mothers.

Even those who perform abortions can find the sight of the unborn troubling. Dr. MacArthur Hill, a physician who performed abortions early in his career, re-evaluated his position on abortion after his experience with the bodies of unborn obtained as the result of suction abortions. He had been assigned to sort through the remains to obtain fetal ovaries for research. "I realized that what I was going through was not just a blob of tissue," he says. "I discovered that I was going through the jumbled remains of a dead human being."[52] Another doctor, who stated having second thoughts after performing "many hundreds" of abortions, writes, "[T]earing a developed fetus apart, limb by limb, is an act of depravity that society should not permit. We cannot afford such a devaluation of human life, nor the desensitization of medical personnel it requires. This is not based on what the fetus might feel but on what we should feel in watching an exquisite, partly formed human being being dismembered. . . . I wish everybody would witness a second-trimester abortion before developing an opinion about it."[53] Even Dr. David Grimes, who has led the push to get more doctors to perform abortions, acknowledges that many doctors who perform abortions find them repulsive.[54]

In a 1978 survey Dr. Warren Hern and a co-author conducted on 15 past and present staff members at Hern's abortion clinic, the reactions of the staff to seeing the aborted remains of the unborn included "shock, dismay, amazement, disgust, fear, and sadness. . . . Attitudes toward the doctor were those of sympathy, wonder at how he could perform the procedure at all, and a desire to protect him from the trauma. Two felt that it must eventually damage him psychologically. . . . Two respondents described dreams in which they had related to the procedure. Both described dreams of vomiting fetuses along with a sense of horror."[55] Though Hern remains adamantly pro-abortion, he and his co-author wrote, "[T]here is no possibility of denial of an act of destruction by the operator. It is before one's eyes. The sensations of dismemberment flow through the forceps like an electric current."[56] (Not surprisingly, given the results of his survey, Hern advises other abortionists not to allow women to view "the products of conception" after their abortions.[57])

Perhaps the most telling illustration of the emotional impact of seeing the unborn comes in a letter Brenda Shafer wrote to her congressman urging him to support legislation against "partial-birth," or "D&X," abortions. Shafer, a registered nurse, assisted in a number of "partial-birth" abortions while working in the Dayton clinic of Dr. Martin Haskell, the abortionist who developed the technique.[58] "I took the assignment," Shafer explains in her letter, "because I was at that time very pro-choice. I had even told my two teenage daughters that if one of them ever got pregnant at a young age, I would make them get an abortion."[59] But she reassessed her views after working several days at the clinic:

It was one of these cases that especially haunts me. The woman was six months pregnant (26½ weeks). A doctor told her that the baby had Down's syndrome and she decided to get an abortion. . . .

Dr. Haskell brought the ultrasound in and hooked it up so that he could see the baby (then 26½ weeks into pregnancy). On the ultrasound screen, I could see the heart beating. I asked Dr. Haskell and he told me that "Yes, that is the heartbeat." As Dr. Haskell watched the baby on the ultrasound screen, he went in with forceps and grabbed the baby's legs and brought them into the birth canal. Then he delivered the body and arms, all the way up to the neck.

At this point, only the baby's head was still inside. The baby's body was moving. His little fingers were clasping together. He was kicking his feet. All the while his little head was still stuck inside. Dr. Haskell took a pair of scissors and inserted them into the back of the baby's head. Then he stuck the high-powered suction tube into the hole and sucked the baby's brains out. I almost threw up as I watched him do these things.

Next, Dr. Haskell delivered the baby's head, cut the umbilical cord and delivered the placenta. He threw the baby in a pan, along with the placenta and the instruments he'd used. I saw the baby move in the pan. I asked another nurse and she said it was just "reflexes."

The woman wanted to see her baby, so they cleaned up the baby and put it in a blanket and handed it to her. She cried the whole time, and she kept saying, "I'm sorry, please forgive me." I was crying too. I couldn't take it. In all my professional years I had never experienced anything like this.

Another case I saw on that third day was a six-month-old (approximately 25 weeks) baby. The mother was over age 40. There was nothing wrong with this baby, she just didn't want it. The doctor used the same procedure. . . . This baby was also alive. I saw the heartbeat on the ultrasound. (Actually every baby that day still had a heartbeat at the time of the procedure.) The second baby was a little smaller than the first baby. I remember thinking how perfect this child was. This mother did not want to see it. . . .

I also saw a third case that day. (I was only assisting in one operating room.) This was a 17–year-old girl. She was approximately 25 weeks. The same procedure was done on this baby.

The Down's syndrome baby was the only baby that had a defect. And that baby with Down's syndrome had the most perfect angelic face I have ever seen. I never realized how perfect these babies are at this point. When you hear the word "fetus," I think a lot of people think as I did of just a blob of cells, or a mass of something. It was very revealing to me. I don't think about abortion the same way anymore. I still have nightmares about what I saw.[60]

As in the case of the Chinese doctor we discussed earlier, Shafer is a trained medical professional, someone who presumably knew what unborn of this age should look like. But it was not until she actually saw the children herself that she re-evaluated her position on abortion. Ironically, the children she saw destroyed might well have survived if only they had the *good fortune to have been born premature.* (As noted earlier in this chapter, more than three quarters of children born after 25 weeks survive at least six months and most of these go on to live healthy, happy lives.) If children of this age are outside the mother, we strive to save them; if they are in the womb, we can kill them. If they are part-way in the birth canal but their head remains in the womb, we can still kill them. There is no logic to these distinctions. They are simply an expedient to allow us to differentiate between what we must see and what we can avoid seeing. Those who believe otherwise must ask themselves "Would we really have the same reaction to the 'partial-birth' abortion procedure if the abortionist waited until the child was outside of the mother before driving the scissors into its head?" Despicable as the deeds are that the Chinese doctors participate in, at least they are willing to do them in the light of day.

IV

Given the fact that the distinction we draw between the *act* of abortion and the *act* of infanticide is arbitrary, we might be tempted to take some solace in the notion that our *reasons* for killing the unborn are more noble than those behind the destruction of newborns. That position, however, does not stand close scrutiny. Those who kill newborns do so for much the same reasons we kill the unborn—if anything, their reasons are better. And, though arbitrary, the distinctions they draw between who has a right to life and who does not are no more arbitrary that those we use.

Consider, for instance, the "humane" reasons we kill the unborn. We often hear that it is better to abort the unborn if they would be born disabled or to a mother unprepared to raise them properly; killing the unborn in such instances is not "cruel"; it is in their best interest. Yet many of those who snuffed out the lives of newborns also were convinced that they were acting in the children's best interest. The destruction of weak and disabled children was an act of kindness, Seneca wrote, not the result of any malice:

Does a man hate the members of his own body when he uses the knife upon them? There is no anger there, but the pitying desire to heal. Mad dogs we knock about the head; sickly sheep we put to the knife to keep them from infecting the flock; unnatural progeny we destroy, we drown even children who at birth are weakly and abnormal. Yet it is not anger but reason which separates the harmful from the sound.[61]

Or consider the "self-defense" arguments made by abortion proponents. We are told that, *even if the unborn are persons*, we are justified in killing them in "self-defense" if delivering the child would interfere with the mother's education, impede her career path, or otherwise impair her "life prospects." The same rationale could be used to justify many instances of infanticide. In 1804, for instance, a missionary who had lived among the Bushmen wrote:

> The Bushmen will kill their children without remorse, on various occasions; as when they are ill-shaped, or when they are in want of food, or when obliged to flee from farmers or others, in which case they will strangle them, smother them, cast them away in the desert or bury them alive. There are instances of parents throwing their tender offspring to the hungry lion, who stands roaring before their cavern, refusing to depart before some peace offering is made.[62]

Most, if not at all, of the examples the missionary cites fall well within the "self-defense" arguments propounded by abortion proponents. Certainly the lion or farmer, or the possibility of starvation, posed a greater threat to these Bushmen than the prospect of giving birth poses to the average American woman today. It might seem cruel to strangle a child or bury it alive, but—if we subscribe to the reasoning of abortion proponents—this is probably preferable to simply abandoning the child, which might prolong its "suffering."

In a great many instances—particularly among the more "primitive" cultures—infants were killed as a means of eliminating a perceived threat to the tribe. The Inuits would place newborns on ice floes when precious resources were scarce.[63] Other cultures sacrificed children to appease deities who, it was thought, might otherwise manifest their displeasure through a plague, famine, or other catastrophe affecting the community as a whole. Peoples struggling simply to survive in hostile environments deemed disabled children a threat because they consumed precious resources without contributing to the tribe's well-being. The difference between these instances of infanticide and the average abortion is that those who killed newborns often did so for reasons larger than themselves—the tribe, the family, their god(s). The reasons we kill the unborn tend to be more selfish.

Some peoples killed their young for reasons which may, on their face, seem remarkably arbitrary. The Bondei, for instance, killed children born headfirst; Madagascar natives exterminated infants delivered in March or April, or on a Wednesday or Friday; the Kamchadals put to death any children born during stormy weather.[64] But these criteria for deciding which children would die are not as arbitrary as they might at first seem. Many tribes killed children born under circumstances the tribe considered ominous.[65] Allowing the children to live might bring some calamity upon their family or community—one which people already lodged in a daily struggle to survive could ill afford to risk. Certainly, killing newborns in such circumstances is no more arbitrary than killing the unborn because of their sex,[66] or because the timing of the pregnancy would interfere with our social lives, schooling, or projected career path. Supreme Court Justice John Paul Stevens betrayed the extent of his naiveté when he wrote, in his dissent in *Planned Parenthood v. Casey*, that "Those who disagree about the legality of abortion agree about one thing: The decision to terminate a pregnancy is profound and difficult. *No person undertakes such a decision lightly.*"[67]

Some people do take the decision to abort seriously, but many do not. One doctor who now refuses to do abortions recalls married couples requesting them because the timing of the birth would interfere with a law firm's partnership track, remodeling their home, their summer travel plans, or the convenience of giving birth in June rather than February.[68] Similarly, "pro-choice" feminist Naomi Wolf reports that, in her high school, abortion was a "rite of passage" for many affluent girls: "the 1970s equivalent of the '50s fraternity pin."[69] And she writes that women she knows have gotten abortions because they were simply trying to find out whether they could get pregnant, to force their partners to become more serious about a relationship, and "to test a boyfriend's character" by seeing whether he would pay for the abortion or accompany her while she got it.[70]

In cultures which practice infanticide, the criteria for determining who has a right to life *are* arbitrary—but no more so than our own. Peoples who kill infants tend to do so soon after birth.[71] The Inuits, for instance, rarely killed children after naming.[72] And exposure was illegal in ancient Greece if a child had been formally adopted as a member of the family, an event which occurred on or before the tenth day after birth.[73] Since we recognize a right to life in our young only from the time they are born, the difference between us now, and the Greeks and the Inuits then, is only a matter of days. A child born two weeks premature in ancient Greece might well be protected before the same child carried to term in the present day United States.

We attempt to minimize any potential feelings of guilt by reminding ourselves that many of the unborn killed in abortion are not viable—they would be unable to survive independently if they were outside the pregnant woman. The implication is that we are not actually *killing* the unborn; we are simply choosing not to aid them. This distinction is utterly false, of course: we kill the unborn both before and after viability, and killing them is the *object*, not merely a consequence, of many abortions. But focusing on the fact that some unborn would be unable to survive outside the womb allows us to convince ourselves that we are not directly responsible for the killing. The cultures engaged in infanticide tend to make a similar distinction between direct and indirect killing. The preferred method of infanticide in many cultures is "exposure"—simply abandoning the child. In Ancient Greece, unwanted infants were typically placed in a large earthenware jar in a location where passers-by could rescue the child if they wanted.[74] "Greek philosophers," writes medical ethicist Earl Shelp, "tended to condone exposure as opposed to the more direct means of killing newborns."[75] The Romans also drew a distinction between direct and indirect killing. Even after the direct killing of infants was finally banned, they still allowed exposure and other indirect means of infanticide.[76]

The tendency to cast abortion as indirect killing is significant in two major respects. First, indirect killing is still killing. To rationalize abortion by saying that the unborn would not survive if outside the mother is like rationalizing the drowning of newborns by saying that they would drown if left in deep water. The fact of the matter is that the unborn are not outside the womb, and newborns are not in deep water, until someone intervenes and puts them there. That individual *kills* the child: one who knowingly moves another from a position of relative safety to one where he or she is virtually sure to perish is responsible for that individual's death. Second, unlike the peoples who practice infanticide, the distinction we make between direct and indirect killing is a false one. We use the notion of viability to mask the fact that we are often engaged in *direct* killing. Consider, for instance, the D&E abortion of an unborn which is not yet viable. The abortionist dismembers the unborn before removing it from the mother. The unborn does not die simply because the abortionist discontinues the aid the mother's body has been providing; it dies as the result of a direct and deliberate act of killing.

V

Ironically, at the same time we give lip service to the idea that all human beings are equal and have inherent rights, many of us have concluded that some human beings have no more intrinsic worth than animals. "Some members of other species are persons;" ethicist Peter Singer writes, "some members of our own species are not. . . . So it seems that killing, say, a chimpanzee is worse than the killing of a gravely defective human being who is not a person."[77]

Michael Tooley, who contends that killing the unborn and newborns is "in no way intrinsically wrong" because they are neither persons nor "quasi-persons," has a different view with respect to the killing of certain non-human animals. He writes, "Members of [some non-human] species would be quasi-persons, and their destruction therefore wrong to a greater or lesser degree. Finally, normal adult members of some species—such as, perhaps, chimpanzees, whales, and dolphins might be persons so that their destruction would be comparable to the destruction of normal adult human beings."[78]

Sue Savage-Rumbaugh, a psychologist at Georgia State University, maintains that gorillas, chimpanzees, and other apes should have semi-human status and deserve the same legal protection as severely retarded children.[79] And animal liberationists argue that apes are equal to humans and have a right not to be "imprisoned" without due process.[80] Strange, is it not, that one would object to animals being kept in cages without due process but accept human beings being killed without it. No doubt when animal rights activists say that apes and humans are equals, they mean apes should be treated as the equivalent of *adult* human beings; if apes were treated as the equivalent of *unborn* humans, they would have no rights at all. (More than just a few people seem to believe that certain animals are worth more than some human beings, incidentally. How many vegetarians and animal rights proponents object to the killing of cattle or poultry or sheep, but have no problems with the destruction of the unborn or newborns with grave birth defects?)

VI

We must decide what we stand for. Currently, we suffer from a strange sort of cognitive dissonance. On the one hand, we say that all human beings have intrinsic worth and inherent rights simply by virtue of being human. On the other, we regard women as having a "fundamental right" to destroy the unborn. Presented with a choice between two irreconcilable positions, we have chosen both.

And so we go on in a strange paradox: extending protection to other animals which we deny to our own flesh and blood; performing life-saving surgery on some sickly unborn yet dismembering others who are perfectly healthy. We profess that all human beings have a right to life, yet we kill a class of them wholesale. We turn to abortion to avoid the responsibility of having children yet end up responsible for killing them.

NOTES

1. *Roe v. Wade*, 410 US at 132.
2. 410 US at 131.
3. Aristotle, *Politics*, VII, 1335b, 20–25, in *Aristotle II*, vol. 9 of the *Great Books of the Western World Series*, ed. Robert Maynard Hutchins (Chicago: Encyclopaedia Britannica, 1952), 540.
4. Plato, *The Republic*, V, 460 in *Great Dialogues of Plato*, trans. W.H.D. Rouse (New York: Mentor Books, 1956), 258.
5. Plato 259 (V, 461).
6. *Planned Parenthood v. Ashcroft*, 462 U.S. 476 (1983).
7. 462 U.S. at 483 n.7. Many abortionists perform abortions far later into pregnancy, some up until the child is full term.
8. Marilee C. Allen, Pamela K. Donahue, and Amy Dusman, "Limit of Viability—Neonatal Outcome of Infants Born at 22 to 25 Weeks Gestation," *The New England Journal of Medicine* 329 (1993): 1597.
9. Allen et al., 1597.
10. Diane M. Gianelli, "Outlawing Abortion Method," *American Medical News*, November 20, 1995: 3.
11. Gianelli, 27.
12. William Raspberry, "Caution Light on Abortion," *Washington Post*, July 13, 1998: A21.
13. Charles Everett Koop, *Koop: The Memoirs of America's Family Doctor* (New York: Random House, 1991), 263.
14. Mary Anne Warren, "On the Moral and Legal Status of Abortion," *Ethical Issues in Modern Medicine*, eds. John Arras and Robert Hunt (Palo Alto, CA: Mayfield, 1977), 175.

15. Peter Singer, *Practical Ethics* (Cambridge, England: Cambridge University Press, 1979), 131–138.

16. Joseph Shapiro, "Who Cares How High Her IQ Really Is?" *U.S. News & World Report*, September 11, 1995: 59.

17. Michael Tooley, *Abortion and Infanticide* (Oxford, England: Clarendon-Oxford University Press, 1983), 411–412.

18. Tooley, 411–412.

19. Tooley, 411–412.

20. Joseph Fletcher, "Euthanasia," in *Humanhood: Essays in Biomedical Ethics* (Buffalo, N.Y.: Prometheus, 1979), 152 (emphasis added).

21. Glanville Williams, *The Sanctity of Life and the Criminal Law*, The 1956 James S. Carpenter Lectures at Columbia Law School (New York: Knopf, 1957), 215. Quoted in James Tunstead Burtchaell, *Rachel Weeping and Other Essays* (Kansas City: Andrews & McMeel, 1982) 200.

22. Jeff Lyon, *Playing God in the Nursery* (New York: Norton, 1985), 61.

23. Lyon, 61.

24. Will Durant, *The Life of Greece* (New York: Simon & Schuster, 1939), 287.

25. Lyon, 62.

26. Lyon, 62.

27. Lyon, 62.

28. Earl E. Shelp, *Born to Die? Deciding the Fate of Critically Ill Newborns* (New York: Free Press, 1986), 160–161.

29. Shelp, 160–161.

30. Lyon, 62.

31. Lyon, 62.

32. Lyon, 63.

33. Lyon, 63.

34. Lyon, 63.

35. Lyon, 63.

36. Lyon, 63.

37. See, for example, "Abandoned," *Eye to Eye*, CBS, WHP-TV, Harrisburg, PA, August 17, 1995.

38. Keith Thomas, *Man and the Natural World: A History of the Modern Sensibility* (New York: Pantheon, 1983), 130.

39. Daniel J. Boorstin, *The Discoverers* (New York: Random House, 1983), 726–730. After Pope Paul III argued that the Indians should not "be treated as dumb brutes created for our service" and that "the Indians are truly men," the conquistadors modified their approach. Invoking Aristotle's view that some men were "natural slaves," they asserted that the Native Americans were by their very nature inferior to Europeans, just as women were to men and children were to adults. Boorstin, 730–733.

40. Robert J. Lifton, *The Nazi Doctors: Medical Killing and the Psychology of Genocide* (New York: Basic Books, 1986), 441 (Wallace); and Stephen Jay Gould, "Flaws in a Victorian Veil," *The Panda's Thumb: More Reflections in Natural History* (New York: Norton, 1980), 170–173 (Agassiz).

41. Gould, "Flaws in a Victorian Veil," 172–173.

42. Quoted in Gould, "Flaws in a Victorian Veil," 173.

43. Gould, "Flaws in a Victorian Veil," 170–171.

44. Eugene Quay, "Justifiable Abortion—Medical and Legal Foundations (Part II)," *Georgetown Law Journal* 49 (1961): 400.

45. Konrad Lorenz, "Part and Parcel in Animal and Human Societies," *Studies in Human and Animal Behaviour*, trans. Robert Martin, vol. 2 (Cambridge, MA: Harvard University Press, 1971), 154–56.

46. Lorenz, 154–155.

47. Lorenz, 154–155.

48. Lorenz, 154–155.

49. Yin Wong, "A Question of Duty," *Reader's Digest*, September 1995: 65–70.

50. Wong, 66.

51. Wong, 66.

52. David R. Boldt, "Not Many Doctors Like the 'Dirty Business of Abortion,' " editorial, *Philadelphia Inquirer*, July 18, 1993: D5. (Norma McCorvey, the "Roe" of *Roe v. Wade*, had a similar reaction. After years of working in abortion clinics, she defected from the abortion movement shortly after seeing her first second-trimester abortion. "Have you ever seen a second-trimester abortion? It's a *baby*," McCorvey said. "It's got a face and a body, and they put him in a freezer and a little container." See David Van Biema, "An Icon in Search Mode," *Time*, August 21, 1995: 36; and Steven Waldman and Ginny Carroll, "Roe v. Roe," *Newsweek*, August 21, 1995: 24.)

53. George Flesh, "Why I No Longer Do Abortions," *Los Angeles Times*, September 12, 1991: B7.

54. Boldt.

55. Quoted in Dave Shiflett, "Dr. Hern and Mr. Clinton," *Weekly Standard*, November 11, 1996: 15.

56. Quoted in Shiflett, 15.

57. Shiflett, 15.

58. Brenda Shafer, "What the Nurse Saw," *National Right to Life News*, July 18, 1995: 23.

59. Shafer.

60. Shafer.

61. Seneca, "De Ira," I, xv, *Moral Essays*, trans. John Basore, vol. 1 (New York: Putnam, 1928), 145. Quoted in Quay, 421.

62. Quoted in Gould, "The Hottentot Venus," in his *The Flamingo's Smile* (New York: W. W. Norton, 1985), 295.

63. Lyon, 63.

64. Will Durant, *Our Oriental Heritage* (New York: Simon & Schuster, 1954), 50.

65. Durant, *Our Oriental Heritage*, 50.

66. Owen D. Jones, writing in the *Harvard Journal of Law and Technology* in 1992, notes that "it is rather widely accepted that no one knows the actual extent of sex-selection abortion in the U.S." Nevertheless, there is good reason to believe that they occur. Jones notes that polls indicate that one out of 10 Americans do not oppose abortion for purposes of selecting the sex of the child. And, since *Roe v. Wade*, the proportion of geneticists willing to perform prenatal diagnosis as a precursor to a sex-selection abortion unrelated to a sex-linked disease, or refer a patient to another geneticist who would, has skyrocketed. Approximately one percent of geneticists would do so in 1973, when *Roe* was issued. The figure rose to 20 percent in 1977 and 62 percent in 1985. It has remained fairly stable since then. See "Sex Selection: Regulating Technology Enabling the Predetermination of Child's Gender," *Harvard Journal of Law and Technology* 6 (1992): 14–16.

67. *Planned Parenthood v. Casey*, 505 U.S. 833, 919 (emphasis added).

68. Flesh.

69. Naomi Wolf, "Our Bodies, Our Souls: Re-thinking Abortion Rhetoric," *New Republic*, October 16, 1995: 32.

70. Wolf, 32.

71. Durant, *Our Oriental Heritage*, 50.

72. Edward Moffat Weyer, *The Eskimos: Their Environment and Folkways* (Hamden, CT: Archon Books, 1969), 63.

73. Durant, *The Life of Greece*, 287.

74. Durant, *The Life of Greece*, 287.

75. Shelp, 160–161.

76. Shelp, 160–161.

77. Singer 97. Quoted in Burleigh, 297–298.

78. Tooley, *Abortion and Infanticide*, 412.

79. Paul Leavitt, "Author Wants Apes Out of Zoos," *USA Today*, October 26, 1994, Washington ed.: 3A.

80. John Leo, "PC: Almost Dead, Still Funny," *U.S. News & World Report*, December 5, 1994: 24.

10

"Hastening Death"

He who contemplates suicide should ask himself whether his action can be consistent with the idea of humanity as an end in itself.
Immanuel Kant, *Fundamental Principles of the Metaphysics of Morals*

When regard for the truth has been broken down or even slightly weakened, all things will remain doubtful.
Saint Augustine, *On Lying*

When the Supreme Court issued its decision in *Roe v. Wade*, abortion proponents insisted that the nation had not embarked on a slippery slope. Abortion, we were told, was a special case; the rules that applied to the unborn did not apply to born human beings. Yet the shadow of *Roe v. Wade* has proven far longer than many had initially anticipated. The reasoning behind the decision has not only been used to justify the destruction of the unborn and newborns; it has also recently been invoked with respect to the seriously ill at the other end of life. As Judge Robert Bork has written:

The systematic killing of unborn children in huge numbers is part of a general disregard for human life that has been growing for some time. Abortion by itself did not cause that disregard, but it certainly deepens and legitimates the nihilism that . . . finds killing for convenience acceptable. We are crossing lines, at first slowly and now with rapidity: killing children for convenience; removing tissue from live fetuses; contemplating creating embryos for destruction in research; considering taking organs from living anencephalic babies; experimenting with assisted suicide; and contemplating euthanasia. Abortion has coarsened us. If it is permissible to kill the unborn human for convenience, it is surely permissible to kill those thought to be soon to die for the same reason. And it is inevitable that any who are not in danger of imminent death will be killed to relieve their families of burdens. Convenience is becoming the theme of our culture. Humans tend to be inconvenient at both ends of their lives.[1]

The current push to legalize assisted suicide and euthanasia shows just how far *Roe's* shadow stretches. In 1996, two Federal circuit courts ruled that some individuals had a *constitutional right* to commit suicide. In *Quill v. Vacco*, the Second Circuit Court of Appeals held that a New York statute which made it a crime to aid in a suicide violated the Equal Protection Clause of the Fourteenth Amendment of the Constitution.[2] According to the Second Circuit, there was no rational basis for New York to distinguish between physicians withdrawing life support upon request (which was legal under the statute) and physicians prescribing lethal doses of drugs upon request (which was illegal). In *Compassion in Dying v. Washington*, the Ninth Circuit Court of Appeals held that a similar Washington statute violated the Due Process Clause of the Fourteenth Amendment because it denied terminally ill individuals their right to "liberty" without due process of law.[3]

The Supreme Court has reversed both cases, but the assisted suicide/euthanasia movement remains alive and well. Although all the members of the Court agreed that the New York and Washington statutes prohibiting assisted suicide were not facially invalid, several suggested that the Constitution may guarantee a right to assisted suicide under other circumstances.[4] Oregon has already enacted legislation authorizing assisted suicide, and nothing prevents other states from doing so in the future. Furthermore, if the Federal circuit court decisions finding a right to assisted suicide are any indication of the sentiment among state judges, courts in many states could recognize a right to assisted suicide under their state constitutions—forcing the state to amend its constitution if it wishes to prohibit the practice.

It might seem at first that assisted suicide threatens no one. After all, if a terminally ill person—or anyone else—finds life so terrible that he is willing to kill himself, who are we to impose our will on him? Who are we to force him to continue suffering? There is a clear moral distinction between a human being taking his own life—or helping another to kill himself—and someone unilaterally killing another.

Yet, while more public support exists for assisted suicide than for "ordinary" suicide, assisted suicide and its cousin—euthanasia—pose a far greater threat to society. "Ordinary" suicide is self-limiting: the killer acts alone, the killing is voluntary, and the killers will not have the opportunity to kill again. Although the death may be a great loss to those who survive, the suicide's death does not threaten the lives of others in any way. Assisted suicide and euthanasia are different. The beguiling end to suffering and control over death that they seem to promise is an apple poisoned with lies, dehumanization, and involuntary killing. They are dangerous because—like abortion—they foster the idea of "humane" killing, they draw others into the destruction process, they loose the strictures of conscience preventing nonconsensual killing, and they tap into notions of relative human worth.

I

As in the case of abortion, much of the support for assisted suicide and euthanasia is built on misconceptions and ignorance. In the minds of many, the typical candidate for assisted suicide is a patient who chooses to die only because it is his only means of escaping unbearable pain. But Dr. Ezekiel Emanuel, professor of medicine and social medicine at Harvard Medical School, observes, "Not a single rigorous study has demonstrated that it is patients in pain who, as a rule, are motivated to seek euthanasia," and that "scientific studies reveal that most patients who seek euthanasia are motivated by psychological factors—often depression—not by unbearable suffering."[5] For instance, a study of Washington state physicians who have participated in assisted suicide or euthanasia (both illegal in Washington) revealed that pain was a factor in the patient's decision to end his or her life in only 35 percent of cases.[6]

Emanuel's own study dealt with cancer victims. It found that patients in pain were no more likely to request euthanasia than those without pain; that they were more likely to find euthanasia *unethical*—even in cases of interminable pain—than patients without pain; that they tended to trust doctors less if they mentioned euthanasia or assisted suicide; and that they were more likely than patients without pain to switch doctors if their physician mentioned euthanasia.[7] Furthermore, in those few cases where doctors are unable to control pain with modern pain-relieving drugs, the terminally ill patients need not suffer—even without assisted suicide. The "double effect" doctrine is widely recognized among bioethicists and the medical community at large.[8] Under that doctrine, doctors may, with a patient's consent, increase his medication to control pain, even if the dose might have the effect of depressing respiration and causing death.[9]

If pain is not the reason, why do so many terminally ill patients want to be killed? There are two answers. First, not many patients in grave condition do want to be killed. Charles Krauthammer has pointed out that, of the approximately 31,000 people who commit suicide each year in the United States, only two to four percent are terminally ill.[10] Second, studies show that those who do want to kill themselves generally want to do so for the same reasons others commit suicide: depression, anxiety, despair, and other psychological factors.[11] The terminally ill are in dire straits by anyone's calculation; they have to contend with the illness itself, the uncertainty of their final days, and the disruption and heartache that their situation causes for their families and finances, among other problems. It should come as no surprise, therefore, that they suffer disproportionately from depression and other psychological maladies. According to some studies, more than 70 percent of terminal patients wrestle with these problems.[12] Studies done on cancer victims who commit suicide have found that about 80 percent suffer from depressive syndromes—the same percentage as people without cancer who commit suicide.[13]

II

Proponents of assisted suicide are fond of pointing out that it differs from other forms of euthanasia because the victim actually kills himself—minimizing the involvement of others in the destruction process and eliminating the threat of involuntary killing. But both claims are suspect. Noting that approximately a quarter of assisted suicides fail, Doctor Edmund Pellegrino has warned that assisted suicide practically requires that doctors have the authority to step in and kill the patient themselves if the patient's attempt is unsuccessful.[14] Thus, legalizing assisted suicide effectively requires that we not only allow doctors to assist in the killing, but that we sometimes allow them to do the killing themselves.

And just how voluntary is a patient's request that he would like to kill himself or be killed? Most patients follow their doctor's advice, and, if their doctor suggests suicide or euthanasia, they may feel they have few options left. Furthermore, as Judge Bork notes, the terminally ill are particularly vulnerable to suggestion:

> The patient who is a candidate for medical termination of his life will be in a greatly weakened physical condition, probably frightened or in despair, which means that his will and his capacity for independent thought will also be weakened. He will be flat on his back with his relatives and the authority figure of the doctor looking down on him. There can be few better subjects and settings for subtle and not-so-subtle psychological coercion. The patient will know, and probably will be informed, that prolonging his existence . . . places an enormous emotional and financial burden on his family. A great many people in this position are likely to accept premature death under coercion. That can hardly be called death with dignity.[15]

The patient's caregivers and relatives need not necessarily have an agenda for his environment to be coercive. In a 1995 article in *The Hastings Center Report*, Herbert Hendin observes:

> Watching someone die can be intolerably painful for those who care for the patient. Their wish to have it over with quickly is understandable. Their feeling can become a form of pressure on the patient and must be separated from what the patient actually wants. The patient who wants to live until the end but senses his family cannot tolerate watching him die is familiar to those who care for the terminally ill. Once those close to the patient decide to assist in the suicide, their desire to have it over with can make the pressure put on the patient many times greater.[16]

And the terminally ill patient's family and caregivers may not be able to objectively assess whether psychological problems are influencing the patient's decision to end his life. The patient's condition exacts a psychological toll on them as well. A recent editorial in *The New England Journal of Medicine* notes, "The literature on suicide is full of evidence that care givers, including health care providers, often collude in the suicides of depressed patients, becoming infected and overwhelmed with their pessimism, helplessness, and dependency."[17]

Furthermore, even when patients say they want to die, that may not really be what they want. Hendin writes, "The patient, who may have said she wants to die in the hope of receiving emotional reassurance that all around her want her to live, may find out that . . . she has set in motion a process whose momentum she cannot control."[18] And he notes that many people express "two conflicting wishes—to live and to die—and [find] support only for the latter."[19]

In other cases, a patient may choose to die, not because she wants to stop living, but because she feels guilty about the emotional or financial costs her condition may impose on those who care for her. The astronomical costs of health care in the twilight of life help drive these feelings of guilt. So does the increasingly common notion that a patient who lingers when his end is near is somehow being "selfish." Former Colorado Governor Richard Lamm, for instance, once suggested the old people have a duty to die, a position amplified by philosopher John Hardwig in a 1997 article in *The Hastings Center Report*.

Hardwig contends that "[t]here can be a duty to die before one's illnesses would cause death" and "there may even be a fairly common duty to die when one would prefer to live."[20] In other words, he thinks many people may have a duty to kill themselves even if they do not want to die. According to Hardwig, the duty arises from the individual's obligations to those close to him: a person suffering from a debilitating disease has a responsibility to kill himself rather than subject his loved ones to the considerable emotional and financial burdens entailed in caring for him.[21] And he writes that one sometimes has a duty to commit suicide sooner, rather than later, if he is in danger of losing the competence or physical ability to kill himself or has "lived a relatively lavish lifestyle instead of saving for illness or old age."[22]

Hardwig also argues that the ill or infirm patient should allow those close to him to help him decide that he has a duty to die—even if the patient himself does not think he has a duty to die: "[T]hose of us with family and loved ones should not define our duties unilaterally, especially not a decision about a duty to die. . . . They should be allowed to speak for themselves about the burdens my life imposes on them and how they feel about bearing those burdens."[23] Hardwig anticipates that "there . . . will be many situations in which it will be very difficult to discern whether one has a duty to die" and that many families will find even talking about death difficult.[24] But he writes, "[E]ven if talking about death is impossible, there are always behavioral clues," and he concludes that "[d]eciding whether you have a duty to die based on these behavioral clues and conversations about them honors your relationships better than deciding on your own."[25]

The most provocative aspect of Hardwig's piece, however, is the question he never asks or answers. If it is immoral for a person to continue living when he becomes a substantial financial and emotional burden, if he has a duty to kill himself and a speedy death would spare our loved ones untold agony and financial ruin, *then what do we do with someone who has a duty to die but is too selfish to act on it?*

For some reason, those receptive to the arguments for assisted suicide and euthanasia tend not to be troubled by the specter of involuntary killing. During the course of its decision in *Quill*, the Second Circuit referred to assisted suicide in the Netherlands, where physician-assisted suicide is legal but involuntary killing is not. Although the Court conceded that Dutch doctors sometimes kill without their patients' consent, it dismissed the problem by saying that such killing was illegal in the Netherlands and that the plaintiffs did not propose legalizing it in the United States.[26] The Court never addressed the concern that liberalized Dutch laws concerning physician-assisted suicide contributed to attitudes among Dutch doctors that made them more receptive to involuntary killing.

The Ninth Circuit was willing to go even further. In its decision in *Compassion in Dying*, the Court emphasized the fact that a court-appointed or patient-appointed surrogate could decide to kill a patient, noting that "the decision of a duly appointed surrogate is for all legal purposes the decision of the patient himself."[27]

The Hemlock Society USA, one the organizations leading the assisted suicide movement, has adopted similar reasoning. In a December 3, 1997, statement, the group's Executive Director, Faye Girsh, maintains that a law only allowing people to kill themselves is inadequate, and that some provision must be made for killing persons who are incompetent to decide to kill themselves.[28] According to Girsh, "A judicial determination should be made when it is necessary to hasten the death of an individual whether it be a demented parent, a suffering, severely disabled spouse or a child."[29] She contends that the law should allow an incompetent person to be killed if his surrogate determines his life is "too burdensome to continue."[30]

It is not difficult to imagine situations where a patient is not legally competent to decide his fate but wants very desperately to live nevertheless. What kind of society allows putting such people to death? And what will it do to our doctors?

III

As in the case of abortion, the notion of "humane" killing figures prominently in the euthanasia movement. Consider the names of the pro-assisted suicide groups mentioned in *Quill* and *Compassion in Dying*: *Compassion* in Dying, Physicians for *Mercy*, Death with *Dignity*. Consider the terms used to refer to the killing: "*mercy* killing," "euthanasia" (which means "fine death"[31]), and "deliverance," among others. As we have seen in previous chapters, once individuals accept the premise that killing can be an act of kindness, even "decent" people can kill.

And the notion of "humane" killing reduces the barriers to involuntary killing as well as assisted suicide. If it is a kindness to help people put themselves out of their misery, then presumably it is also a kindness to "end the suffering" of those unable to make such a request. Would it not be natural for medical personnel attending incompetent patients suffering from terminal illnesses to ask, "*Why should my charge continue to suffer simply because she is incompetent? She has suffered every bit as much as the mentally-competent patients in my care—probably more. Would it not be more humane to 'release' her from her unfortunate torture? Surely she would have made that request beforehand had she appreciated what lay in store for her. Why should she be subjected to this misery simply because her surrogate is unfeeling?*"

Wouldn't these doctors and nurses be inclined to persuade the patient's surrogate to consent to "hasten" the patient's death? Might not some even be tempted to take action themselves to "deliver" her, rather than being an accomplice in "prolonging her suffering"?

Of course, those attending individuals with chronic, debilitating, and painful—but non-terminal—disabilities might ask themselves similar questions. If it is better to be killed than to live suffering, why should their charges be forced to endure misery for thirty or forty years when the terminally ill can commit suicide to escape much shorter suffering? Why should their patients be condemned to a lifetime of suffering simply because their surrogates are unfeeling or have antiquated views about euthanasia? Perhaps they can prevail on the surrogate to see the light. It would spare the patient, the family, and the staff. Surely the patient would herself request to "hasten" her death if only she had the ability.

IV

Once killing is legalized, it becomes difficult to contain. Oregon enacted the nation's only assisted-suicide law, the so-called "Death with Dignity Act," in 1994.[32] Although the law did not become effective for three years because of court challenges, there has been at least one suicide—and perhaps several other suicides—under it already.[33] Advocates of assisted suicide look to the Oregon law as a model of legislation they would like to see enacted in other states and insist that it shows that a state can legalize physician-assisted suicide while restricting it to competent individuals with less than six months to live.

In practice, however, the killing would not be so limited. Although the Oregon law limits physician-assisted suicide to persons with less than six months to live, 50 percent of Oregon physicians doubt whether they can determine that a patient has that little time remaining.[34] There are similar problems with the Oregon law's psychological safeguard. Under the law, doctors must refer patients to a psychiatrist or psychologist if they think that the patient suffers from depression or another psychological problem which may be influencing the patient's request for assisted suicide. However, studies have shown that primary care physicians miss between 45 and 90 percent of psychiatric disorders in their patients.[35] And 94 percent of Oregon psychiatrists doubt whether they can determine if a person seeking assisted suicide is competent in a single evaluation.[36]

The experience of the Netherlands with assisted suicide provides even more compelling evidence of the dangers of allowing the camel's nose into the tent. A 1997 article in the *Journal of the American Medical Association* notes, "During the past two decades, the Netherlands has moved from considering assisted suicide . . . to giving legal sanction to both physician-assisted suicide and euthanasia, from euthanasia for terminally ill patients to euthanasia for those who are chronically ill, from euthanasia for physical illness to euthanasia for psychological distress, and from voluntary euthanasia to nonvoluntary and involuntary euthanasia."[37] It also observes, "Virtually every guideline set up by the Dutch—a voluntary, well-considered, persistent request; intolerable suffering that cannot be relieved; consultation; and reporting of cases—has failed to protect patients or has been modified or violated."[38]

Approximately 4.7 percent of all deaths in the Netherlands result from physician-assisted suicide or the physician deliberately killing the patient.[39] Pain is the sole motivating factor in only 5 percent of the euthanasia deaths.[40] The leading reason is loss of "dignity."[41] Fifty percent of Dutch physicians consider it appropriate to suggest euthanasia to their patients, and 59 percent fail to report their euthanasia cases though required to do so.[42] Of the euthanasia cases not reported, 89 percent are done without consulting another physician—another violation of the guidelines.[43]

The Dutch candidate for assisted suicide or euthanasia need not be terminally ill or even suffering from physical problems. In 1994, the Dutch Supreme Court ruled that physician-assisted suicide may be justifiable for patients with mental suffering but no physical problems.[44] When a healthy 50-year-old woman became depressed about her son's death, her psychiatrist helped her commit suicide though her son had died only four months previously.[45] More than two-thirds of Dutch psychiatrists believe it acceptable to assist in the suicide of patients even if the patients' suffering results solely from mental—not physical—problems.[46] There is virtually no inquiry into whether depression or some other psychological problem might be influencing patients' requests to die. Dutch physicians ask for a psychiatric evaluation in only 3 percent of cases where the patient requests assisted suicide.[47]

Involuntary euthanasia is not legally sanctioned in the Netherlands but is commonplace nevertheless. One quarter of Dutch physicians have killed patients without an "explicit request," and an additional third have said they could consider doing so.[48] More than a fifth of those killed without an explicit request were mentally competent at the time they were killed.[49]

To illustrate why it was often necessary for physicians to kill competent patients without their consent, an attorney for a Dutch pro-euthanasia group pointed to a nun whose physician killed her a few days before she would have died because she was in great pain but her religious beliefs prevented her from asking to be killed.[50] (Ironically, the attorney represented the Dutch *Voluntary* Euthanasia Society.) Another doctor who killed a patient who did not want euthanasia explained, "It could have taken another week before she died. I just needed this bed."[51]

David C. Thomasma has written that assisted suicide and euthanasia would be even harder to contain in the United States than in the Netherlands. He notes that the Dutch have a comprehensive national health care plan (and, consequently, the Dutch need not worry that a patient's care might bankrupt his relatives), while the proportion of the elderly in the U.S. population will balloon in coming decades, dramatically increasing the intense pressure to control American health care costs.[52] In a 1997 article in *U.S. News & World Report*, one Oregon doctor explained that she renounced her support for physician-assisted suicide after an elderly patient dying of cancer asked her for help committing suicide because the patient was suffering terribly from nausea and her HMO refused to pay for anti-nausea medication.[53]

V

Should anyone doubt the connection between abortion and assisted suicide/euthanasia, he need only look to the two 1996 Federal circuit court cases which held that there was a constitutional right to physician-assisted suicide. Both *Quill* and *Compassion in Dying* identified the Supreme Court's abortion case law as the lodestar for their holdings. In *Quill*, the Second Circuit concluded that New York had no interest in preventing mentally competent, terminally ill individuals from committing suicide. In support of that proposition, the Court pointed to language from the Supreme Court's recent abortion decision *Planned Parenthood v. Casey* which said, "At the heart of liberty is the right to define one's own concept of existence, of meaning, of the universe, and of the mystery of human life."[54]

The Supreme Court's abortion decisions figured even more prominently in the Ninth Circuit's reasoning in *Compassion in Dying*. In his opinion for the majority of the court, Judge Stephen Reinhardt wrote, "In deciding right-to-die cases, we are guided by the Court's approach to the abortion cases," and he referred to the "compelling similarities" between the two.[55] As in *Quill*, the Ninth Circuit turned to the Supreme Court's abortion decision in *Casey* in its quest to determine whether there is a right to assisted suicide as part of the right to "liberty." Quoting *Casey*, Judge Reinhardt wrote:

These matters, involving the most intimate and personal choices a person may make in a lifetime, choices central to personal dignity and autonomy, are central to the liberty protected by the Fourteenth Amendment. At the heart of liberty is the right to define one's own concept of existence, of meaning, of the universe, and of the mystery of human life. Beliefs about these matters could not define the attributes of personhood were they formed under compulsion of the State.[56]

The Ninth Circuit also noted that its approach for defining the "liberty" interest in assisted suicide was "identical to the approach used by the Supreme Court in the abortion cases,"[57] and explained, "Like the decision of whether or not to have an abortion, the decision how and when to die is one of 'the most intimate and personal choices a person may make in a lifetime,' a choice 'central to personal dignity and autonomy.' "[58]

The Ninth Circuit even sought to destigmatize suicide in the same manner the Supreme Court sought to destigmatize abortion in *Roe*: by pointing to Greek and Roman acceptance of the practice. The court wrote that among the Greeks and Romans, "suicide was often considered commendable in literature, mythology, and practice."[59] And it pointed to several "literary suicides"[60] from Greek mythology where self-destruction "is made to seem praiseworthy"[61] and even "natural and heroic."[62]

VI

Like abortion supporters, the proponents of assisted suicide and euthanasia cloak their position in euphemisms. The definitions of words mean less than their connotations. It may well be that the proponents of euthanasia and assisted suicide can defend one person "killing" another or helping the other to "kill" himself. But they virtually never defend it that way. Rather than acknowledge the act as "killing," "suicide," or—in the case of involuntary killing—"murder," and defending it under the circumstances, those sympathetic to assisted suicide and euthanasia disguise their end with seemingly innocuous code-words: for instance, "aid-in-dying," "death with dignity," "hastening death," and "assisting to die." ("Mercy killing," popular during the 1970s and 1980s, has lost favor because it acknowledges that the act involves "killing.")

The two circuit courts that found a constitutional right to physician-assisted suicide proved receptive to such euphemisms. In *Quill*, the Second Circuit wrote approvingly of guidelines for physician-assisted suicide which refer to the physician assisting in the suicide as an "obitiatrist" and the suicide itself as "patholysis," a term coined by the notorious Dr. Jack Kevorkian.[63] In *Compassion in Dying*, meanwhile, the Ninth Circuit wrote:

> While some people refer to the liberty interest implicated in right-to-die cases as a liberty interest in committing suicide, we do not describe it that way. We use the broader and more accurate terms, "the right to die," "determining the time and manner of one's death," and "hastening one's death" for an important reason. The liberty interest we examine encompasses a whole range of acts that are generally not considered to constitute "suicide." . . . [W]e believe that the broader terms—"the right to die," "controlling the time and manner of one's death," and "hastening one's death"—more accurately describe the liberty interest at issue here.[64]

Indeed, the Ninth Circuit refused even to consider physician-assisted suicide as "suicide." The Court explained, "[W]e are doubtful that deaths resulting from terminally ill patients taking medication prescribed by their doctors [for the express purpose of the patients killing themselves] should be classified as 'suicide'. . . . Thus, notwithstanding the generally accepted use of the term 'physician-assisted suicide,' we have serious doubt that the state's interest in preventing suicide is even implicated in this case."[65]

This tendency to call killing something other than "killing" in the hope of gaining acceptance for assisted suicide and euthanasia is dangerous. As noted in the previous chapter, such euphemisms loose the strictures of conscience because they allow people to kill without ever having to confront their involvement in "killing." The vocabulary of the assisted-suicide/euthanasia movement is also dangerous because the language itself tends to exert subtle pressure on the patient and health care personnel. Consider one of the movement's favorite euphemisms for assisted suicide: "death with dignity." The implication is that some patients are "undignified" if they do not choose to kill themselves. These patients must already wrestle with their illness and the effect of their condition on the lives and finances of those close to them. Should we subject patients to this additional psychological pressure when they are particularly vulnerable to suggestion and depression? Furthermore, if the alternative to a patient killing himself is "death with*out* dignity," then medical personnel could rationalize the killing of patients who are unable to kill themselves as in the patient's best inter-est—whether the patient requested that he be killed or not.

VII

The assisted-suicide/euthanasia movement is particularly dangerous because it will likely incorporate some of the notions of relative human worth that have already become accepted as part of the abortion move-ment. Many of the definitions of "person" advanced by abortion pro-ponents exclude some individuals who are seriously ill. For instance, abortion proponent and bioethicist Joseph Fletcher writes, "There are, as physicians know so well, some human beings who either will never become, *or have ceased to be*, persons."[66] Mary Anne Warren, another prominent defender of abortion, also writes of human beings who are no longer "persons."[67] If, as these individuals suggest, some human be-ings are not "persons" and only "persons" have a right to life, then it follows that one may kill human beings who are no longer "persons." This reasoning is perilous because it would allow the acceptance of as-sisted suicide and voluntary euthanasia to mutate rather quickly into ac-ceptance of *involuntary* euthanasia.

The tendency to regard some human lives as worth less than others also played a role in the circuit court decisions in *Quill* and *Compassion in Dying*. Although the reasoning the courts used would seem to ex-tend to virtually *any* mentally competent individual who wants to com-mit suicide, the courts shrank from actually going that far. Instead, both the Second Circuit and the Ninth Circuit were careful to limit their holdings to the terminally ill. They did this, not by holding that the terminally ill had more of a right to kill themselves than others, but by holding that *the state had less of an interest in preserving their lives*. In *Quill*, for instance, the Second Circuit wrote:

[W]hat interest can the state possibly have in requiring the pro-longation of a life that is all but ended? Surely, the state's interest lessens as the potential for life diminishes. . . . What concern prompts the state to interfere with a mentally competent patient's "right to define [his] own concept of existence, of meaning, of the universe, and of the mystery of human life"? The greatly reduced interest of the state in preserving life compels the answer to these questions: "None."[68]

Similarly, in *Compassion in Dying*, the Ninth Circuit wrote that "the relative strength of the competing interests changes as physical, medical, or related circumstances vary"[69] and that "the outcome of the balancing test may differ at different points along the life cycle as a person's physical or medical condition deteriorates."[70]

VIII

Like abortion, assisted suicide and euthanasia violate long-accepted standards of medical ethics. As the Ninth Circuit itself acknowledged in *Compassion in Dying*, the Hippocratic Oath forbids physician-assisted suicide.[71] Under the Oath, doctors swear: "I will neither give a deadly drug to anybody if asked for it, nor will I make a suggestion to this effect."[72] Furthermore, the American Medical Association has argued that "the societal risk of involving physicians in medical interventions to cause patients' death is too great in this culture to condone euthanasia or physician-assisted suicide at this time."[73]

The canons of medical ethics will not stop assisted suicide or euthanasia, however. Having held that the Hippocratic Oath was meaningless when it banned abortion, the courts cannot accord it much weight with respect to other killing. Indeed, in its decision in *Compassion in Dying*, the Ninth Circuit stated that *Roe v. Wade* showed that doctors should not take the Hippocratic Oath "literally." It wrote:

> Twenty years ago, the [American Medical Association] contended that performing abortions violated the Hippocratic Oath; today, it claims that assisting terminally ill patients to hasten their death does likewise. Clearly, the Hippocratic Oath can have no greater import in deciding the constitutionality of physician-assisted suicide than it did in determining whether women had a constitutional right to have an abortion. . . . *As Roe shows, a literalist reading of the Hippocratic Oath does not represent the best or final word on medical or legal controversies today.*[74]

Rather than relying on the Hippocratic Oath or some other ethical standard for the medical community, the Ninth Circuit chose to place its faith in the judgment of the individual medical personnel attending the patient:

We believe that most, if not all, doctors would not assist a terminally ill patient to hasten his death as long as there were any reasonable chance of alleviating the patient's suffering or enabling him to live under tolerable conditions. We also believe that physicians would not assist a patient to end his life if there were any significant doubt about the patient's true wishes. To do so would be contrary to the physicians' fundamental training, their conservative nature, and the ethics of their profession.[75]

Yet, if we can trust the individual judgment of medical professionals, why do we have any ethical standards in medicine? They would seem to be utterly superfluous. Furthermore, if physicians did not sometimes act "contrary to [their] fundamental training, their conservative nature, and the ethics of their profession," no physicians would be willing to engage in assisted suicide even now: It is contrary to their fundamental training, the conservative nature of the profession, and the Hippocratic Oath, and is even illegal in most states.[76] Yet surveys of physicians indicate that one out of every five doctors has helped patients kill themselves already—as the Ninth Circuit itself noted in its opinion.[77] Evidently, a great many doctors are already willing to act "contrary to [their] fundamental training, their conservative nature, and the ethics of their profession." How much of a safeguard will standards of medical ethics prove if, as the Ninth Circuit suggests, *Roe v. Wade* shows that they *are not to be taken literally?*

We should be especially wary of assisted suicide and euthanasia. We have seen that patients who want to kill themselves or be killed are often motivated by depression or other psychological problems rather than pain. We have seen that, even where a patient requests assisted suicide, the request is often not purely voluntary. We have seen that assisted suicide will likely lead to euthanasia, and that voluntary killing will likely lead to involuntary killing. And we have seen that our acceptance of abortion has fostered notions of relative human worth and "humane" killing that facilitate involuntary killing. When Germany first considered legalizing assisted suicide for the terminally ill in the early decades of this century, many doctors put up no resistance. One, however, objected in terms as relevant today as they were then. He said, "I . . . believe that this would be the first step, but whether it would be the last appears to me to be very doubtful. . . . Once respect for the sanctity of human life has been diminished by introducing voluntary mercy killing for the mentally-healthy incurably ill, and involuntary killing for the mentally ill, *who is going to ensure that matters stop there?*"[78]

NOTES

1. Robert H. Bork, *Slouching Towards Gomorrah: Modern Liberalism and American Decline* (New York: ReganBooks-Harper, 1996), 192.

2. *Quill v. Vacco*, 80 F.3d 716 (2d Cir.1996), *reversed* ___ U.S. ___, 117 S.Ct. 2293 (1997).

3. *Compassion in Dying v. Washington*, 79 F.3d 790 (9th Cir.1996), *reversed sub nom. Washington v. Glucksberg*, ___U.S.___, 117 S.Ct. 2258 (1997).

4. See Justice Stevens' concurring opinion to *Washington v. Glucksberg*, ___ U.S. at ___, 117 S.Ct. 2302, 2304, 2310, and Justice Souter's concurring opinion in *Washington v. Glucksberg*, ___ U.S. ___, 117 S.Ct. 2258, 2290.

5. Ezekiel J. Emanuel, "The Painful Truth about Euthanasia," *Wall Street Journal*, January 7, 1997: A16.

6. Emanuel.

7. Emanuel.

8. Report from the New York State Task Force on Life and the Law, "When Death Is Sought: Assisted Suicide and Euthanasia in the Medical Context," May 1994, 163 n. 6.

9. "Report of the Council on Ethical and Judicial Affairs of the American Medical Association," *Issues in Law and Medicine* 10 (1994): 92.

10. Charles Krauthammer, "Traveling Executioner," *Washington Post*, December 3, 1993: A29.

11. Emanuel.

12. Emanuel.

13. Linda Ganzini and Melinda A. Lee, editorial, "Psychiatry and Assisted Suicide in the United States," *New England Journal of Medicine* 336 (1997): 1825.

14. Edmund D. Pellegrino, "Ethics," *Journal of the American Medical Association* 274 (1995): 1674–1675.

15. Bork, 188.

16. Herbert Hendin, "Selling Death with Dignity," *Hastings Center Report*, May/June 1995: 22–23.

17. Ganzini and Lee, 1826.

18. Hendin, 23.

19. Hendin, 22.

20. John Hardwig, "Is There a Duty to Die?" *Hastings Center Report*, March/April 1997: 35.

21. Hardwig, 36.

22. Hardwig, 39.

23. Hardwig, 38.

24. Hardwig, 38.

25. Hardwig, 38.

26. 80 F.3d at 730.

27. 79 F.3d at 832 n.120.

28. "Hemlock Society Endorses Nonvoluntary Direct Killing," *National Right to Life News*, December 9, 1997: 16. Girsh has since attempted to back away from the statement. See "Hemlock Executive Director Seeks to Pull Back from Endorsement of Nonvoluntary Euthanasia," *National Right to Life News*, February 11, 1998: 15+.

29. "Hemlock Society Endorses Nonvoluntary Direct Killing."

30. "Hemlock Society Endorses Nonvoluntary Direct Killing."

31. Michael Burleigh, *Death and Deliverance: Euthanasia in Germany 1900–1945* (New York: Cambridge University Press, 1994), 12.

32. Oregon Revised Statutes, §§ 127.800–127.897 (1996).

33. Timothy Egan, "First Death under an Assisted-Suicide Law," *New York Times*, March 26, 1998: late ed. : A14. Only one person has made her decision to commit suicide under the law public. Others may have decided to commit physician-assisted suicide privately. State officials are not required to state how many individuals choose physician-assisted suicide, but have said they will release a report on the Death Dignity Act when at least ten people exercise that option.

34. Joseph P. Shapiro, "On Second Thought," *U.S. News & World Report*, September 1, 1997: 62.

35. Leon Eisenberg, "Treating Depression and Anxiety in Primary Care: Closing the Gap between Knowledge and Practice," *New England Journal of Medicine* 326 (1992): 1081.

36. Shapiro, 62.

37. Herbert Hendin, Chris Rutenfrans, and Zbigniew Zylicz, "Physician-Assisted Suicide and Euthanasia in the Netherlands: Lessons from the Dutch," *Journal of the American Medical Association* 277 (1997): 1720.

38. Hendin et al., 1721.

39. Hendin et al., 1720.

40. Emanuel.

41. Emanuel.

42. Hendin et al., 1721.

43. Hendin et al., 1721.

44. Johanna H. Groenewoud et al., "Physician-Assisted Death in Psychiatric Practice in the Netherlands," *New England Journal of Medicine* 336 (1997): 1795.

45. Hendin et al., 1722.

46. Groenewoud et al., 1795.

47. Groenewoud et al., 1795.

48. Hendin et al., 1721. The authors note, "The use of the word 'explicit' is somewhat inaccurate, since in 48% of these cases there was no request of any kind, and in the others there were mainly references to patients' earlier statements of not wanting to suffer."

49. Hendin et al., 1721.

50. Hendin et al., 1721–1722.

51. Hendin et al., 1721.

52. "Euthanasia as Power and Empowerment," in *Medicine Unbound: The Human Body and the Limits of Medical Intervention*, eds. Robert H. Blank and Andrea L. Bonnicksen (New York: Columbia University Press, 1994), 210–227.

53. Shapiro.

54. 80 F.3d at 730, quoting *Planned Parenthood v. Casey*, 505 U.S. 833, 851 (1992).

55. 79 F.3d at 801, 800.

56. 79 F.3d at 801.

57. 79 F.3d at 801.

58. 79 F.3d at 813–814.

59. 79 F.3d at 806.

60. 79 F.3d at 806.

61. 79 F.3d at 806.

62. 79 F.3d at 806.

63. 80 F.3d at 731 n.4.

64. 79 F.3d at 802.

65. 79 F.3d at 802.

66. Joseph Fletcher, "Humanness," in *Humanhood: Essays in Biomedical Ethics* (Buffalo, N.Y.: Prometheus, 1979), 11 (emphasis added).

67. Mary Anne Warren, "On the Moral and Legal Status of Abortion," in *Ethical Issues in Modern Medicine*, eds. John Arras and Robert Hunt (Palo Alto, CA: Mayfield, 1977), 171.

68. 80 F.3d at 729–730.

69. 79 F.3d at 800.

70. 79 F.3d at 800.

71. 80 F.3d at 730.

72. 80 F.3d at 730, quoting one of the translations used in *Roe v. Wade*, 410 U.S. 113, 131 (1973).

73. 79 F.3d at 829 n.108.

74. 79 F.3d at 829 (emphasis added).

75. 79 F.3d at 827.

76. Julia Pugliese, Note, "Don't Ask—Don't Tell: The Secret Practice of Physician-Assisted Suicide," *Hastings Law Journal* 44 (1993): 1295.

77. 79 F.3d at 811. The Ninth Circuit also pointed out that in some specialties the rate is considerably higher. It noted, for instance, that a 1995 study of San Francisco Bay Area AIDS physicians found that more than half of the 188 doctors polled had helped patients commit suicide. 79 F.3d at 811 n.57.

78. Burleigh, 15.

11

The House of Atreus?

Behold ye—yonder on the palace roof
The specter-children sitting—look, such things
As dreams are made of, phantoms as of babes
Horrible shadows that a kinsman's hand
Hath marked with murder, and their arms are full—
A rueful burden—see, they hold them up,
The entrails upon which their fathers fed!

Aeschylus, *Agamemnon*

Murder most foul, as in the best it is;
But this most foul, strange and unnatural.

Shakespeare, *Hamlet*

Twenty-five centuries ago, Aeschylus composed *The House of Atreus*, a trilogy depicting the misfortunes that befell Agamemnon and his family upon the Greek leader's triumphant return from the expedition against Troy. Aeschylus focused on just part of the history of one of the most complex and troubled families in ancient Greek mythology: the House of Atreus. The legend of that family remains important today—and not simply because it provided the inspiration for Aeschylus's dramatic masterpiece. If there is a metaphor for the role of abortion in our society—where mothers routinely destroy their young, where doctors routinely kill—it may well be the story of the House of Atreus.

THE MYTH

Most readers will be familiar with some aspects of the saga of Atreus and his kindred. Atreus and his family were cursed because of an outrage committed long before by his grandfather, Tantalus. Tantalus had been skeptical of the powers of the gods and decided to put them to the test. He invited the immortals to a lavish banquet, then served them meat prepared from his only son to see whether they would recognize what they ate. The ploy failed to deceive most of the immortals, but Demeter was distracted and ate before she realized what she had been served.

Tantalus's depravity and deception infuriated the Olympians, who condemned him to spend eternity starving amidst plenty. The gods also restored Tantalus's son, Pelops. But Tantalus would not be the only one to suffer for his crime. In the minds of the ancient Greeks, the sins of parents could be passed on to their children. Tantalus's depravity had doomed his descendants. Pelops himself was spared, but his line was cursed with abominations for generations.

The first occurred when three of Pelops's sons murdered their half-brother. Later two of the sons—Atreus and Thyestes—turned on each other. After Atreus became king of Mycenae, Thyestes seduced his queen. Atreus banished him, but Thyestes soon concocted a scheme to get revenge. He had raised one of Atreus's sons as his own, and the young man thought Thyestes was his father. Thyestes sent him to murder Atreus. Atreus foiled the plot and—not knowing that the would-be assassin was his son—killed him.

Atreus was devastated when he discovered that he had killed his son. Resolving to even the score with his brother, Atreus pretended to make amends with Thyestes and invited him to Mycenae for a magnificent feast. After Thyestes finished eating, Atreus told him that the meal consisted of the flesh of Thyestes's sons, whom Atreus had butchered.

Thyestes had no sons left to avenge him, but he resorted to his daughter in a mad quest to sire another. She married Atreus shortly after she conceived, and he mistakenly believed that he had fathered the son she bore, named Aegisthus.

Aegisthus grew up in Atreus's household with Agamemnon and Menelaus—sons of Atreus by a prior marriage. One day after Aegisthus had reached adulthood, Agamemnon and Menelaus discovered Thyestes hiding in Mycenae and imprisoned him. They chose Aegisthus to kill him. At the last moment, however, Aegisthus and his father discovered one another's true identity. Aegisthus freed Thyestes, and together they slew Atreus, seized the throne, and forced Agamemnon and Menelaus into exile.

Nevertheless, Agamemnon and Menelaus both managed to become prominent leaders. When a Trojan prince absconded with Menelaus's wife, Helen, Agamemnon led the Greek campaign to retrieve her. But the expedition encountered trouble even before leaving Greece. Some of the Greeks had offended the goddess Artemis, and, as a result, the Greeks were denied the winds necessary to sail to Troy. Agamemnon could secure the winds only if he offered his daughter Iphigenia as a human sacrifice. Reluctantly, he did so.

The sacrifice of Iphigenia did not sit well with Agamemnon's wife, Clytemnestra. While her husband and the Greeks lay siege to Troy, she carried on an adulterous affair with Aegisthus. She also conspired to avenge the death of her daughter. Clytemnestra and Aegisthus were waiting for Agamemnon when he made his triumphant return from Troy. While Agamemnon sat in his palace distracted by his homecoming feast, Aegisthus stole up behind the banquet table and struck him down.

Agamemnon's children, Orestes and Electra, avenged his death. With his sister's help, Orestes put his mother and Aegisthus to the sword. The Furies, immortals from the underworld who administer justice, tormented Orestes relentlessly for killing his mother and cousin. Ultimately, however, the gods took pity on Orestes, absolved him of his crime, and lifted the curse from the family.

THE METAPHOR

At first glance, an ancient Greek tale of incest, parricide, adultery, and cannibalism may seem to have little relevance to contemporary America. But the story of the House of Atreus is relevant today. It is more than a simple parable about corruption. It is, in many respects, a metaphor for our abortion-minded society.

We have fallen into the same pattern of indiscriminate and almost habitual killing that plagued Atreus and his family. We kill our unborn young because they are male instead of female. We kill because we have second thoughts about becoming parents or because the pregnancy is the fruit of a failed relationship. We kill because a child could impede our career or social life, or compromise our standing in the community. We Americans abort approximately 1.5 million of our young each year—38 abortions for every 100 live births.[1] At current rates, there will be 78 abortions for every 100 women by the time the women reach the end of their child-bearing years.[2] (In our nation's capital, the figure is *414* abortions for every 100 women by the time the women reach the end of their child-bearing years.[3]) Of the women getting abortions, 47 percent have had at least one previously; 19 percent have had two or more.[4] Half of all women are likely to have an abortion at some point in their lives.[5]

Like Tantalus, Thyestes, and Agamemnon, we relentlessly pursue our own concerns, blind to the consequences for our young. Tantalus wanted human flesh to test the gods, so he turned upon his son; Thyestes wanted another son, so he impregnated his daughter; Agamemnon desired favorable winds to sail to Troy, so he sacrificed his daughter in exchange for them. We indulge our own interests even if it costs the lives of our unborn young. There is no room in the moral calculus of abortion to weigh the interests of the unborn. Only the interests of the mother matter. If she decides to give birth, that is her prerogative. But if she decides to get an abortion, so much the better—one less body polluting the environment, one less competitor for limited resources, one less potential juvenile delinquent. We insist that the mother has freedom to "choose," but warn her that she is "irresponsible" if she chooses life.

Tantalus, Thyestes, and Agamemnon used their children's bodies to effect their own ends. We exploit the bodies of our young by using their aborted remains for scientific research and tissue transplants. A panel appointed by the National Institutes of Health has suggested that human embryos be created in the laboratory so that scientists could perform experiments on them which kill them.[6] Fertility clinics custom-design, create, and sell "ready-made" human embryos to would-be parents.[7] To ensure that their clients become pregnant, many fertility clinics also hedge their bets by using techniques which result in multiple embryos implanting in the uterus, calculating that, once the woman becomes pregnant, she can abort any "extras" (a "selective termination" or "fetal reduction"). Indeed, we are even starting to regard our young precisely in the same way Thyestes regarded his daughter: as simply a source for the eggs necessary to create other offspring. Already some in the medical community are willing to remove the eggs from the aborted bodies of unborn females (human females produce all of their eggs within ten weeks of conception) and put them in grown women whose own eggs are inadequate.[8] Thyestes was father and grandfather to Aegisthus; by transplanting the eggs of aborted females, we would create mothers who were never daughters and grandmothers who were never mothers.

The relationship between Thyestes and his daughter was just one of the unnatural relationships in the House of Atreus. Atreus's family is crowded with individuals who are, to borrow Hamlet's phrase, "A little more than kin, and less than kind."[9] Atreus marries his niece; Clytemnestra carries on an adulterous affair with her husband's cousin; Thyestes impregnates his daughter and seduces his brother's wife. Tantalus kills his son; Atreus and his brothers murder their half-brother; Atreus murders his nephews and slays his son, then is himself dispatched by his brother and the nephew he thought to be his son; Agamemnon offers up his daughter as a sacrifice, then is murdered by his wife and cousin; Orestes puts his mother and his father's cousin to the sword.

These perversions can be understood as metaphors for abortion at two levels. Taken alone, the parricides are metaphors for the role of the mother—and, in many instances, the father—in abortion. Ordinarily, family members nurture, protect, and make sacrifices for one another. But in abortion, as in the House of Atreus, the most elemental relationships between human beings are turned inside out. The ultimate threat comes from inside the family, not outside of it. The nurturers kill; the creators destroy. If there is a sacrifice to be made, the child is sacrificed.

The parallel can be drawn at an even broader level if one considers the illicit sexual relationships in the House of Atreus in addition to the parricides. Both types of perversions are metaphors for nature turned on its head. In our abortion-minded society, the womb has been transformed from a place of special safety to one of special danger; the beginning of life is the end of life; healers are killers; human beings are human for some purposes, but not for others.

Indeed, even the cannibalism in the House of Atreus is, in a sense, a metaphor for abortion. We abort the unborn, in many instances, because to us they are simply the unintended consequence of our quest for sexual fulfillment or a threat to our preferred lifestyle. Thyestes and Demeter ate human flesh. We insist upon satisfying our appetites and tastes even if the unborn are consumed in the process. We treat the bodies of the unborn as a means of sustenance, scavenging their aborted remains for tissue that might enhance our health, then cannibalizing it for use in our own bodies. And, like Demeter and Thyestes, we partake in the Thyestean banquet only because we do not know the true nature of the offering. Demeter and Thyestes did not realize they were eating human beings; we fail to realize that, through abortion, we are killing them.

Curiously, Aeschylus himself drew a parallel between the killing of unborn young and the victims of Atreus's family. In Aeschylus's trilogy, the Greeks see an omen before they embark for Troy. Two eagles swoop down upon a pregnant hare, devouring it and its unborn young. A seer who witnesses the event proclaims that the eagles represent Atreus's two sons—Agamemnon and Menelaus—and warns the two leaders that their actions will anger the goddess Artemis:

> For the virgin Artemis bears jealous hate
>   Against the royal house, the eagle pair,
> Who rend the unborn brood insatiate—
>   Yea, loathes their banquet on the quivering hare.[10]

The hare's unborn offspring represent the victims of Agamemnon and Menelaus. In *A Companion to Greek Tragedy*, classicist John Ferguson writes that Agamemnon and Menelaus incur the wrath of the goddess simply "because they tear the innocent."[11] "A pregnant animal," Ferguson explains, "contains unborn innocent young. In one sense, the hare is Troy and the embryos the innocents who have suffered in an expedition that Zeus ordained against Paris; in another, the rending is the whole work of the expedition and the unborn leverets represent the innocent Iphigenia."[12]

Atreus's sons figuratively "rended the unborn brood insatiate." We do so literally. As the destruction of the unborn was once a metaphor for the House of Atreus, the House of Atreus now appears to be a metaphor for the destruction of the unborn.

Curiously, even some defenders of abortion have seized upon the metaphor. In *The Sacrament of Abortion*, Ginette Paris compares abortion to the slaying of Iphigenia and argues that it may be understood as "sacrifice to Artemis": a "sacrament" necessary "for the gift of life to remain pure."[13] Brenda Peterson expresses similar sentiments in an October 1993 article in the *New Age Journal*. She writes that women need to "make sacred the sacrifice" of "those sisters who have chosen . . . abortion," and adds, "[W]e'll initiate our daughters into the women's mysteries . . . , remembering the midwives' herbs and potions; and perhaps with spiritual dignity we'll ritualize the RU486 pill with prayers to Artemis or the Divine Mother, She who gives and takes life."[14]

Feminist Naomi Wolf, an opponent of abortion restrictions, unwittingly invoked another metaphor from the House of Atreus in her influential *New Republic* article, "Our Bodies, Our Souls." In the article, Wolf describes a woman she calls "Clare"—a baby-boomer, Democrat, cardiologist, and ardent "abortion rights" supporter—whom Wolf characterizes as the epitome of the abortion movement. Yet, Wolf quotes Clare as saying, "I had an abortion when I was a single mother. . . . I would do it again. *But you know how in the Greek myths when you kill a relative you are pursued by furies? For months, it was as if baby furies were pursuing me.*"[15]

NOTES

1. United States Bureau of the Census, *Statistical Abstract of the United States, 1997* (Washington: Government Printing Office, 1997), 83, 86.

2. *Statistical Abstract of the United States, 1997*, 86. There are 2.6 abortions each year for every 100 women in their childbearing years (between the ages of 15 and 44). (Based on 1992 data, the most recent year for which accurate data are available.)

3. *Statistical Abstract of the United States, 1997*, 87. There are 13.8 abortions each year for every 100 women in their childbearing years (between the ages of 15 and 44) in Washington, D.C. (Based on 1992 data, the most recent year for which accurate data are available.)

4. *Statistical Abstract of the United States, 1997*, 86.

5. Julie Rovner, "U.S. Abortion Survey Produces Surprise Statistics," *Lancet* 348 (1996): 469.

6. Robert H. Bork, *Slouching Towards Gomorrah: Modern Liberalism and American Decline* (New York: ReganBooks-Harper, 1996), 183.

7. Gina Kolata, "Clinics Selling Embryos Made for 'Adoption,' " *New York Times*, November 23, 1997: A-1+.

8. Gina Kolata, "Fetal Ovary Transplant Envisioned," *New York Times*, January 6, 1994: A-16.

9. Shakespeare, *Hamlet* 1.2.65, in *The Unabridged William Shakespeare*, William George Clark and William Aldis Wright, eds. (Philadelphia: Running Press, 1989), 1010.

10. Aeschylus, *Agamemnon*, in *The Harvard Classics*, gen. ed. Charles W. Eliot, vol. 8, *Nine Greek Dramas* (New York: Collier and Son, 1937), 12.

11. John Ferguson, *A Companion to Greek Tragedy* (Austin: University of Texas Press, 1972), 77.

12. Ferguson, 77–78.

13. Ginette Paris, *The Sacrament of Abortion*, trans. Joanna Mott (Dallas: Spring, 1992), 34–41, 107.

14. Brenda Peterson, "Sister Against Sister," *New Age Journal*, September/October 1993: 144.

15. Naomi Wolf, "Our Bodies, Our Souls: Re-thinking Abortion Rhetoric," *New Republic*, October 16, 1995: 26 (emphasis added).

Epilogue

Justice Sandra Day O'Connor, before she had her latest change of heart, once declared *Roe v. Wade* was on a "collision course with itself."[1] She was right but did not go far enough. *Roe* is not only on a collision course with itself; it is on a collision course with the Hippocratic Oath, the Declaration of Independence, and some of our most important international human rights treaties. It is on a collision course with truth and science and our best aspirations of ourselves. It is on a collision course with any society that recognizes the inherent dignity, worth, and potential of *all* human beings.

The Supreme Court held in *Roe* that the unborn had no right to life because they were not persons within the meaning of the Due Process Clause of the 14th Amendment. (The Due Process Clause, remember, states that no "person" shall be deprived of life, liberty, or property without due process of law.) The irony is that, while the Court does not consider the Amendment to protect fetuses, the Amendment was drafted to protect blacks, and *blacks were regarded as fetuses at the time the Amendment was drafted and ratified.*

The 14th Amendment was drafted and ratified in the wake of the Civil War to ensure that fundamental rights of blacks were protected in the former slave states. Even after "the war to end slavery," most whites regarded blacks much as Justice Taney referred to them in his opinion in *Dred Scott*: as "beings of an entirely inferior order."[2] During Reconstruction, Phillip Paludan writes, "Americans clung firmly to a belief in the basic inferiority of the Negro race, a belief supported by the preponderance of nineteenth-century scientific evidence."[3]

Foremost among the "scientific" arguments cited in support of these racist views was the theory, held by many scientists and intellectuals, that white Europeans had accelerated development compared to other races.[4] According to this theory—prevalent even before the 1859 publication of Darwin's theory of natural selection—development in whites passed through and beyond the adult stages of other races, while the adults of other races developed only to the level of a typical white child.[5] Thus, Dr. John Down, the English physician who described Down's syndrome in 1866, dubbed the condition "Mongolian idiocy" because he assumed that the condition arrested the development of whites at the level normally associated with Oriental adults.[6] (Down also identified cases of "idiocy" in which the development of whites was retarded to a level which characterized other "primitive" peoples, among them Native Americans, Malaysians, and blacks.[7])

Blacks were regarded as the most primitive and retarded of the "lower" races. D. G. Brinton wrote, "The adult who retains the more numerous fetal, [or] infantile . . . traits is unquestionably inferior to him whose development has progressed beyond them. Measured by these criteria, the European or white race stands at the head of the list, the African or negro at its foot."[8] In 1864, Carl Vogt detailed similarities between the brains of blacks and those of white children and fetuses.[9] Louis Agassiz—a slavery opponent, Harvard professor, and America's leading biologist in the mid-nineteenth century—was even more forthcoming. He declared, "*The brain of the Negro is that of the imperfect brain of a seven month's old infant in the womb of the white.*"[10]

When the framers decided to protect the lives of blacks in the 14th Amendment, therefore, they extended protection to individuals regarded as equivalent to white unborn. When they drafted the Amendment to read that no "person" shall be deprived of life without due process of law, the framers no doubt meant to protect the lives of black children as well as black adults. And, if black *adults* were regarded as equivalent to an unborn white seven months into pregnancy (or even just to a white child), then wouldn't we have to go far earlier into pregnancy before we found what was regarded as the white equivalent of a black *newborn*?

Since blacks were regarded as having retarded development compared to whites, when the framers drafted the protections in the 14th Amendment for "persons," they must have:

1. meant to extend protection to the lives of blacks thought to be less developed than certain whites not protected (i.e., black babies versus white unborn);
2. meant to extend protection to white young while they were still within the womb but black young only upon birth; or
3. meant to protect the lives of all human beings, regardless of their state of development.

Only the third alternative is reasonable. Given the widespread antipathy to recognizing blacks as totally equal, even in the midst of Reconstruction, it is highly improbable that the Amendment was drafted to protect the lives of blacks thought less developed than whites left unprotected. The second alternative is patently ridiculous (and also inconsistent with *Roe v. Wade*, since this reading would confer a right to life upon some white unborn).

This is just one of the idiosyncrasies underlying the abortion movement. We have examined many others in previous chapters. We have explored the problems inherent in declaring that the unborn are not living or human beings or persons. We have examined the perils that can follow from refusing to recognize the right to life of any class of human beings, from refusing to recognize human beings as human, and from permissive attitudes about killing. And, though abortion proponents insist that the arguments against abortion are all rooted in theology, we have done it all without touching on religion.

Indeed, in one sense it is the *defenders* of abortion who rely on theology. Time and time again we hear them argue that the unborn are not "human beings" or not "persons." They do not use any of the commonly accepted definitions for these terms, nor do they agree on the definitions they do use. And a close examination of their arguments reveals that they are not really talking about biology or medicine or the like. They are talking about the intangible and indefinable essence which separates us from "mere beasts"; they are talking about *souls*.

We have, as a society, grown increasingly accustomed to thinking that we intuitively recognize who is human, and that it is permissible to kill so long as the killer does not regard his or her victim as human. We have even come to regard our permissive attitudes about abortion as an indication of how enlightened we are and have tried to export our attitudes to countries with "antiquated" notions about protecting the lives of their unborn as well as born young.

How much have we learned from history? In the last century, Bushmen were regarded as subhuman. An 1847 newspaper article described a Bushman family on display at the Egyptian Hall in London as "little above a monkey tribe," adding, "They are continually crouching, warming themselves by the fire, chatting or growling. . . . They are sullen, silent, and savage—mere animals in propensity, and worse than animals in appearance."[11] Indeed, the tendency to regard Bushmen as animals was so deep-rooted that one party of European settlers, out on a hunting expedition, shot and ate a Bushman assuming that he was the African equivalent of an orangutan.)[12]

Strange, is it not, that these settlers could kill and eat a man yet never realize that their victim was human? The settlers were probably good people, people with a sense of right and wrong, people who regarded themselves as "civilized" and enlightened. Yet their hubris, their ignorance, and their narrow understanding of who is "human" allowed them to engage in conduct as abominable as that of any "savage." The settlers were not terrible people, but they did a terrible thing.

As we have seen in previous chapters, we are capable of doing some terrible things ourselves. We deny that some human beings are human and that all human beings have a right to life. We dismember our young and cannibalize their remains for scientific research. We have embraced notions of relative human worth and "humane" killing which threaten the born as well as the unborn. We have enshrined a constitutional right to kill.

The truth about abortion is painful, and we have a propensity for seeing what we want to see. The sizable percentage of people who doubt that the Holocaust occurred attests to the lengths that we will go to deny reality. It would be much *easier* to believe that abortion does not snuff out the lives of a million and a half human beings each year, but it would be wrong. As Henri Frederic Amiel once observed, "A belief is not true because it is useful."[13]

Yet even amidst the disturbing truth about abortion there is reason for hope. I have outlined the shadows of things as they *are*, but not as they *need be*. Because we live in a democracy, changing the course of the country is as easy (or as difficult) as persuading people to change their minds. The future of abortion in the United States ultimately depends on the attitudes of our judges, elected officials, health care personnel, and the public in general. Most people who support abortion are still within reach. They still have compassion; they still subscribe to the idea that every human being has intrinsic worth and a right to life. The facts are on the side of protecting the unborn. If those who currently support abortion can only be persuaded to seriously re-evaluate their position, many will change their minds.

Shortly before he left office in 1994, Pennsylvania Governor Robert Casey spoke eloquently about the reasons he was optimistic that the tide in America is now turning against abortion:

I believe we are now living through a period in our nation's history that will one day be recognized as an era of hope, the time of a new beginning. For today, hidden in the confusion of public debate, in the hurly-burly of partisan politics, in the mad rush of news-of-the-day, there is a great story waiting to be written.

America is returning to its senses. There is a reawakening throughout the land, a rediscovery of the vital importance of spiritual values, a renewed conviction that we must return to the moral principles that made this nation great. And *that*, I am convinced, is where the future lies. . . .

It is my conviction—and it is an empirical conviction, not a wish—that abortion has not taken, and never will take, a permanent place in our culture. In a country whose whole reason for being is to affirm the goodness and equality of all human life, how could such a thing ever fit in?

Indeed, I will even say this: our grandchildren will study *Roe v. Wade* with bewilderment, as a sad, mysterious chapter in American history, when a great nation briefly lost its way.

For those with eyes to see, reasons for optimism abound. Quietly, slowly, painfully, inexorably, the American people are coming to the conclusion: We cannot live with abortion. We know there is a better way. . . . Nothing could be more foreign to the American experience—which is an ongoing story of expanding the circle of the commonly protected. Abortion is inconsistent with our national character—with all that we have done, with everything we hope to be.

Abortion is un-American. That is why I am so confident that legal abortion is destined for the scrap-heap of history. The American people did not ask for it. They have not accepted it. And in the end, they will reject it.

I say there is already a pro-life consensus. But if it is to be effectively reflected in our national debate, in our public life, and in our laws, I believe that this pro-life consensus requires two things: first, it needs to find its voice; and second, it needs to find the courage of its convictions. . . .

I'm talking about moral leadership of the highest order, leadership that is as compassionate as it is principled. That means support for alternatives to abortion—above all, a serious push to encourage adoption, which has never really been tried—and a generous recognition of our societal obligations towards mothers and children. . . .

We need leaders who present the protection of the unborn child for what it truly is: an imperative that flows naturally from the social justice mission of America, an imperative that is consistent with the historic teachings not only of the Catholic religion but of all religions—and, above all, consistent with who we are as a people, a nation dedicated to the proposition that all are created equal and endowed with an inalienable right to life. This is the message that the American people are waiting to hear. . . .

This is a challenge worthy of a great nation.[14]

We have a choice before us, a choice about how we value the lives of our young. On one hand, we have the view of the Marquis de Sade:

And so that is what murder is: a little matter disorganized, a few combinations changed, some atoms broken and returned to nature's crucible from whence they shall return in a few days in another form; where is the evil in that? Are women or children more precious to Nature than flies or worms? If I take life from the one, I give it to the other; where is the crime in what I do?[15]

The alternative is the view expressed by Ben Jonson:

It is not growing like a tree
In bulk, doth make Man better be;
Or standing long an oak, three hundred year,
To fall a log at last, dry, bald, and sere:
A lily of a day

Is fairer far in May,
Although it fall and die that night—
It was the plant and flower of Light.
In small proportions we just beauties see;
And in short measures life may perfect be.[16]

It will not be easy to make our society one in accord with Jonson's view, one which accommodates the right to life of even the weakest and most helpless. But we cannot lower our goal on that account. The Founding Fathers did not content themselves with a goal that it would be easy for the country to attain. They founded the United States on the principle that all human beings were created equal, and that each had inherent rights—including a right to life. By doing so, as Abraham Lincoln explained, "They meant to set up a standard maxim for a free society, which should be familiar to all, and revered by all; constantly looked to, constantly labored for, and even though never perfectly attained, constantly approximated, and thereby constantly spreading and deepening its influence and augmenting the happiness and value of life to all people of all colors everywhere."[17]

We have had difficulty living up to the high ideals expressed in the Declaration of Independence before, but we have not renounced them. We should not—and I believe we will not—do so now.

NOTES

1. *Akron v. Akron Center for Reproductive Health, Inc.*, 462 U.S. 416, 458 (1983).
2. *Dred Scott v. Sandford*, 60 U.S. (19 How.) 393, 407 (1857).
3. Phillip S. Paludan, *A Covenant with Death* (Urbana: University of Illinois Press, 1975), 54. Quoted in Raoul Berger, *Government by Judiciary: The Transformation of the Fourteenth Amendment* (Cambridge, MA: Harvard University Press, 1977), 13.
4. Stephen Jay Gould, *Ontogeny and Phylogeny* (Cambridge, MA: Belknap–Harvard University Press, 1977), 126–129.
5. Gould, *Ontogeny and Phylogeny*, 127–128.
6. Gould, "Dr. Down's Syndrome," in *The Panda's Thumb: More Reflections in Natural History* (New York: Norton, 1980) 160–168.
7. Gould, "Dr. Down's Syndrome," 160–168.
8. D. G. Brinton, *Races and Peoples* (New York: Hodges, 1890), 48. Quoted in Gould, *Ontogeny and Phylogeny*, 128.
9. Carl Vogt, *Lectures on Man* (London: Longman, 1864), 183.

10. Quoted in Gould, *Ontogeny and Phylogeny*, 127 (emphasis added).

11. Quoted in Gould, "The Hottentot Venus," in *The Flamingo's Smile: Reflections in Natural History* (New York: Norton, 1985), 294.

12. Gould, "The Hottentot Venus," 294.

13. Henri Frederic Amiel, *Amiel's Journal*, trans. Mrs. Humphrey Ward (n.p.: Macmillan, 1893), 234.

14. Robert Casey, "America Is Returning to Its Senses," *National Right to Life News*, January 1995: 16+.

15. Geoffrey Gorer, *The Marquis de Sade* (New York: Liveright, 1934), 232. Quoted in Eugene Quay, "Justifiable Abortion—Medical and Legal Foundations (Part II)," *Georgetown Law Journal* 49 (1961): 444.

16. Ben Jonson, "It Is Not Growing Like a Tree," *Immortal Poems of the English Language*, ed. Oscar Williams (New York: Pocket Books, 1952), 79.

17. Earl W. Wiley, *Abraham Lincoln: Portrait of a Speaker* (New York: Vantage, 1970), 155.

Selected Bibliography

BOOKS

Adler, Mortimer J. *We Hold These Truths: Understanding the Ideas and Ideals of the Constitution.* New York: Macmillan, 1987.

Arras, J., and Robert Hunt, eds. *Ethical Issues in Modern Medicine.* Palo Alto, CA: Mayfield, 1977.

Baird, Robert M., and Stuart Rosenbaum, eds. *The Ethics of Abortion.* Buffalo, N.Y.: Prometheus, 1989.

Bauman, Zygmunt. *Modernity and the Holocaust.* Ithaca, NY: Cornell University Press, 1989.

Berger, Raoul. *Government by Judiciary: The Transformation of the Fourteenth Amendment.* Cambridge, MA: Harvard University Press, 1977.

Bork, Robert H. *Slouching Towards Gomorrah: Modern Liberalism and American Decline.* New York: ReganBooks-Harper, 1996.

———. *The Tempting of America: The Political Seduction of the Law.* New York: Free Press, 1990.

Breitman, Richard. *The Architect of Genocide: Himmler and the Final Solution.* New York: Knopf, 1991.

Burleigh, Michael. *Death and Deliverance: "Euthanasia" in Germany 1900–1945.* Cambridge, England: Cambridge University Press, 1994.

Burtchaell, James Tunstead. *Rachel Weeping and Other Essays.* Kansas City: Andrews & McMeel, 1982.

Condit, Celeste Michelle. *Decoding Abortion Rhetoric: Communicating Social Change.* Urbana: University of Illinois Press, 1990.

Cooke, Robert E., et al. *The Terrible Choice.* New York: Bantam, 1968.

Dower, John W. *War without Mercy: Race and Power in the Pacific War.* New York: Pantheon, 1986.

Eliot, Charles W., gen. ed. *The Harvard Classics.* Vol. 8: *Nine Greek Dramas.* New York: Collier, 1937.

Farley, John. *The Spontaneous Generation Controversy from Descartes to Oparin.* Baltimore: Johns Hopkins University Press, 1977.

Feder, Lillian. *Crowell's Handbook of Classical Literature.* New York: Crowell, 1964.

Fleming, Gerald. *Hitler and the Final Solution.* Berkeley: University of California Press, 1984.

Fletcher, Joseph. *Humanhood: Essays in Biomedical Ethics.* Buffalo, N.Y.: Prometheus, 1979.

Garvey, John H., and T. Alexander Aleinikoff, eds. *Modern Constitutional Theory: A Reader,* 2d ed. St. Paul: West, 1991.

Gasman, Daniel. *The Scientific Origins of National Socialism: Social Darwinism in Ernst Haeckel and the German Monist League.* New York: American Elsevier, 1971.

Gould, Stephen J. *The Flamingo's Smile: Reflections in Natural History.* New York: Norton, 1985.

—— *The Panda's Thumb: More Reflections in Natural History.* New York: Norton, 1980.

—— *Ever Since Darwin: Reflections in Natural History.* New York: Norton, 1977.

—— *Ontogeny and Phylogeny.* Cambridge, MA: Belknap–Harvard University Press, 1977.

Haller, John S., Jr. *Outcasts from Evolution: Scientific Attitudes of Racial Inferiority, 1859–1900.* Urbana: University of Illinois Press, 1971.

Haller, Mark H. *Eugenics: Hereditarian Attitudes in American Thought.* New Brunswick, NJ: Rutgers University Press, 1989.

Hamilton, Edith. *Mythology.* New York: Mentor Books, 1969.

Hilberg, Raul. *The Destruction of the European Jews,* rev. and definitive ed. New York: Holmes & Meiers, 1985.

Höhne, Heinz. *The Order of the Death's Head: The Story of Hitler's SS.* Trans. Richard Barry. New York: Ballantine, 1969.

Howatson, M. C. *The Oxford Companion to Classical Literature.* 2d ed. New York: Oxford University Press, 1989.

Ide, Arthur Frederick. *Abortion Handbook: The History, Legal Process, Practice and Psychology of Abortion.* 3rd ed. Las Calinas, TX: Liberal Press, 1988.

Kempf, Edward J. *Abraham Lincoln's Philosophy of Common Sense: An Analytical Biography of a Great Mind.* New York: New York Academy of Sciences, 1965.

Kevles, Daniel J. *In the Name of Eugenics.* New York: Knopf, 1985.

Koop, Charles Everett. *Koop: The Memoirs of America's Family Doctor.* New York: Random House, 1991.

Kren, George M., and Leon Rappoport. *The Holocaust and the Crisis of Human Behavior.* New York: Holmes & Meier, 1980.

Kuhse, Helga, and Peter Singer. *Should the Baby Live? The Problem of Handicapped Infants.* New York: Oxford University Press, 1985.

Lawson, Edward, ed. *Encyclopedia of Human Rights.* New York: Taylor and Francis Institute, 1991.

Lifton, Robert J. *The Nazi Doctors: Medical Killing and the Psychology of Genocide.* New York: Basic Books, 1986.

Lyon, Jeff. *Playing God in the Nursery.* New York: Norton, 1985.

Manney, James, and John C. Blattner. *Death in the Nursery: The Secret Crime of Infanticide.* Ann Arbor, MI: Servant Books, 1984.

Paris, Ginette. *The Sacrament of Abortion.* Trans. Joanna Mott. Dallas: Spring, 1992.

Pickens, Donald K. *Eugenics and the Progressives.* Nashville: Vanderbilt University Press, 1968.

Reiser, Stanley Joel; Arthur J. Dyck; and William J. Curran, eds. *Ethics in Medicine: Historical Perspectives and Contemporary Concerns.* Cambridge, MA: MIT Press, 1977.

Rhode, Deborah L. *Justice and Gender.* Cambridge, MA: Harvard University Press, 1989.

Shelp, Earl E. *Born to Die? Deciding the Fate of Critically Ill Newborns.* New York: Free Press, 1986.

Singer, Peter. *Practical Ethics.* Cambridge, England: Cambridge University Press, 1979.

Smith, J. David. *Minds Made Feeble: The Myth and Legacy of the Kallikaks.* Rockville, MD: Aspen, 1985.

Stover, Eric, and Elena O. Nightingale, eds. *The Breaking of Bodies and Minds: Torture, Psychiatric Abuse and the Health Professions.* New York: W. H. Freeman, 1985.

Tooley, Michael. *Abortion and Infanticide.* Oxford, England: Clarendon-Oxford University Press, 1983.

Wenz, Peter. *Abortion Rights as Religious Freedom.* Philadelphia: Temple University Press, 1992.

Wheaton, Eliot Barculo. *Prelude to Calamity: The Nazi Revolution 1933–35.* Garden City, NY: Doubleday, 1968.

JOURNAL AND MAGAZINE ARTICLES

Allen, Marilee C., Pamela K. Donahue; and Amy Dusman. "Limit of Viability—Neonatal Outcome of Inf,nts Born at 22 to 25 Weeks' Gestation." *The New England Journal of Medicine* 329 (1993): 1597–1601.

Friedman, Jay A. "Taking the Camel by the Nose: The Anencephalic as a Source for Pediatric Organ Transplants." *Columbia Law Review* 90 (1990): 917–978.

Glasson, John, et al. "The Use of Anencephalic Neonates as Organ Donors," *Journal of the American Medical Association* 273 (1995): 1614–1618.

Hardwig, John. "Is There a Duty to Die?" *Hastings Center Report*, March/April 1997: 34–42.

Hendin, Herbert. "Selling Death with Dignity." *Hastings Center Report*, May/June 1995: 19–23.

Hendin, Herbert, Chris Rutenfrans, and Zbigniew Zylicz. "Physician-Assisted Suicide and Euthanasia in the Netherlands: Lessons from the Dutch." *Journal of the American Medical Association* 277 (1997): 1720–1722.

Johnsen, Dawn, and Marcy J. Wilder. "*Webster* and Women's Equality." *American Journal of Law and Medicine* 15 (1989): 178–184.

Jonas, Robert E., and John D. Gorby, trans. "West German Abortion Decision: A Contrast to *Roe v. Wade*." *John Marshall Journal of Practice and Procedure* 9 (1976): 605–684.

Noonan, John T., Jr. "The Root and Branch of *Roe v. Wade*." *Nebraska Law Review* 63 (1984): 668–679.

Peterson, Brenda. "Sister Against Sister." *New Age Journal*, September/October 1993: 64+.

Quay, Eugene. "Justifiable Abortion—Medical and Legal Foundations (Part II)." *Georgetown Law Journal* 49 (1961): 395–538.

Redman, D. "The Choices." *Mother Jones*, January/February 1994: 32–35.

Rhoden, Nancy K. "The New Neonatal Dilemma: Live Births from Late Abortions." *Georgetown Law Journal* 72 (1984): 1451–1509.

Shiflett, Dave. "Dr. Hern and Mr. Clinton." *Weekly Standard*, November 11, 1996: 14–15.

Waldman, Steven, Elise Ackerman, and Rita Rubin. "Abortions in America." *U.S. News & World Report*, January 19, 1998: 20–25.

Wall, Stephen N., and John Colin Partridge. "Death in the Intensive Care Nursery: Physician Practice of Withdrawing and Withholding Life Support." *Pediatrics* 99 (1997): 64–70.

Wiesel, Elie. "One Must Not Forget." *U.S. News & World Report*, October 27, 1986: 68.

Wolf, Naomi. "Our Bodies, Our Souls: Re-thinking Abortion Rhetoric."
    New Republic, October 16, 1995: 26–35.
Wong, Yin. "A Question of Duty." *Reader's Digest*, September 1995:
    65–70.

NEWSPAPER ARTICLES

Casey, Robert. "America Is Returning to Its Senses." *National Right to Life
    News*, January 1995: 16+.
Emanuel, Ezekiel J. "The Painful Truth about Euthanasia." *Wall Street Jour-
    nal*, January 7, 1997: A16.
Flesh, George. "Why I No Longer Do Abortions." *Los Angeles Times*, Sep-
    tember 12, 1991: B7.
Kolata, Gina. "Fetal Ovary Transplant Envisioned." *New York Times*, Janu-
    ary 6, 1994: A16.
Neuhaus, Richard John. "Don't Cross This Threshhold." *Wall Street Jour-
    nal*, October 27, 1994: A20.
Schumacher, Edward. "Feminists Stage Abortions." *New York Times*, No-
    vember 10, 1985, sec. I:7.
Shafer, Brenda. "What the Nurse Saw." *National Right to Life News*, July 18,
    1995: 23.
Stout, David. "An Abortion Rights Advocate Says He Lied about Proce-
    dure." *New York Times*, February 26, 1997: A12.

COURT CASES

Akron v. Akron Center for Reproductive Health, Inc., 462 U.S. 416 (1983).
Buck v. Bell, 274 U.S. 200 (1927).
Compassion in Dying v. Washington, 79 F.3d 790 (9th Cir.1996), *reversed
    sub nom.* Washington v. Glucksberg, ___ U.S. ___, 117 S.Ct. 2258
    (1997).
Davis v. Davis, 842 S.W.2d 588 (Tenn. 1992), *cert. denied sub nom.* Stowe v.
    Davis, 507 U.S. 911 (1993).
Doe v. Israel, 359 F.Supp. 1193 (D.R.I.), *aff'd* 482 F.2d 156 (1st Cir.
    1973), *cert. denied*, 416 U.S. 993 (1974).
Judgment of February 25, 1975, 39 BVerfGE 1, trans. in Robert E. Jonas
    and John D. Gorby, "West German Abortion Decision: A Contrast
    to *Roe v. Wade*." *John Marshall Journal of Practice and Procedure* 9
    (1976): 605–684.
Planned Parenthood, v. Casey, 505 U.S. 833 (1992).
Quill v. Vacco, 80 F.3d 716 (2d Cir.1996), *reversed* ___ U.S. ___, 117 S.Ct.
    2293 (1997).
Roe v. Wade, 410 U.S. 113 (1973).

Rosen v. Louisiana State Board of Medical Examiners, 318 F. Supp. 1217 (1970 E.D. La.), *vacated* 412 U.S. 902 (1972).
Vacco v. Quill, ___U.S.___, 117 S.Ct. 2293 (1997).
Washington v. Glucksberg, ___U.S.___, 117 S.Ct. 2258 (1997).
Webster v. Reproductive Health Care Services, 492 U.S. 490 (1989).

Index

About the Author

JAMES F. BOHAN is an attorney in Pennsylvania.